Our Country/Whose Country?

Our Country/Whose Country?

Early Westerns and Travel Films as Stories of Settler Colonialism

RICHARD ABEL

OXFORD
UNIVERSITY PRESS

Oxford University Press is a department of the University of Oxford. It furthers the University's objective of excellence in research, scholarship, and education by publishing worldwide. Oxford is a registered trade mark of Oxford University Press in the UK and certain other countries.

Published in the United States of America by Oxford University Press
198 Madison Avenue, New York, NY 10016, United States of America.

© Oxford University Press 2023

All rights reserved. No part of this publication may be reproduced, stored in a retrieval system, or transmitted, in any form or by any means, without the prior permission in writing of Oxford University Press, or as expressly permitted by law, by license, or under terms agreed with the appropriate reproduction rights organization. Inquiries concerning reproduction outside the scope of the above should be sent to the Rights Department, Oxford University Press, at the address above.

You must not circulate this work in any other form
and you must impose this same condition on any acquirer.

Library of Congress Cataloging-in-Publication Data
Names: Abel, Richard, 1941– author.
Title: Our country/whose country? : early Westerns and travel films as stories of settler colonialism/ Richard Abel.
Description: New York : Oxford University Press, 2023. |
Includes bibliographical references and index.
Identifiers: LCCN 2023019521 (print) | LCCN 2023019522 (ebook) |
ISBN 9780197744055 (paperback) | ISBN 9780197744048 (hardback) |
ISBN 9780197744062 (epub) | ISBN 9780197744086
Subjects: LCSH: Western films—United States—History and criticism. |
Silent films—United States—History and criticism. | Pioneers in motion pictures. |
Colonies in motion pictures. | Indigenous peoples in motion pictures.
Classification: LCC PN1995.9.W4 A25 2023 (print) | LCC PN1995.9.W4 (ebook) |
DDC 791.43/6278—dc23/eng/20230613
LC record available at https://lccn.loc.gov/2023019521
LC ebook record available at https://lccn.loc.gov/2023019522

DOI: 10.1093/oso/9780197744048.001.0001

Paperback printed by Marquis Book Printing, Canada
Hardback printed by Bridgeport National Bindery, Inc., United States of America

As a descendant of white settlers, I wish to acknowledge the Indigenous peoples who long ago inhabited ancestral territories where I later resided most of my life: the Erie and Shawnee in northeastern Ohio, the Ioway and Sauk in central Iowa, and the Council of Three Fires—the Mississauga Ojibwe, Odawa (Ottawa), and Potawatomi—in southeast Michigan.

Contents

Acknowledgments	ix
List of Illustrations	xiii
Introduction	1
1. Wild West Subjects to 1910	12
Touring the West 1	33
2. Single-Reel Westerns, 1910–1913	38
Touring the West 2	67
3. Multiple-Reel Westerns, 1912–1914	72
Touring the West 3	94
4. William S. Hart, "The Man with the Face That Talks"	97
Touring the West 4	123
5. Harry Carey, Tom Mix, and Douglas Fairbanks	127
Afterword: Looking Backward to Look Ahead	159
Notes	167
Bibliography	221
Index	225

Acknowledgments

Normally, I would be thanking archives and libraries for allowing me to screen film prints and study paper and microfilm materials on site. But the COVID-19 pandemic has made the past few years far from normal. Instead, like many other historians, I have depended so gratefully on the recent efforts of more and more archives to digitize great numbers of their film prints and stream them as digital files for viewing. In terms of my specific research, the EYE Museum (Amsterdam), US Library of Congress, and George Eastman Museum (Rochester) have been unusually helpful. But so too has Jay Weissberg, director of the Giornate del cinema muto, who asked even more archives to digitize their rare prints of westerns for several series of festival programs that I curated or co-curated (with Diane and Richard Kosarski) in Pordenone, Italy. Also crucial to this research was the Media History Digital Library for its extensive holdings of trade press materials as well as websites such as genealogybank.com and newspapers.com for their wealth of digitized US newspapers. In the case of film prints still unavailable for streaming, I dug through old folders to find more or less readable notes taken long ago on site at those named as well as other archives. Historical research involves difficult archaeological work, but the pandemic more than doubled that difficulty for this project.

Writing history always has to be a collaborative project. For collaborators, I am deeply indebted to Elif Rongen and others at the EYE Museum (formerly Nederlands Film Museum); to Paolo Cherchi Usai, Sophia Lorent, and others at the George Eastman Museum (formerly George Eastman House); to David Pierce and others at the US Library of Congress; to David Kehr and others at the Museum of Modern Art; to Bryony Dixon at the National Film Archive (London); and to Eric Hoyt at the Media History Digital Library. James Akerman, Curator of Maps at the Newberry Library (Chicago), Ryan Brubacher, Reference Librarian at the Boston Public Library, Riche Sorensen at the Smithsonian American Art Museum, and Mary Pedley in the Maps Division at the Clements Library (University of Michigan) were invaluable in suggesting specific maps to use as relevant illustrations and in sharing information on lithograph permissions.

X ACKNOWLEDGMENTS

The COVID-19 pandemic, unfortunately, also limited the number of colleagues who could read all or parts of the manuscript. I found an early anonymous reviewer's suggestions invaluable, leading me to consult important recent scholarship on the representation of Native Americans and Mexicans in early films as well as recent studies of Indigenous peoples and Mexicans in American history. I am especially grateful to Giorgio Bertellini for reading the Introduction multiple times, raising excellent questions, giving me crucial ideas for its reframing and helping reword the book's subtitle. Others have recommended more sources and/or offered pertinent points for revising other parts of the text at various points: Vibeke Petersen, Jennifer Lynn Peterson, Raina Polivka, Joseph Schneider, and Valerie Traub. For many of the frame grabs from specific film prints I am greatly indebted in particular to Vincent Longo at the University of Michigan as well as to Elif Rongen and Bryony Dixon.

At Oxford University Press, I could not be more surprised and pleased by Norm Hirschy's encouragement, as Acquisitions Editor, and his unflagging interest in what this book could become. Together with the Editorial Board, he offered valuable ideas for revising the final version of the manuscript. As did the anonymous reviewers, one of whom wrote an especially astute, detailed evaluation and another who insisted I consult several relevant studies of early Indian pictures. Thanks to Editorial Assistant Alastair Motylinksi for organizing all the documents required for the contractual agreement. Special thanks to the Press's Project Editor Zara Cannon-Mohammed, the Press's Senior Production Editor Leslie Johnson, who oversaw the production process, and to Kavitha Yuvaraj at the Press's partner company, Newgen Knowledge Works, who so efficiently handled the full production schedule of copy editing, page proofing, and indexing. Equally special thanks to copy editor Jennifer Sharpe, whose meticulous reading, pertinent questions, and excellent suggestions for revision greatly improved the text. Finally, thanks to Brady McNamara for syncing the lithograph of "American Progress" with the title/subtitle and designing such a stunning front cover for the book.

For years, I have drawn on, yet could never match, Barbara Hodgdon's unique elegance and wry intelligence in writing on performed Shakespeare as a model for my own. Now, I find that she has become another kind of model. During the six long years she lived with lung cancer and COPD, Barbara continued to work tirelessly on several essays and a final book. Unable to attend live performances or enter distant archives, she was forced to restrict the range of her research: mining her own archive of collected materials in the past, viewing dozens of digitized versions of Shakespeare performances, and requesting permission from a number of colleagues and friends to study and reproduce little known photographs and documents in their own private collections. During the COVID-19 pandemic as well as my own months of living with stomach cancer, fortunately resolved, I too have had to confine my research to digitized documents and a limited number of streamed archive film prints as well as my own collection of materials amassed in the past. I could not be more indebted to such an extraordinary and marvelous partner.

Illustrations

I.1. John Gast, *American Progress*, 1873 chromolithograph (US Library of Congress Prints and Photographs Division) — 3

I.2. Railroad land grant map, 1878 (Norman B. Leventhal Map Center, Boston Public Library) — 5

I.3. Emanuel Leutze, *Westward the Course of Empire Takes Its Way [Westward Ho!]*, 1861 mural study (Smithsonian American Art Museum, Bequest of Sara Carr Upton) — 7

1.1. *The Fighting Trapper, Kit Carson to the Rescue*, 1874 (*The House of Beadle and Adams*, 1950) — 14

1.2. AM&B, *From Leadville to Aspen: Hold-Up in the Rockies*, 1906 (George Eastman Museum, Rochester, New York) — 18

1.3. Selig, *The Cattle Rustlers*, 1908 (National Film Archive, London) — 24

1.4. Biograph, *The Mended Lute*, 1909 (US Library of Congress, Washington, DC) — 27

W1.1 *Moving Picture World* (August 10, 1907): front cover — 36

2.1. *Nickelodeon* (March 4, 1911): 246 — 39

2.2. Selig, *The Sergeant*, 1910 (Academy of Motion Picture Arts and Sciences, Los Angeles, California) — 42

2.3. Pathé, *The Legend of Lake Desolation*, 1911, *Moving Picture World* (July 29, 1911) — 47

2.4. Vitagraph, *The Better Man*, 1912 (George Eastman Museum, Rochester, New York) — 49

2.5. American Film, *The Ranchman's Vengeance*, 1911 (EYE Museum, Amsterdam) — 50

2.6. *Mexican Joan of Arc*, 1911, *Moving Picture World* (July 15, 1911): 19 — 52

2.7. Pathé, *For the Squaw*, 1911 (EYE Museum, Amsterdam), *Film Index* (June 17, 1911): 13 — 55

2.8. Essanay, *A Pal's Oath*, 1911 (US Library of Congress, Washington, DC) — 60

2.9. Essanay, *A Wife of the Hills*, 1912 (EYE Museum, Amsterdam) — 61

2.10. Essanay, *Broncho Billy's Christmas Dinner*, 1911 (EYE Museum, Amsterdam), *Moving Picture World* (December 30, 1911): 1082 — 63

xiv ILLUSTRATIONS

2.11. Vitagraph, *The Craven*, 1912 (EYE Museum, Amsterdam)   64

2.12. Vitagraph, *How States Are Made*, 1912 (EYE Museum, Amsterdam)   65

W2.1. *Life on the Circle Ranch in California*, 1912 (UCLA Film & Television Archive, Los Angeles, California)   69

W2.2. Northern Pacific Railroad map, 1885 (Norman B. Leventhal Map Center, Boston Public Library)   70

3.1. Bison-101, *The Lieutenant's Last Fight*, 1912 (EYE Museum, Amsterdam)   74

3.2. Bison-101, *The Indian Massacre*, 1912 (David Shepard, Film Preservation Associates)   76

3.3. Bison-101, *The Invaders*, 1912 (US Library of Congress, Washington, DC)   77

3.4. Kay-Bee, *Custer's Last Fight*, 1912, *Moving Picture World* (June 22, 1912): 1116   78

3.5. American Film, *The Fall of Black Hawk*, 1912, *Moving Picture World* (July 6, 1912)   80

3.6. Universal-Bison, *The Massacre of the Fourth Cavalry*, 1912, *Moving Picture World* (November 23, 1912)   81

3.7. Kay-Bee, *The Last of the Line*, 1914 (Museum of Modern Art, New York)   85

3.8. Famous Players–Lasky, *The Squaw Man*, 1914, *Moving Picture World* (February 28, 1914)   91

W3.1. Edward A. Salisbury, *Wild Animal Life in America*, 1915 (Academy of Motion Picture Arts and Sciences, Los Angeles, California)   96

4.1. Paramount-Artcraft, *The Silent Man*, 1917 (US Library of Congress, Washington, DC)   99

4.2. "In the Frame of Public Favor," *Chicago Sunday Tribune* (December 12, 1915): 5.3   106

4.3. Triangle, *Hell's Hinges*, 1916 (EYE Museum, Amsterdam)   107

4.4. Triangle ad, *Moving Picture World*, October 21, 1916   109

4.5. Paramount-Artcraft, *The Narrow Trail*, 1917 (George Eastman Museum, Rochester, New York)   114

4.6. Paramount-Artcraft, *The Narrow Trail*, 1917 (George Eastman Museum, Rochester, New York)   115

4.7. Triangle, *The Aryan*, 1916 (Museo dei Cine Pablo C. Ducrós Hicken, Buenos Aires, Argentina)   119

4.8. Triangle, *The Aryan*, 1916 (Museo dei Cine Pablo C. Ducrós Hicken, Buenos Aires, Argentina)   120

W4.1. Essanay, *Lake Tahoe, Land of the Sky*, 1916 (US Library of Congress, Washington, DC)   125

5.1.	Fox, *Straight Shooting*, 1917 (Kino Lorber/Universal)	130
5.2.	Fox, *Straight Shooting*, 1917 (Kino Lorber/Universal)	132
5.3.	Fox, *Hell Bent*, 1918 (Kino Lorber/Universal)	136
5.4.	Selig, *Legal Advice*, 1916 (US Library of Congress, Washington, DC)	141
5.5.	Selig ad, *Moving Picture World*, July 24, 1915	143
5.6.	Tom Mix in Fox, *Treat 'Em Rough*, 1919, (*Illinois State Journal* [January 12, 1919])	146
5.7.	Triangle, *The Good Bad-Man*, 1916 (San Francisco Film Festival/ Cinémathèque française/)	151
5.8.	Triangle, *The Half-Breed*, 1916 (San Francisco Film Festival/Cinémathèque française)	154
5.9.	Triangle, *The Half-Breed*, 1916 (San Francisco Film Festival/Cinémathèque française)	155
A1.1.	Biograph, *The Tourists*, 1912 (Museum of Modern Art, New York)	161

Introduction

"Today we are dividing the lands of the native Indians into States, counties, and townships. We are driving off from their property the game upon which they live, by railroads. We tell them plainly they must give up their homes and property, and live upon corners of their own territories, because they are in the way of our civilization."

Ex-Governor Horatio Seymour, "Letter to the Working Men at Rochester," *New York Times* (6 August 1870), 5

"It [US policy toward Indigenous people] is among the heinous sins of this nation, for which I believe God will one day bring them to judgement."

Diary entry [1841], *Memoirs of John Quincy Adams* (Philadelphia, 1876), 10.492

"There was a West worth knowing. There is a West better worth knowing. Those who were there thirty years ago understand what this means. Those who have been there recently understand full well that the present is quite as seriously misunderstood as the time long since passed. The West is a state of mind which requires adjustment, no matter whether the author is indulging in reminiscence or is reproducing facts which belong to the present. The real result, misleading and untrue to life, is almost invariably the same."

"The Wild West," *Moving Picture World* (24 February 1912): 21

More than 20 years ago, in "Our Country/Whose Country?," the last chapter of *The Red Rooster Scare*, I explored one surprising way the emerging US movie industry tried to compete with French films that were so dominant in exhibition by producing, promoting, and exploiting a set of distinctive films.[1] Those were Wild West films, which *Moving Picture World* claimed, in 1909,

Our Country/Whose Country?. Richard Abel, Oxford University Press. © Oxford University Press 2023.
DOI: 10.1093/oso/9780197744048.003.0001

2 INTRODUCTION

the quintessential "American subject."[2] In two chapters of *Americanizing the Movies and "Movie Mad" Audiences*, I extended this exploration to the Wild West films that proved immensely popular in the first few years of the 1910s.[3] Those now proliferated in a loose grouping of cowboy films, cowgirl films, and Indian pictures that were coalescing into the genre of the *western* (from now on, I'll use this term to cover all of these films).[4] Recently I began to think about how I might take up, revise, and extend this line of research.

Spurring this move initially were three series of programs on early westerns I curated for the Giornate del cinema muto (2015–2017) and another series, co-curated with Diane and Richard Koszarski, devoted to William S. Hart's westerns (2019). The crucial provocation, however, came in my discovery of Roxanne Dunbar-Ortiz's *An Indigenous Peoples' History of the United States*, which led to further readings about the forced removal of Native Americans in the face of settlers encroaching on their traditional lands.[5] Those readings also prodded me to search for maps sketching the shifting locations of Indian tribes as well as the major scouting and pioneer trails going west in the 19th century—all in order to get a better handle on the volatile, violent history of the not-always-unequal confrontation between waves of white settlers and resisting Indigenous peoples on the North American continent. In *The Red Rooster Scare*, "Our Country/Whose Country?" raised this question: Who would win out in the transnational competition between the young US film industry and the many imported French films that initially filled nickelodeons on the American market? For the current book, however, "Our Country/Whose Country?" shifts the focus to the emerging American nation-state. Now the same terms define a radically different question: How did early westerns embody the long years of internal conflict as to who would dominate the continent—the original inhabitants or the European emigrants and their descendants whose expansion westward was being justified by the myth of "American Progress"?

That myth, I now argue, must be reframed as a virulent, unacknowledged form of *settler colonialism*. The concept, in Lorenzo Veracini's abstract definition, involves "the permanent movement and reproduction of communities and the dominance of an exogenous agency over an indigenous one."[6] It is "intimately related to," he argues, but "structurally distinct from . . . both colonialism and migration."[7] The "primary object of settler colonialism," the late Patrick Wolfe asserted more succinctly "is the land itself" or a "ceaseless expansion" governed by an "insatiable dynamic" of the need for more and more land.[8] And that dynamism assumed the *dispensability* of Indigenous peoples and a different vision of their land. In the words of Mark Rifkin, it also meant "recoding land formerly beyond the purview of the U.S. government as intimately embedded in national space" and coercing Indigenous peoples to accept their place in the newly national life of that land.[9] Settler colonialism may not have been unique to the United States, but it arguably served to structure the country's formation through the persistent invasion by Europeans of an immense continent already inhabited by millions of Indigenous peoples. Furthermore, I want to extend the time frame beyond the early Wild West subjects to take in the diverse body of reconfigured westerns released through the late 1910s. Early westerns and their reconfiguration, I argue, provided a narratively cogent justification of settler colonialism that, during Hollywood's emergence as the dominant form of popular culture, could be sold to Americans and non-Americans alike. At the same time, I want to enlarge the lens to include nonfiction travel films, particularly those that depicted tourists journeying into wild areas of the West, specifically the recently established national parks previously inhabited by Indigenous peoples. So, what are the chief tenets of settler colonialism?

(See Figure I.1.) In the early 20th century, continual progress generally was accepted as the dominant narrative of American history, often inflated into

Figure I.1. John Gast, *American Progress*, 1873 chromolithograph (US Library of Congress Prints and Photographs Division)

4   INTRODUCTION

an origin story, the grand narrative of "Manifest Destiny." John L. O'Sullivan may have coined the latter term in 1845, and George H. Hill, as "Yankee Hill," popularized it a year later in a stage routine.[10] But its classic articulation came decades later in Frederick Jackson Turner's "Significance of the Frontier in American History" (1893).[11] For Turner, put far too simply, white emigrants moved westward across the North American continent, crossing one frontier after another, transformed in the process into new Americans allegedly "born of a free land." Walter Prescott Webb, in *The Great Plains* (1931), then gave Turner's thesis a more specific location in the Midwest and West, describing how new technologies—from railroads and irrigation systems to repeating rifles and revolvers and steel plows—supported by the 1863 Homestead Act, allowed ranchers, farmers, and other settlers to subdue, enclose, and "civilize" the "blank space" of what often seemed a hostile landscape.[12] (See Figure I.2.) The 1862 Railroad Act was equally crucial because it granted to railroad companies huge swaths of land that displaced native peoples, could be sold to speculators and then to settlers, and "tipped the balance of power" in the "desperate struggle of control of the West."[13] For an iconic painting, a stunningly condensed vision of this westward expansion, see John Gast's *American Progress* (1872), commissioned originally for George A. Crofutt's travel guides (1878–1879).[14] A dark version of this progress narrative envisioned an eventual environmental decline and drew at least partly, according to William Cronon, on the emerging concept of scientific ecology.[15] An early pioneer in the field, Frederic Clements, in *Plant Succession* (1916), for instance, foresaw that decline, describing the grasslands of the Great Plains as a "climax community" disrupted so severely by those new Americans, not only turning "native flora and fauna into a dwindling resource" for Indigenous peoples but also creating conditions that eventually would lead to the Dust Bowl of the 1930s.[16] This attention to the ecology of the land certainly marks westerns that pitted different groups of settlers against one another in their expropriation of a rich, supposedly "empty land," but it is strikingly absent in most travel films.

More specifically, what questions and issues provoked by settler colonialism are particularly relevant for this study of early American films? Patricia Nelson Limerick posed a crucial one: What exactly do we mean by the West? In the pages that follow, I generally accept her own answer: "the trans-Mississippi West."[17] That is, half of the North American continent stretching from the Mississippi River to the West Coast, but especially focused on the Great Plains and Rocky Mountains region. At the same time,

Figure I.2. Railroad land grant map, 1878 (Norman B. Leventhal Map Center, Boston Public Library)

6 INTRODUCTION

the films selected for analysis in this study will involve forays into other regions: the colonial West, the trans-Appalachian West, the Old Northwest, the Old Southwest, and California. For Native Americans and Mexicans, however, the "West" was a meaningless concept for a land they knew as "home." And that home encompassed "a remarkable convergence of languages" and peoples.[18] One group, in John Mack Faragher's words, included "thousands of indigenous communities in a variety of finely tuned adaptations to environmental possibilities and constraints, with over two hundred distinct languages and thousands of dialects."[19] Another, according to Jay Gitlin, was the French *métis* culture based on "a network of Indian alliances" to support its principal commerce, fur trading, in the Great Lakes and Mississippi Valley region.[20] A third was the network of Spanish-Mexican settlements in the Southwest, comprising villages and towns, Faragher added, with "a strong collective sense of community," unlike the scattered homesteads of most English settlements that encouraged individualism.[21] In each case, the boundaries between these settlements created what Gitlin called "alternate" frontiers.[22]

Like Turner's idea of a singular frontier, the mainstream of American culture in the late 19th and early 20th centuries reduced and condensed this historical multiplicity into more or less stable concepts. Perhaps the most significant of those, according to the tenets of "race theory" at the time,[23] assumed the supremacy of white male European emigrants as a new breed of Anglo-Saxon and a culminating figure in "race-history."[24] In an 1823 Supreme Court decision, Chief Justice John Marshall codified those tenets in *legal* terms, defined as the "Christian doctrine of discovery."[25] That, in turn, meant the elimination of the incredibly diverse Indigenous peoples through outright extermination, severely limited legal rights, deportation to reservations, and the "civilizing" strictures of forced assimilation through boarding school "education" and religious conversion.[26] From a white settler perspective, the infinity of bands, clans, villages, and people was subsumed within a single generic category, *Indian*.[27] Similarly, that "theory" meant the subordination of early Spanish landowners and especially Mexicans who, harassed by the Diaz regime, migrated in ever greater numbers into the American Southwest as an underclass of laborers in the late 19th and early 20th centuries.[28] It also meant the demonization of other "races," notably Chinese immigrants taken in as cheap expendable labor (prior to the Exclusion Act of 1882), especially for work on building the western half of the continental railroad.[29] At the same time, it often simply erased the presence of African American cowboys, who, perhaps lured by the dismantling of Reconstruction and the rise of Jim Crow laws, numbered at least 5,000 of all those herding cattle on the plains in the late 19th century.[30] Presuming that Indigenous peoples did not work "but depended instead on the spontaneous production of nature to supply almost all their wants,"[31] the 1863 Homestead Act transformed much of the land they shared or fought over, actually a form of "commons," into property for settlers to possess, enclose, and inhabit.[32] The "unimaginable natural wealth" of that newly freed land was then open to exploitation from farming and ranching to profiting from fur trading, logging, gold mining, and oil extraction.[33] (See Figure I.3.) For an iconic image of this "paradise" of wealth, see Emanuel Leutze's mural in the US Capitol, "Westward the Course of Empire Takes Its Way [Westward Ho!]" (1862).[34] This mural was so familiar that an 1898 poster for Buffalo Bill's Wild West inserted the legendary showman as its central figure.[35] What wilderness remained, especially in the newly legislated national parks, all

Figure I.3. Emanuel Leutze, *Westward the Course of Empire Takes Its Way [Westward Ho!]*, 1861 mural study (Smithsonian American Art Museum, Bequest of Sara Carr Upton)

8   INTRODUCTION

formerly occupied by Indigenous peoples, now became spectacular scenic landscapes for tourists to consume as marvelous vistas.

So, what happens to our sense of early American cinema history if we put "civilized" white settlers, confronting both external and internal threats, at the center of Wild West subjects? My argument is that early westerns constituted a singular collection of artifacts, products, and symptoms of early 20th-century American culture for they staged a remarkably contested vision of *our country*'s westward expansion across the continent during the 19th century. Moreover, they revealed a historical transformation in American culture by recapitulating what American Progress came to mean in three different stages, one marked by continuity, the others by a break.[36] In the first two stages in particular, they indulged in a kind of nostalgia for a Jeffersonian ideal of settlers as independent, self-sufficient people "civilizing" the resource-rich land of a "New World."

Initially, early westerns tracked settlers moving westward across the Appalachians, the Great Plains, and the Rockies to California. Their often illegal seizure of "empty land" provoked the continual resistance of Indigenous peoples and later Mexicans.[37] Some even began to indulge in the entrenched notion of nostalgic empathy for the Indian as the "Vanishing American."[38] In the early 1910s, increasingly popular westerns spun ever more diverse tales, articulating, as Nanna Verhoeff writes, the fraught relations of "a temporal frontier between, on the one hand, a past that is closed off and therefore instantaneously becomes the object of idealization and mythification, and, on the other hand, the uncertain future."[39] In Indian pictures, Indigenous peoples ranged from cruel devious savages or their opposite, "Noble Savages," to victims of violent attacks by whites, with others acting as "in-between" figures unable to survive in the clash of opposing cultures and fewer as "mixed-descent peoples" partnered for the purposes of security and/or advantage.[40] Mexicans—and, in rare instances, Chinese—tended to take positions across a similar spectrum.[41] In cowboy and cowgirl films, while "ordinary" characters became heroes and heroines fighting outlaws, a bandit like Broncho Billy could undergo a transformation into a "good badman." The mid to late 1910s, then, saw the most crucial shift, even a kind of rupture, as Indian pictures and cowgirl films nearly disappeared and white male figures, embodied by movie stars, dominated several popular series, from shorts to features. In different ways, William S. Hart and Harry Carey reinvented the "good badman" as a stoic, if sometimes troubled, figure of virile masculinity. By contrast, in cowboy stories of often comic romance, Tom Mix not only indulged in dangerous stunts as an expert horseman but also donned costumes that made him a fashionable icon for an emerging consumer society. In just a few films, Douglas Fairbanks turned the myth of American Progress on its head in ramshackle parodies, ever sporting a nonchalant grin of effortless self-confidence. However diverse were these latter stories, nearly all assumed the context of a settled white community, only occasionally still harassed by Indians or Mexicans; instead, most of those now served as secondary characters or crowds of extras. Throughout these decades, and often in parallel, travel films increasingly imagined a vision of the West, especially the allegedly virgin wildernesses of the national parks, that consistently now created a fantasy space of escape for spectators as virtual tourists as well as for those who could afford to travel.[42]

A note is needed for the primary sources for this book's argument, which the COVID-19 pandemic limited to some extent. For the secondary sources consulted, please see the Bibliography. With on-site research compromised, certain archives were particularly important for their recent efforts to digitize prints and, as primary sources in this study, for their generosity in giving access to digital files of numerous early westerns. Complementing those digital files were DVDs of relevant film titles, both westerns and travel films, notably in the *Treasures* series produced by the National Film Preservation Foundation. Useful supplements to those were my own detailed notes on archive prints screened at various times in the past. In terms of paper documents, the Media History Digital Library gave ready access to articles, reviews, and ads dealing with early westerns and travel pictures published in the trade press at the time. Less useful—especially for any sense of actual movie audience reception—were local and regional newspapers, that is, until reviews of and articles on films began to appear with some frequency and regularity in the mid-1910s. Finally, because so many of these early westerns, as well as travel films, did not survive, recovering them for "viewing" and analysis through the plethora of synopses from trade press publicity material, reviews, and exhibitor comments became a notable feature of this book.

I have carved the sections of this book into two interconnected pathways. The primary path links together five chapters that analyze early western films framed by the concept of settler colonialism. The first chapter surveys the initial westerns produced from 1903 to 1910 as "white supremacist entertainments"[43] within the historical context of 19th-century dime novels, paintings, Wild West shows, plays, world's fairs, and photographs, all of which constitute a rich storehouse of stories and images. It sketches

10 INTRODUCTION

out a series of tropes, including the nostalgic concept of the "Vanishing American," most of which soon came to characterize westerns. The second chapter analyzes the many one-reel cowboy films, cowgirl films, and Indian pictures that were so popular from 1910 to 1913. The tropes introduced previously, along with another introducing the "good badman," serve to organize and examine what can only be a representative selection of those countless films. This selection includes a wide variety of narratives as well as some surprising counternarratives, such as those envisioning interracial marriage, to the myth of American Progress that excluded threatening non-white "aliens." The third chapter shifts the focus to early multiple-reel westerns, from 1912 through 1914, with Indian pictures particularly conspicuous. While some offered a rationale for Native American resistance to the advancing settlers, a few even admitted that the latter were invading and illegally seizing Indian lands.

The fourth chapter marks a significant break, as films featuring both Indians and Mexicans as well as central female characters tended to disappear. Instead, westerns with white male movie stars promoted the ideology of not only white supremacy but also superior white masculinity. Epitomizing this break was Williams S. Hart, one of the top five stars between 1914 and 1918. Concluding this critique of Hart's reconfigured "good badman" of sometimes cruel authority is the analysis of a restored print of the long-thought-lost film, *The Aryan* (1916)." The fifth chapter extends that analysis, taking up the contemporaneous, but contrasting westerns of Harry Carey, Tom Mix, and Douglas Fairbanks from 1915 to 1918. In one way or another, nearly all of their films are set in settled white communities, and both heroic cowboys and non-white "aliens" could be sent up in comedies or parodies. The second pathway links together four short sidebars that examine early travel films within the same conceptual frame and often form close links with westerns. During the first two decades of the 20th century, whether in shorts or features, these films offered virtual tours coincident with the "See America First" movement.

"History permits us to be responsible," Timothy Snyder writes, perhaps not for everything but at least for something.[44] If settler colonialism offers an invaluable lens for re-viewing early westerns as a uniquely American cultural form that sharply exposed the complexities and contradictions of "Manifest Destiny" in the 19th and early 20th centuries, then this book's aim is to urge a radical reconsideration of our conception of early American cinema. It seeks to prod historians and other researchers to return to the ideological foundations of *our* national cinema and sift through the silt of forgetting to find new ways to argue for the incomparable significance of early westerns as well as travel films in the history of American culture. The aim also, in the current troubled times, is to provoke a teachable moment for all those interested in learning how to think more critically about United States history and culture and to question who was and who still may be included and excluded in the term *our*. That moment, I have to confess, includes a more grounded understanding of my own position in *our* history. For the well-worn tracks of early pioneers moving westward certainly lured me from a home in northeastern Ohio to an initial undergraduate study of forestry and wildlife management in Utah and then to five summers of work for the US Forest Service in the Rocky Mountains and California Sierras. Yet hardly ever was I aware that Indigenous peoples and Mexicans once inhabited the landscapes I grew to love. In writing this book, then, "Our Country/Whose Country?" also became personal in this equally concise reformulation: "Who was/am I?"

1

Wild West Subjects to 1910

Even in the earliest Wild West subjects, the lens of settler colonialism reveals major tropes that will become characteristic of westerns in their portrayal of the expansion of *our country* across the North American continent. Single and split-reel fiction films initially may not have captured the vistas of plains and mountains depicted in the large historical paintings and murals described in the Introduction. After all, up to 1904, those companies producing motion pictures for sale or rental were located chiefly in or around New York (Edison, AM&B), Philadelphia (Lubin), and Chicago (Selig Polyscope). Moreover, their cameras, especially the bulky Biograph camera (using 68mm filmstock until 1903), kept them from venturing beyond their spartan studios, except for shooting travel films. The stories and characters that had long circulated in popular dime novels, however, proved a welcome source of inspiration.

One figure was particularly notable. Kit Carson (1809–1868) was known as a trail-blazing hunter, trapper, scout, and Indian fighter whose frontier adventures led him frequently across the plains and into the western mountains in the mid-19th century. He had guided John Charles Frémont on no fewer than three expeditions (1842, 1843, 1845) through the Rocky Mountains into California on the Oregon and Santa Fe trails.[1] Together they mounted an uprising against Mexico and prepared the way for California to become a state. Later the frontiersman led several campaigns against the Apaches, Navajos, and Kiowas in what became New Mexico.[2] Carson's legendary stature as an American pioneer came largely from dime novels such as *Kit Carson, the Prince of the Gold Hunters* (1849) and *The Prairie Flower, or the Adventures of the Far West* (1849) as well as his "memoir," *The Life and Adventures of Kit Carson, the Nestor of the Rocky Mountains* (1858).[3] Scores of novels featuring his fictional exploits were published and republished through the turn of the century. Even in its book cover design, *The Fighting Trapper, Kit Carson to the Rescue* (1874), for instance, graphically depicts

Our Country/Whose Country?. Richard Abel, Oxford University Press. © Oxford University Press 2023.
DOI: 10.1093/oso/9780197744048.003.0002

his skill at hand-to-hand combat (see Figure 1.1).[4] Perhaps it is no wonder that AM&B made him the hero of its early story films, *Kit Carson* and *The Pioneers* (both 1903), shot with a more standardized camera (using 35mm filmstock) in the Adirondack Mountains, "amid scenery of the wildest natural beauty and enacted with the greatest fidelity to the original."[5]

Kit Carson tells an oft repeated tale of multiple captures and escapes in 10 tableaux.[6] A "band of painted Indians" follow the trail of Carson and a companion while the latter are trapping in an unspecified western wilderness.[7] The Indians attack at night, kill the other trapper, and seize Carson. Crossing a fallen log over a stream, he leaps into the water and escapes. Fleeing the Indians in a canoe, he is ambushed downstream and taken to the Indians' village, where he is tied to a tree and endures threats and tortures. At night an "Indian maiden, moved to compassion," frees him to escape a second time. The last tableau simply has Carson return to his wife and children and their "rude log cabin." Common stereotypes abound in this long familiar story of the repeated capture and rescue of whites. Carson and his companion assume the right to invade this wilderness territory inhabited by Indians; the generic Indian warriors are hostile, devious, and cruel; but a young Indian woman betrays her people and frees the white man. What happens to her is of no apparent interest and left unclear. In a move typical of mythmaking, the tale ignores the historical record. Specifically, it elides Carson's real-life attacks on Indigenous peoples: he especially hated the Blackfeet, even before leading campaigns against native peoples in the Southwest. But it also erases his relations with Indigenous women. For, historically, he was married to two Indian wives and one "elite Hispano" wife who survived him.[8] When Carson returns home in the film, however, it cannot be to an Indian or Mexican family but to a white family at the center of American "civilization."

The Pioneers tells an even more gruesome story, shortened into six tableaux.[9] It begins with the domestic scene of a settler family living in a log cabin on land carved out of an anomalous wooded wilderness—rarely do any of these films mention from whence these settlers have come. A band of Indians attack the cabin, set it on fire, and then murder all of the family except for a little girl, who is taken captive. Kit Carson and several companions chance upon "the ruins of the cabin and the mutilated bodies, and vow an oath of vengeance." They track the Indians across the mountains, engage them in a fierce fight, and rescue the little girl. This film depicts the settlers

Figure 1.1 *The Fighting Trapper, Kit Carson to the Rescue*, 1874 (*The House of Beadle and Adams*, 1950)

as an "innocent," unthreatening domestic white family. The Indians, however, seem to appear out of nowhere, attack allegedly without motive, and kill the family with unusual cruelty—the use of the term *mutilation* likely implies scalping. That cruelty seems to justify Carson's retaliatory vengeance, although, from the 17th century on, white settlers in the British colonies engaged in scalping noncombatants as often as did Indigenous peoples. Not only does the film ignore what happens to the little girl after her rescue, but it also assumes, despite historical evidence, that Carson and his fellows are equally "innocent," even though they likely were acting as scouts preparing the way for more settlers to encroach on and "civilize" a territory, a form of commons, already inhabited and often shared by Indigenous peoples.

An even earlier frontiersman often featured in dime novels was Daniel Boone (1734–1820). Boone was best known for opening a trail through Maryland's Cumberland Gap in the Appalachians,[10] but less known for being "hired by land speculators," after he had served in the Seven Years War, to encourage settlers to invade the commons of traditional Indian hunting grounds in Ohio Country and, specifically, what became Kentucky.[11] During the Revolutionary War, as many Indian tribes now were allied with the British in Kentucky, Boone had to rescue his daughter Jemima who was captured by a Cherokee-Shawnee war party.[12] Less than two years later, on a hunting expedition, he himself was captured by Shawnees and adopted (a common practice that also could include enslavement, even in intertribal conflicts, especially after the forced migration of tribes in the East into the Great Lakes region and eventually onto the Great Plains)[13] but eventually escaped to defend his Boonesboro settlement against an Indian siege.[14] Dime novels such as *Life & Times of Col. Daniel Boone* (1859) and *Boone, the Hunter* (1873) recounted some of these and other episodes.[15] In short, Boone was a perfect example of the "free white men," writes Jon Coleman, who "pursued game, land, profit, and celebrity in the name of agrarian domesticity."[16] In late 1906, Edison began filming *Daniel Boone* (1907), from a scenario based on these dime novel stories by way of the 19th-century stage play, *Daniel Boone: on the Trail*, that a stock company at the time was still performing to packed houses in the South.[17] Shot in Bronx Park in the dead of winter, the film tells a complicated story that has Boone off on a hunting expedition while Indians attack his cabin and abduct his two daughters.[18] While Boone and a friend search separately for the girls, an "Indian maiden" (whom one daughter had aided in the opening scene) helps that daughter to ride away and find her father's

16 OUR COUNTRY/WHOSE COUNTRY?

friend. Meanwhile, the enraged Indians capture Boone, tie him to a tree, and torture him. While his friend arrives to scare off most of the Indians, Boone rescues his other daughter and kills the chief in hand-to-hand combat. In the end, however, this story of frontier captivity and escape leaves open the question of what kind of settler family remains after the men and two girls are reunited.[19] In the context of the early 20th century, it also focuses solely on the Indians as "savages" and excludes any mention of the British with whom they were allied in 1778.

Even though the filming location ranged from the Adirondacks to a New York City borough, *Kit Carson, The Pioneers,* and *Daniel Boone* all told stories of early frontiersmen leading settlers westward across the continent in the face of Indian resistance. Soon, a new figure replaced such historical frontiersmen: the cowboy.[20] Initially ignored in large historical paintings,[21] the cowboy had emerged as a crucial white hero in fiction by the 1890s, namely in Owen Wister's essay, "The Evolution of the Cowpuncher."[22] Only the "Anglo-Saxon" male, wrote Wister, had "the spirit of adventure, courage, and self-sufficiency" needed to survive in the American West. Among the early westerns with recognizable cowboy heroes, the most intriguing was Edison's *The Life of a Cowboy* (1906). Probably based on a stage play, it was filmed on Staten Island but promoted as having "real cowboys and Indians" in a "stirring western drama."[23] The opening scene in the Big Horn saloon introduces an unusual mix of characters: a Mexican at the bar, an "old Indian" whose daughter keeps him from drinking, a cowboy who kicks the Mexican out of the saloon, and rowdy cowboys who make a "tenderfoot" dance and force him to give money to a Salvation Army girl.[24] The next scene begins to develop a story as a stagecoach stops by a ranch, the cowboy welcomes a young lady that he knows, and he again shoves aside the Mexican who has taken an interest in her. But the film pauses here to stage a spectacle of "cowboy sports": trick riding, lassoing (the tenderfoot is humiliated again), and wrestling. The story resumes after the stagecoach leaves the ranch, as Indians attack and wound the driver, and the Mexican and his gang quickly follow and abduct the young lady. Alerted by the driver, the cowboy leads a posse in pursuit of the Indians and then rescues the woman, whom the Mexican has set on a galloping horse. In the final scene, the Mexican stalks the couple and is about to shoot the cowboy when the Indian girl reappears and plugs him with her own pistol. This film creates a rather contradictory world that condenses past and present into an entertaining palimpsest as well as the geographical regions of the northern plains and Southwest. Here, a "civilized" white community (the Salvation Army girl and tenderfoot, the ranch with its cowboy sports) is still threatened by hostile Indians but even more so by Mexicans. It also repeats the familiar plot device of having an "Indian maiden," strangely separate from the marauding Indians, save the central white figures, in this case a romantic couple.[25]

Now, along with the cowboy, another trope began to emerge in westerns as well: actual location filming in the mountains of the West. The company responsible was Selig Polyscope, whose western agent, H. H. Buckwalter, shot several story films around Colorado Springs. One, *The Hold-Up of the Leadville Stage* (1905), the company claimed, reenacted an actual robbery of a stagecoach strongbox (presumably filled with a mine company's profits) from 25 years before.[26] The story involves an outlaw gang planning and executing the hold-up, gunning down a child who tries to flee, their pursuit by a posse, and their capture. All of the robbers are shot and killed, except for one survivor. Much of the first part of the film, however, tracks the stagecoach (in a dozen shots) into and through the mountains toward the mining town and, according to a Selig circular, offers a tour of Colorado scenery already familiar in the company's earlier travel films (see Touring the West 1). Consequently, in the context of what Glenn Adamson notes was an emerging "cult of authenticity,"[27] *The Hold-Up of the Leadville Stage* promoted a double sense of authenticity or truth claims. While it depicted the "true events that made Colorado famous," it also insisted that the company took the trouble to film those events in the very landscape of the robbery.[28] Yet, perhaps even more important, this unusual attention to spectacular scenery turned the recent history of a sensational crime into an analogous kind of tourist attraction.[29] (See Figure 1.2.) Buckwalter himself claimed that he wanted to shoot "just enough of Ute Pass . . . Cheyenne Canon and Bear Creek to awaken a desire to see the scenery in reality."[30]

For the next year or two, Buckwalter, along with G. M. Anderson, continued to produce western subjects for Selig in Colorado. *The Bandit King* (1907), for instance, has an outlaw gang first rob a stagecoach of its Wells Fargo mining gold and then steal more gold and treasury notes from a bank.[31] A horseback ride through steep mountains leads to the initial robbery, a lengthy chase by a sheriff's posse, and then the second theft, which ends in the outlaws' deaths. Shot in similar locations around the town of Golden, *The Girl from Montana* (1907), however, introduces a twist on the usual story

Figure 1.2 AM&B, *From Leadville to Aspen: Hold-Up in the Rockies*, 1906 (George Eastman Museum, Rochester, New York)

that will become a trope in later films.[32] Here, it is a cowgirl (played by the horsewoman Pansy Perry) who comes to the rescue, saving her cowboy lover from death and holding off an angry mob with her guns.[33] In *Western Justice* (1907), a "real old-fashioned Bad Man" shoots a town marshal who tries to arrest him. The latter's daughter (probably Pansy Perry again) finds her father left dead in the street and gathers a posse of ranching friends and neighbors to pursue the killer. Led by the young woman, the posse follows the Bad Man into the mountains on a "rocky and precipitous trail" and finally corners him in a deserted shepherd's hut, where he is shot through the heart.[34] In ads for *Western Justice*, Selig boasted that rival companies like Edison could not come close to matching its "magnificent scenic effects," scornfully noting they were confined to "some backyards in the East."[35]

Of the tropes introduced in these Wild West subjects, hardly any of which survive except in prints of poor quality, a number bear further analysis. One has to do with how the North American continent was defined and who would win out in the violent struggles over control of the land. In several early films, the landscape appeared as an untamed wilderness in which Indians as non-white aliens resisted frontiersmen and settlers, especially in captivity narratives, as the latter fought to clear and subdue the land and to exploit its resources. That land may already have been tamed and settled in *The Life of a Cowboy*, but Mexicans, along with Indians, still could threaten. In other westerns, the effort to reproduce something similar to those 19th-century paintings and murals discussed in the Introduction led Selig to engage in filming on location in the West. Especially telling in all of its films shot in Colorado, however, Indigenous peoples had already vanished. The wilderness they once inhabited now served, for whites, a double purpose. First, as a supposedly uninhabited natural landscape, it could lure an audience of virtual tourists, as in some early travel films, to immerse themselves in its spectacular scenery. Second, it could be envisioned as a wide-open, empty space for expropriation. Settlers (from wherever) built more or less stable small communities, extracted gold from mines, herded cattle on ranches, and, as cowboys and cowgirls, took to skillfully riding horses and wielding revolvers and rifles, threatened mainly by renegade outlaws.

Another trope has to do with how the central figures were defined in this ongoing struggle over land. Whites appeared as sympathetic settler families and couples who had every right to take over land previously inhabited by Indians. Whether frontiersmen, cowboys, lawmen, or vigilantes, leading male figures acted as fathers, lovers, and avengers. Leading female figures, by contrast, acted as daughters as well as lovers. In either case, closely linked to families, they all deflected attention to or awareness of the brutal expropriation of Indigenous peoples' lands. Abetting that deflection were either "bad men" who preyed on supposedly legitimate miners or illegitimate mobs who threatened "innocent" law-abiding communities. Indians, by contrast, were not defined in terms of families—nor were Mexicans.[36] Instead, Indians were either vicious male warriors attacking the invading whites or else an Indian maiden acting alone and separately from those warriors. As in prior captivity fiction, the Indian maiden betrayed her own people to rescue captured whites and restore them to their settler communities. Unlike others of her tribe, she showed compassion for both white men and women, especially girls of her own age. Yet, however selfless and dangerous were her actions, they served to maintain the assumed superiority of the white "race." In short, at least in these early films, only the settlers were depicted as families taking shape through the contestation over land.[37] If Indian and Mexican men seemed not to have

20   OUR COUNTRY/WHOSE COUNTRY?

families, Indian maidens guaranteed a future for white families. Finally, per-sistent, often extreme violence marked the fraught relations between whites and Indians or Mexicans. Yet it also animated the conflicts among whites that pitted good men and women against "bad men." In short, hardly ever ab-sent from these Wild West subjects, violence was a crucial determining force usually masked in the myth of "Manifest Destiny"—and long a fundamental tenet of American national identity.[38]

The Landscape and Its Peoples Expand

In early 1908, Selig claimed that western subjects were ever more alluring attractions for movie audiences: "The popularity of Western romance will never exhaust itself. The increasing population of the West is causing a gradual extrication of daring adventure and makes a reproduction of actual occurrences all the more valuable."[39] Over the course of the next two years, western subjects proliferated, with those from Selig and Essanay notable for being filmed on location in the West and those from Biograph for featuring Indians as the main characters. Typically, the stories were familiar and full of melodramatic conflict, occasionally with touches of originality. White characters, not surprisingly, usually were central and identified as cowboys, cowgirls (in ever greater numbers), ranchers, miners, or other kinds of settlers. They also often had good Anglo-Saxon names. Yet Indigenous peo-ples now could play important roles and not only as hostiles. In the context of their historical eradication or subjugation, nostalgically idealized as the Vanishing American, they also could act as uneasy models of assimilation (e.g., Indian maidens) that still ensured the superiority of whites.[40] With rare exceptions, especially in films where pioneers were attacked crossing the Great Plains, the hostiles simply became generic male warriors.[41] Mexicans or Mexican Americans also appeared more frequently, typically as jealous, violent villains. They also had no specific identity beyond stereotypical names like Pedro. Despite a long history of oppression by whites, the latter—Wister's "small, deceitful aliens"—remained a nasty threat. And that threat loomed ever larger in the few years leading up to the Mexican Revolution that broke out in 1910. Finally, a new figure emerged, that of the US Cavalry, already prominent in Buffalo Bill's Wild West, an icon of federal power that could supersede the local authority of a lawful sheriff or a vengeful band of vigilantes.

An increasingly prominent subject was the pioneer story of a captured white woman and her escape or rescue. In Edison's *Pioneers Crossing the Plains in '49* (1908), a young woman joins her family in a prairie schooner traveling westward in search of gold.[42] Perhaps drawing on paintings such as Carl Wimar's *The Attack on an Emigrant Train* (1856), this film has Indians attack the prairie schooner and seize the woman, after killing everyone else.[43] When news reaches her lover, who has had to stay behind in the East, he goes in search of her but is captured and (ala Mazeppa) tied to a wild horse.[44] Meanwhile the woman escapes the Indian camp and now rides to his rescue and their reunion. Although praised more for its scenery than its action,[45] this film was not shot in the West, unlike Selig's *The Cowboy's Baby* (1908), which followed Buckwalter's earlier production methods in Colorado.[46] After hostile Indian warriors attack and overwhelm a wagon train on the western plains, a band of cowboys drives them off into the mountains, and one, Joe Dayton, finds a baby as the lone pioneer survivor. Soon Joe marries his neighbor's daughter, who agrees to become the orphan's mother. A "wealthy Mexican" who has been courting her, however, has hirelings steal the baby from the negligent care of a Chinese servant. Joe and his cowboys pursue the Mexicans, rescue the crying baby after the infant is tossed into a river, and then "mete out swift Western justice." That this film piles on one set of villains after another is remarkable, even if all three non-white "aliens" cannot escape their roles as familiar cultural stereotypes. Yet historically, whether Indian, Mexican (rich and poor), or Chinese, each did pose an obstacle to whites' efforts to control and exploit the land. Moreover, *The Cowboy's Baby* made custody of the orphaned child crucial to the formation of a newly restructured settler family.

Also shot in the East, Vitagraph's *Children of the Plains* (1909) tells a different, more surprising story of reunion.[47] Again, Indians massacre a wagon train and capture a surviving little girl; US Army soldiers soon find her sister alive and take her to their fort. Twelve years later, the same Indians happen to seize the rescued young woman who, in their camp, recognizes the locket of her long-lost sister. After the two young women escape and reach the fort in the nick of time, the film strangely ignores the question of how the first sister so quickly could recover an inner white identity.[48] That white characters could so easily slough off "Indianness" as a masquerade created a striking parallel to the white actors, on stage as well as in films, who also could simply remove blackface makeup.[49] Aiding in that transformation, of course, was the casting of an unknown white actress who, after her rescue, perhaps

22   OUR COUNTRY/WHOSE COUNTRY?

lightened her redface makeup.[50] Yet, in another instance of how a frontier myth could mask historical practice, evidence suggested that captured white settlers, especially when young, more often than not later chose to remain with their Indian abductors rather than return to a white community that now seemed alien.[51]

Several other Selig films had white settlers or ranchers already claiming and inhabiting Indian territory. *In Old Arizona* (1909) settles a rancher, not in Wister's "clean cattle country," but "in the very heart of the Apache country" in the Southwest.[52] Here, it is a Mexican horse trader who provokes the native inhabitants to go on the warpath.[53] The Apaches attack a band of cowboys protecting the rancher's daughter, but the cavalry arrives in time to scatter them and drag the Mexican back to the fort for punishment. *On the Warpath* (1909) has two white families settled in forested foothills, with the son of one, Jim Wayman, in love with the daughter of the other, Betty Price.[54] A "half-breed Indian scout," Bill Horn, tries to court Betty and is rebuffed; full of "all the hatred and jealous rage of his Indian nature" (according to Selig's description), he tries to seize Betty but "her Indian maid," like others before her, thwarts him.[55] When Horn then persuades "a band of real Sioux" to attack the settlers,[56] Jim's own "friendly Indian" learns of their plan and joins the two families in defending one of the log cabins. Jim and his friend escape and bring a nearby troop of cavalry to rescue the whites. "With a perfect whirlwind of fire pouring from their carbines," the cavalry "completely annihilates the murderous band of bloodthirsty savages." This time, however, Selig's racist publicity says nothing about what happens to either the "friendly Indian" or "Indian maid" and merely implies that Jim and Betty will be married.[57] Both of these films, much like their predecessors, assumed that whites had every right to stake claims on Indian territory and that Indian resistance was nefarious and futile.

That resistance was anything but futile, however, in Selig's *On the Little Big Horn* (1909). Just 15 years earlier, Buffalo Bill's Wild West had begun to include "Custer's Last Stand" as one of its spectacle entertainments, and lithographs of Cassilly Adams's massive painting of the same name hung prominently in saloons across the country.[58] But the Selig film was the first effort to reenact and rewrite the popular memory of this historic event in motion pictures. Led by the "wily 'Rain-in-the-Face,'" the Sioux warriors lure Custer's cavalry into a trap and, despite their escape to higher ground, "the red circle of death closes in about them."[59] Having been arrested two years earlier, "Rain-in-the-Face" now has his revenge. Because it can hardly celebrate this unexpected Indian victory over whites, however, the film introduces a romance involving the Fort Lincoln commander's daughter and a Lt. Glenn, one of Custer's subalterns. In a letter, the daughter pleads with Custer to send Glenn back to the fort for needed supplies, and, although delayed briefly by a roving band of Sioux, he returns with his uniform in shreds and covered in dust to discover that news of the massacre has preceded him. An ambitious production, the climactic battle was staged at the state fairgrounds near Pierre, South Dakota.[60] According to its publicity, the company recruited "more than 400 Indians and two companies of national guardsmen" to perform what amounted to an entertaining reenactment before thousands of spectators. Whether the romance subplot could ever compensate for the US Cavalry's stunning defeat is unclear from Selig's own description, the only thing that remains of this lost film.

If hostile Indians seemed to rise out of the landscape in these Selig films,[61] they continued to be absent in outlaw stories such as Essanay's *The Road Agent* (1909).[62] Here, an Englishman (a Wister hero "gone wrong") and a Mexican are an unlikely pair of stagecoach robbers.[63] After one heist, supposedly based on "a once famous California hold-up," they quarrel over the loot, and the Mexican shoots his fellow thief. Before dying, the Englishman struggles to intercept a sheriff and his posse who have been hunting them. A chase ensues through mountain and desert, until the Mexican, lacking any sense of honor, is "lassoed from his horse and brought to justice."[64] A more "ambitious out-door production," according to the trade press, was Selig's *The Cattle Rustlers* (1908), filmed in and around a big valley in the Rockies.[65] It begins in a saloon with a white rancher offering a reward for the capture of a band of rustlers. Believing they are invulnerable, the rustlers steal more of the rancher's cattle and start rebranding them. Alerted by a girl on horseback, the rancher and his cowboys chase the rustlers into the forest and capture them. The leader escapes to his mountain cabin, where he is followed, badly wounded, and brought to jail—but dies during the night. The Colorado landscape plays a major role in this otherwise familiar story. There are repeated shots of the rustlers' camp beside a swiftly flowing stream, *actualité* footage of rounding up and branding the cattle, and a climactic shoot-out at a log cabin, isolated on a treeless ridge and backed by distant foothills (see Figure 1.3). Identifying several key figures, Seilg's publicity reveals that this landscape is not really empty of Indigenous people: the leader is a "half breed" named Cherokee; the rustlers' camp cook is Mexican; and Cherokee's "Indian sweetheart" is called Wahnita.[66] Yet the film counters, ever so slightly, the

Figure 1.3 Selig, *The Cattle Rustlers*, 1908 (National Film Archive, London)

stereotyping of those hostile to the whites by ending with Wahnita alone with her dead outlaw lover, bewailing her loss.

As these and a few already cited western subjects attest, Mexicans increasingly appeared as "greasers" threatening or threatened by the central white characters.[67] Examples could include Biograph's *Fight for Freedom* (1908) and Essanay's *The Indian Trailer* (1909).[68] The most intriguing of these by far was Biograph's *The Red Girl* (1908), which unites a white and an Indian character who are threatened by a Mexican.[69] And, surprisingly, all three are women. Here, Kate Nelson is a miner who stakes a profitable claim, only to have a Mexican woman steal her gold. The latter comes upon the river campsite of the Red Girl and her "half breed" husband who hide her from a posse. The Mexican then seduces the "half breed," and "they sadistically" tie up the Red Girl and hang her from a large tree overarching the water. Using an ornament on her necklace, she frees herself and meets up with Kate and her friends. They pursue the thieves in separate canoes, capture the Mexican woman, and the Red Girl repulses the "half breed" who had betrayed her. The final tableau is stunning: Kate and the Red Girl stand on a cliff, "enfolded in each other's arms, bathed in the golden rays of a setting sun." This picturesque image might represent the potential union of whites and Indians in the figures of two women (not a man and a woman), seemingly bonded as sisters.[70] The setting sun, from today's perspective, however, could just as easily mark that union as a "vanishing" fantasy. Moreover, might the sunset's golden glow remind audiences of the gold Kate has plundered from the land?

As for Mexicans, they too could be rescued from vigilante injustice and, in turn, later save their white rescuers. In Biograph's *Greaser's Gauntlet* (1908), set in a border town full of white cowboys, miners, and railway engineers, José is falsely accused of theft and threatened with hanging.[71] Mildred, an engineer's wife, discovers that a Chinaman is the real thief, saves José's life, and he gives her a gauntlet his mother has embroidered with a cross. Later, after a disillusioned José becomes a drunk, another engineer abducts Mildred, and now José rescues her when he recognizes the gauntlet on her wrist. If José can be redeemed, that comes at the expense of another "alien," the Chinaman. A variation on this grateful exchange occurs in Essanay's *A Mexican's Gratitude* (1909), after a "bad man of the West" steals a ranchman's horse, which then runs off while he is in a saloon.[72] A Mexican spots, pursues, and captures the horse, but cowboy vigilantes seize him and prepare for a lynching. A sheriff saves the innocent man, however, and the grateful Mexican gives him "a half card on which is written 'Gratitude.'" Five years later, a cowboy cooks up a scheme to falsely accuse the former sheriff in front of his "sweetheart" (whom he too loves). Despite being forced to confess, the cowboy gets several Mexicans to help him imprison the couple. Now one of the Mexicans, looking for tobacco in the former sheriff's pocket, discovers the card, and unties his old rescuer, who starts choking the cowboy until his sweetheart begs him to stop. While one trade press review has the two lovers go off together, it says nothing about what happens to the cowboy or the Mexican.[73] Despite its title, perhaps the film has to privilege the reunion of the white lovers at the latter's expense.

For more than a year, from late 1908 on, D.W. Griffith produced at least half a dozen Indian pictures that he apparently found so popular with audiences.[74] Yet the descriptions of the Indian characters in these films revealed just how contradictory the prevailing attitudes toward Indigenous peoples had become at the time. Biograph's publicity introduces *Call of the Wild* (1908), not unlike Selig's later *On the Warpath*, for instance, with an explicitly racist generalization about the "Redman": "Civilization and education cannot bleach his tawny epidermis, and that will always prove an unsurmountable barrier to social distinction. . . . 'Lo the poor Indian' . . . for his condition is indeed deplorable."[75] This film's hero is George Redfeather, a

26 OUR COUNTRY/WHOSE COUNTRY?

top graduate of Carlisle Indian Industrial School in Pennsylvania (modeled on the Hampton Normal and Agricultural Institute for southern Blacks) and a football star (like Jim Thorpe who was just gaining national attention at Carlisle, which handily defeated leading university teams).[76] But, at a banquet in his honor, a lieutenant's daughter, Gladys, angrily rejects his love. Now "his long-suppressed nature asserts itself and he hears the call of the wild." He dons his former Indian garb, returns to his old village, guzzling whiskey, and plans revenge. Surprising Gladys out horseback riding, he seizes her as a captive, but she appeals to him, "calling to his mind the presence of the All Powerful Master above." On hearing "this Higher Voice," he relents, "watches her ride off homeward," "kiss[es] away the daughter's handkerchief," and sits dejected on his horse, "with no place to go."[77] Why this call of a Great Spirit or a vaguely Christian God should suddenly override and suppress the "call of the wild" in Redfeather's "deplorable" nature may today seem scarcely plausible. Moreover, the transformation comes in sharp contrast to the no less plausible recovery of a young woman's white identity in Vitagraph's slightly later *Children of the Plains*. If, as Gregory S. Jay writes, "Redfeather ultimately recognizes the superior purity of white womanhood" and his exclusion from "civilization,"[78] the ending not only avoids the threat of miscegenation but also may leave him excluded from his own tribe.

In the summer of 1909, Griffith began producing a series of Indian pictures near Cuddebackville, New York, nearly 50 miles northwest of Fort Lee. Biograph's publicity for the first of these, *The Mended Lute* (1909), was radically different from that for *The Call of the Wild*.[79] It begins with a "history lesson" that located the Dakota Sioux Indians in northern Minnesota in the 17th century before the French claimed their lands.[80] During the later Indian wars, they were driven south and west and became roving "tepee dwellers, expert horsemen and canoeists," and, in quasi-ethnographic stereotyping, a "highly emotional and poetic" people. The film's story was "laid in the neighborhood of Spirit Lake, Iowa," just prior to an outbreak of hostilities caused by the federal government's failure to "meet the stipulations of land purchases." Yet that history seems to have no bearing on this drama of two rival Indian men seeking to marry a chief's daughter.[81] Although Little Bear and Rising Moon are in love, her father promises her to the richer suitor, Standing Rock.[82] Rising Moon convinces her father of her love, and he lets her join Little Bear and go off in a canoe. Standing Rock gathers his warriors to pursue, finds and kills the chief, and hunts down the two lovers. Now he tortures Little Bear, whose "stoic courage" causes Standing Rock to free

Figure 1.4 Biograph, *The Mended Lute*, 1909 (US Library of Congress, Washington, DC)

his rival, give him "a coveted eagle feather taken from his own headband as a sign of honor," and lets the lovers go free (see Figure 1.4). The resolution of the two Indians' rivalry was shaped by the long-held concept of the Noble Savage, epitomized in Henry Wadsworth Longfellow's "The Song of Hiawatha," frequently depicted in novels and stage melodramas, and already evidenced in the less than plausible ending of *The Call of the Wild*. Perhaps most striking, however, was the film's presumption, much like Longfellow's alleged "Native storytelling" and Edward Sheriff Curtis's promotion of Native American "authenticity," that an American film company could create an allegedly authentic world that predated the white invasion of the Indigenous peoples' territories on the North American continent.[83]

Supposedly set in the Black Hills, Biograph's *Comata the Sioux* (1909) was framed with a similar view of the Indian. While he "is the soul of honor, where his own is concerned at least," too often he has been deceived by the "white man's unscrupulousness."[84] Comata is in love with Clear Eyes, a Sioux chief's daughter, but a white cowboy, Bud Watkins, persuades her to live with him in the mountains.[85] Once she has a "papoose," however, he

28 OUR COUNTRY/WHOSE COUNTRY?

abandons her and courts Nellie Howe, a white woman. Comata discovers Bud's villainy, reveals the truth to Clear Eyes (ironically, she has been blind to this), and shows the papoose to Nellie, who confronts Bud. When Comata takes Clear Eyes to Nellie, her father orders Bud away, and the child is returned to the mother. As "the heartbroken squaw . . . resumes her native attire" and starts back to her own father's home, Bud tries to intervene, but Comata disarms him. As they walk through the mountains, Comata begs Clear Eyes to marry him—"he will be a father to the child"—and she now agrees. Unfamiliar with the Black Hills, an exhibitor complained that the Sioux were Plains Indians and rarely went into the mountains.[86] Not only did the distant vistas present "an ironic contrast to the wretchedness of the Indians' fate," Ben Brewster writes, but the "romantic landscapes" backing the courtship scenes also contrasted with the "more nondescript country-side" where the white characters live.[87] That Comata is less an active hero than an observer, Brewster argues, makes him a "good Indian" or a kind of chorus, interpreting the actions of the other characters, especially the whites, "morally for the audience."[88] Unlike Selig's *On the Warpath*, it is worth noting, *Comata the Sioux* did not avoid miscegenation but roundly condemned sexual relations between the "races."[89] Unclear, however, is whether the papoose born of a white man and Indian woman will ever become tarred with the label of a "half-breed."

In late 1909, Biograph released one more Indian picture, *The Redman's View*, which continued to pity the persecution of the Indians. This time it was the Kiowas who were forced to "trek from place to place by the march of progress," that is, by the coming of the white men who seized their land.[90] Just as Silver Eagle becomes engaged to Minnewanna, white men appear and force the tribe to move on.[91] The whites detain Minnewanna as a slave, but Silver Eagle's sense of duty makes him accompany the chief, his father, who is old and feeble, on their migration. After the old chief dies and the Indians perform an elaborate platform burial, Silver Eagle returns to rescue Minnewanna, but the whites thwart their escape. A "more altruistic" white intervenes and "bids the young brave take his squaw and go in peace." In the end, the couple stands "with bowed heads at the bier of the chief." As Tom Gunning notes, the film sharply distinguishes the white men, "a primal horde with no women," from the Indians with their devotion to family and marriage traditions.[92] In a rare exception to the familiar figure of the "Indian maiden," here it is a white man who frees the Indian couple—and apparently goes unpunished. Several reviewers described *The Redman's View* as unusually "poetic," more "allegorical and symbolic" than an argument against injustice.[93] The sense of allegory is especially strong in evoking the long-accepted concept of the Vanishing American. That cannot be missed in the final tableau of the Indian couple mourning the dead chief, accentuated by the setting sun. This tableau is more definite in its implications than the hopeful one of the two women embracing in *The Red Girl*. But the allegory also appears elsewhere, as Gunning writes, in "a recurring image, the long line of Indians searching for a new homeland," a reimagining of the Cherokee "Trail of Tears" as well as many other violently forced deportations of Indigenous peoples.

If most of these Wild West subjects either avoided or condemned miscegenation, at least two films dared to embrace the interracial marriage of whites and Indians.[94] One was Edison's *Pocahontas, Child of the Forest*, adapted from a play by Will Rising, produced to be shown at the 1907 Jamestown Exposition, and released commercially the following year.[95] This film situated Pocahontas within a melodramatic story of John Smith and then John Rolfe as romantic rivals against a fictional Kunder-Wacha. Accepting the superiority of English culture, she tends Smith's wounds after a fight with the jealous Indian and, once Smith returns to England, marries Rolfe, his successful replacement. The film ends with Pocahontas, long known as the most legendary Indian maiden who betrays her native tribe, in a wedding blessed by both colonizer and colonized.[96] This interracial marriage depended on the widely circulating myth or "perplex" of her "elevated status as 'a princess,'" the daughter of a chief.[97] It also ignored her historical entry into England as a spectacle of exoticism, followed soon by her death. Unimpressed, *Variety* dismissed the film in an overtly racist review: the Indians "look like Chinese ballet girls" and the Colonists "resemble a crowd of Hebrew impersonators."[98] By contrast, Selig's *The Squawman's Daughter* (1908), according to the company's publicity, reenacted a "thrilling romance which actually occurred" and was filmed partly in a Colorado prairie landscape "that reach[ed] as far as the eye can see."[99] Here, the white father of the title tries to sell his daughter to a "villainous desperado," but her Indian mother intervenes. The daughter meets her "cowboy sweetheart," and together they return to her home, rebuke the father, and force him and the villain to leave. The latter then return with a sheriff, seize and bind the cowboy, and take him away. Now the daughter leads his fellow cowboys in pursuit, and they capture all the white men who plotted against the lovers. Intriguingly, this film replaces one troubled interracial marriage with another much praised and

30   OUR COUNTRY/WHOSE COUNTRY?

ends with a scene, one year later, that "includes a baby." Unlike earlier films, moreover, this daughter of "mixed descent," now a wife and mother, is never described as a "half-breed."

In November 1909, *Moving Picture World* summed up the increasing importance of these latter westerns: "the most popular subjects of [motion picture] audiences are those which deal with Indian or Wild West themes."[100] Again, what more does the lens of settler colonialism reveal about these "popular subjects"? Selig and Essanay in particular sought to place their stories in "authentic" natural landscapes by continuing to film on location in Colorado. Even Biograph followed their lead by finding more or less similar locations, especially in the hilly regions on the border of New York and New Jersey. With such "wild" landscapes as an alluring background, however, the films' stories stood out in sharp contrast for their violent conflicts that typically pitted whites against Indians and/or Mexicans or against one another. The stories of settlers contesting with Indians tended to align the control of lands once inhabited by Indigenous peoples with the control over child custody and sometimes the extraction of gold, all of which worked to guarantee the future of white people. By contrast, the stories of law-abiding whites, or sometimes vigilantes, who fought with outlaws worked to determine the "proper" ways that settler communities should exploit the "natural wealth" of the lands they had seized. In either case, extreme violence continued to mark the westward expansion of settlers that came to define *our country*.

Particularly striking now was the troubled characterization of Indians and Mexicans in so many of these westerns. The perspective on these non-white "aliens" had grown more and more ambiguous, even contradictory. At one end of a spectrum, hostile Indians kept attacking, killing, and abducting white settlers—and overwhelming Custer's cavalry at Little Big Horn—in numerous films by Edison, Selig, Vitagraph, and even Biograph. Likewise, whether as single individuals or small gangs, villainous Mexicans continued stealing gold, robbing stagecoaches, and kidnapping babies from settlers. At the opposite end, more often than not, Biograph's Indian pictures staged stories in which, as Michelle Raheja writes, Indigenous people were seen, however problematically, as "commensurable and sympathetic to white spectatorship."[101] That is, they become human and humane characters and, unlike before, defined in terms of families, yet now often "broken." In *Call of the Wild*, Redfeather overcomes his supposedly "suppressed nature" to act compassionately toward the white woman who rejects him; in *Comata the Sioux*, the lead character exposes the villainy of a white man who has betrayed the Indian woman he himself loves. Similarly, in a few Biograph and Essanay films, several Mexicans, after being falsely accused, reciprocally rescue the whites who had earlier saved them. To be sure, all of the actions by those sympathetic characters in Biograph's Indian pictures are framed by another kind of nostalgia, a guilty nostalgia for "lo, the poor Indian"—that is, the Vanishing American.

The claim of authenticity in the production of "real frontier life" also rested on costumes, gestures, and props in westerns that Raheja compared with reservations or living dioramas, "where tourists could putatively step outside of time and space to see . . . what passed for the 'real' in the settler nation's national mythology."[102] Wild West shows, Joanna Hearne writes, already had made some of those costumes highly visible and popular: "the Plains warbonnet, the cavalry uniform, and the cowboy's outfit."[103] One could add the horses, wagons, and weapons as well as the hand signals associated with Indians. Indeed, Hearne argues, costuming involved a "close association with racial identity," even reducing "Indianness" to "an accretion of objects."[104] This was especially the case in Biograph's "sympathetic" Indian pictures, most notably in *Call of the Wild*. In this early narrative of education or "the plight of Native Americans upon graduation from federal boarding schools,"[105] Redfeather undergoes a double change of costumes and props, first on his move from his tribal village to Carlisle and then on his return, where he dresses again in his native garb and indulges in a stereotypical bottle of whiskey. This kind of exchange of clothes and props, Hearne astutely argues, creates a "fluidity of identity" that counters most westerns' "ostensible messages about maintaining racial boundaries. . . . Both whiteness and Indianness, then, are revealed as unstable performances."[106] And that opens a potential space for westerns to confuse, unravel, and even reverse the visual politics of racial identity. Indians in particular, Paul Chaat Smith pointedly remarks, consequently become "shape-shifters in the national consciousness, accidental survivors, unwanted reminders of disagreeable events."[107]

At least two other western tropes offer the possibility of compromising supposedly stable categories. Despite its commonly disreputable meaning at the time, the "half-breed" occupied an intriguingly fraught position. In *The Cattle Rustlers*, *On the Warpath*, and *The Red Girl*, the half-breed acts as an outlaw, a deceptive lover, or a rejected jealous rival. However, also in *On the Warpath* as well as, implicitly, in *Comata The Sioux* and *The Squawman's Daughter*, a parallel half-breed serves as an assimilated "friendly" or as a child accepted without question by either an Indian couple or a "mixed-descent" couple. To movie-goers at the time, could the latter half-breed also have suggested a tentative alternative to the widespread virulent fear of miscegenation based on the Dawes Act's legal boundaries separating allegedly superior and inferior "races"? In contrast to *The Call of the Wild, The Squawman's Daughter* seems especially relevant because it ends with a "mixed-descent" marriage that not only counters the authority figures of a white father and a sheriff but also turns the married couple into a family with a child.[108] As Hearne writes of westerns in the early 1910s (the subject of the next chapter), "sympathetic images of interracial romance and child custody can also facilitate representational space for dissent on screen."[109] *The Red Girl* is equally relevant, but in a very different way. Despite the evident ambiguities in its concluding tableau, the film does promote the union of a white woman and an Indian woman. That union, of course, is not explicitly one of marriage but rather of sisterly friendship and even affection. Yet, within the context of our own time, could some now read their union as more than sisterly love and claim to recover or at least posit a potential repressed lesbian relationship?

Touring the West 1

> "I / hear it every— / where. The earth / said remember
> me. I am the / earth it said. Re- / member me."
>
> Jorie Graham, *Runaway: New Poems* (2020)

From early on, settler colonialism and the myth of American progress marked many travel films, in parallel with western films. They circulated as one set of nonfiction—actualities, news films, industrials, advertising films, sports films—that American manufacturers produced in large numbers for the programs of vaudeville houses, traveling showmen, summer tent shows, and eventually nickelodeons. Much like the Eastern Westerns, some explored more or less familiar areas in the Northeast, such as Edison's *Waterfall in the Catskills* (1897).[1] The most interesting for this study, however, came from cameramen sent into the West, following the tracks of white settlers, from the Great Plains to the Rocky Mountains and Pacific Coast. Relying on railroads for transportation, they sometimes shot footage for films such as Edison's *Phantom Ride on Canadian Pacific* (1903).[2] Mostly, however, they gave motion picture audiences views of major world's fairs and the spectacular vistas of national parks, both of which were beyond the means of "ordinary" Americans.

Some of their films also explicitly promoted the migration of new settlers into the West, such as Edison's *California Orange Groves, Panoramic View* (1897) that was "taken from the front end of a train passing through endless expanses of orange trees."[3] Not unlike their counterparts among early westerns, these travel films explored landscapes in which Indigenous people usually were absent, as if already eradicated. A rare exception, Edison's *Indian Day School* (1898), benignly marches boys and girls in and out of the Isalat Indian School in New Mexico.[4] The film's implication that they hardly differ from white children attending a school masks the historically forced removal from their families and the erasure of their native culture—language, dress,

---

Our Country/Whose Country?. Richard Abel, Oxford University Press. © Oxford University Press 2023.
DOI: 10.1093/oso/9780197744048.003.0003

34   OUR COUNTRY/WHOSE COUNTRY?

traditions. Likewise, in these travel films, no threats came from Mexicans, and African Americans remained out of sight. There also was little sense that settler migration and the disappearance of Indian cultures were creating any danger to the natural environment.

Early travel films tended to take up at least three loosely related subjects. One was the world's fairs that followed the famous Chicago World's Columbian Exposition of 1893: the Pan-American Exposition in Buffalo (1901) and the Louisiana Purchase Exposition in St. Louis (1904). Although located far from western landscapes, the Pan-American Exposition did aim to promote American progress during the past century, and it gained crucial financial backing from corporate interests in railroads, along with lumbering, coal mining, and banking.[5] Edison produced a series of short films that showed very selective views of specific attractions. Besides one offering a canal trip around the exposition grounds, two films depicted the Electric Tower, "the high C of the entire architectural symphony."[6] The 475-foot tower celebrated the technological advances in electricity (dear to Edison), and the most popular films showcasing those advances were the *Pan-American Exposition at Night* and the *Panorama of the Esplanade by Night*.[7] The magic of electricity also was displayed in the rainbow color scheme that crafted an allegory of "the nation's successful struggle with nature and forecast a future where racial fitness would determine prosperity."[8] What the Edison films ignored were images of racial unfitness in the Midway, from the Esquimaux and Japanese villages to the Filipino Village, an enclosure separating white spectators safely from "natives."[9]

Yet one film did stage the racial hierarchy in a "sham battle" that favored a US infantry unit against Indians from no less than six tribes.[10] The St. Louis Exposition celebrated the 100th anniversary of the Louisiana Purchase, which had expanded the country for future white settlement westward into the Great Plains and Rocky Mountains.[11] Although two surviving AM&B films focused on the opening ceremonies and a parade of floats, *Asia in America* crowded together people riding camels and a host of men parading in a variety of costumes.[12] Ignored again was the infamous recreation of an even larger Filipino reservation and the spectacle of others less "racially fit."[13] Intriguingly, the exposition eliminated any trace of the Indigenous peoples of the plains and western mountains, just as the "purchase" itself seemed to erase them from a vast territory of "empty lands."

Another subject involved a low form of technological experimentation for an amusement ride linked more directly with railroads. This was Hale's Tours, a popular, if short-lived ride, which appeared in amusement parks and some indoor installations from 1905 to 1907.[14] Here, spectators boarded a special train car that simulated the motion and sound of traveling on a railroad track, with a screen high in the front wall on which was projected one or more travel films. The company that licensed Hale's Tours secured films of foreign lands from Pathé, Kleine, and its own freelance cameramen. Those devoted to American landscapes came largely from Selig. A commercial photographer in Denver, H. H. Buckwalter, shot a series of these films in Colorado to promote both the state and its railroads: *Red Rock Canyon*, *Panoramic View of Royal Gorge*, *Ute Pass*, and *Georgetown Loop*.[15] Others, whether or not shot by Buckwalter, included *Trip Through the Black Hills* [South Dakota], *Trip Through Utah*, *Trip Through the Coeur d'Alene Mountains* [Idaho], and *Columbia River* [Oregon].[16] According to Selig's 1906 catalog, *Ute Pass* was one of many multiple-shot films that changed camera positions from the front to the back of a train; others could change the locale being viewed and/or leave the railroad track for a city scene or a staged scene inside a train car.[17] *Trip Through the Black Hills* includes one of the latter: "Panorama climbing the Mountains, *stopping for a comic scene showing the difficulties of trying to dress in a Pullman berth*, closing the trip by arriving in a station [italics added]."[18]

The third subject of these early travel films, the recently established national parks in the West,[19] probably was spurred by several popular books, large paintings evoking the West's "unimaginable wealth," and photographs, particularly of Yosemite Valley.[20] All of which often erased Indigenous peoples, except peripherally, who had occupied those lands for centuries.[21] Yellowstone Park already was another favorite tourist spot, and Edison released four single-shot films with views of the Park by 1899: *Tourists Going Around Yellowstone Park* and *Coaches Arriving at Mammoth Hot Springs*, both digitized by the US Library of Congress.[22] AM&B soon followed, using its large, bulky camera, to shoot half a dozen short films of the Rocky Mountains, such as *The Gap, Entrance to Rocky Mountains, Frazer Canon*, and *Devil's Slide* (1901–1902), as well as *Coaching Party Yosemite Valley* (1902), also digitized by the Library of Congress.[23] That year Selig also released short films of the Rockies that later would be sold to Hale's Tours operators and another of Grand Canyon National Park.[24] In 1904, AM&B produced a total of 21 films of "American Indians" (Moqui, Zuni, Navajo, Crow) sponsored by "the U.S. Interior Department for exhibition at the St. Louis Exposition."[25] If screened at the exposition, these pseudo-ethnographic films would have

36   OUR COUNTRY/WHOSE COUNTRY?

been attractions not unlike the physical enclosures of the "racially unfit." Indian activities singled out were dances, sports, and other skills.

Among these films, however, were five separate views of Yellowstone and the Grand Canyon.[26] In 1907, those two parks once more became special movie attractions. Selig came first with its "newest scenic," *A Trip Through*

Figure W1.1 *Moving Picture World* (August 10, 1907): front cover

Yellowstone Park, which ran 660 feet.[27] Not to be outdone, Edison released its own *A Trip Through the Yellowstone Park, U.S.A.*, an even longer film of eight scenes that were described in some detail in *Moving Picture World*.[28] The title insisted that this tour explored an American territory of spectacular natural beauty: "America's holiest shrines," writes Spence, more than equivalent to European cathedrals such as Canterbury.[29] Months later Selig heavily promoted another scenic subject, *Grand Canyon of Arizona and the Cliff Dwellers*.[30] (See Figure W1.1.) Not only did this film showcase "the grandest and most astounding feature of nature in the known world," but it also took in the nearby "Petrified Forest of Stone." While Selig did shoot scenes of "native blanket weavers and silversmiths," it particularly highlighted the absence of Indians in scenes of "The Curious Homes of the Aboriginal Cliff Dwellers." These later travel films of the West likely got a big boost from the newly emerging "See America First" Movement.

2

Single-Reel Westerns, 1910–1913

Western subjects grew ever more popular with audiences as 1909 turned into 1910. By that year, Robert Anderson estimated "one out of every five pictures produced by American manufacturers was a western."[1] According to trade press listings of licensed Motion Picture Patents Company (MPPC) films, Essanay, the "indisputable originators of cowboy films,"[2] was releasing at least one film featuring a white cowboy or outlaw each week throughout the year. Matching that output, Selig boasted that "there has been and always will be a demand for the Selig Wild West pictures."[3] For its part, Biograph was producing a dozen Indian pictures, mostly now shot in California. By mid-1910, Kalem was releasing an Indian picture each week, and Pathé was putting out one Indian picture every two weeks or so, all staged in the East by James Young Deer.[4] In April and May 1911, *Motion Picture News* categorized the films released in New York City by the independent companies into four tracks: *dramatic, comedy, educational,* and *western*.[5] The latter, the *News* proclaimed, "abound in the life, snap, and vigor that mean so much to M.P. audiences." At the same time, trade press listings for the rival independent films showed that a new company, American Film, quickly ramped up to produce two Flying A cowboy films each week, also shot in California, while New York Motion Picture (NYMP), still restricted to its Eastern locations, released a Bison Indian picture and cowboy film weekly as well. Especially noteworthy is how many Indian pictures now were an unusually major portion of many companies' output. This is evidence of what Fatimah Tobing Rony provocatively labels "fascinating cannibalism"—that is, the "obsessive consumption of images of a racialized Other as the Primitive."[6]

Many theater managers viewed these western subjects as popular with audiences, profitable, and also worthy of praise. One, for instance, commended Essanay's *The Bad Man's Last Deed* (1910) for its interest "in the development of character shown and the typical Western setting," that is, actual locations.[7] Another wrote the following about the same company's

Our Country/Whose Country?. Richard Abel, Oxford University Press. © Oxford University Press 2023.
DOI: 10.1093/oso/9780197744048.003.0004

Figure 2.1 *Nickelodeon* (March 4, 1911): 246

The Bearded Bandit (1910): it is "an excellent study of character . . . that one enters into its very spirit and forgets for the time that it is only a picture."[8] Such praise, by contrast, was now much less true in the trade press. *Variety* repeatedly condemned "wooly westerns," damning Selig's *Girls on the Range* (1910) with sarcasm: was this the sort of thing to lure "women who drop into a picture show after a shopping trip"?[9] Within a year, such disgust would culminate in attacks from opposite angles (See Figure 2.1.) The first, based on protests from Shoshone, Cheyenne, and Arapahoe chiefs to President Taft about movie depictions of Indians,[10] derided ugly stereotypes that parodied the language of a Chief Big Bear and Chief Big Buck: "Pictures show Injun men bad men and do heap bad thing all time. Injun men in pictures heap lie."[11] The other was headlined "The Indian and the Cowboy (By One Who Does Not Like Them)."[12] Not only did the writer argue that "there are far, far too many of these pictures"[13] and the public is weary of them, but also that exchanges and exhibitors were daft to believe that "children demand them," as a New York Child Welfare Committee survey assumed.[14] Instead, he imagined an "intelligent . . . small boy" who (much like himself) knew better: "Indians and Cowboys [were] nasty, dirty, uncomfortable, unpleasant people." Within weeks, *Nickelodeon* proclaimed "the Western photoplay [had] run its course of usefulness and [was] slated for an early demise" partly because its "old thrills [were] exhausted."[15] By the end of 1911, *Moving Picture World* sounded exasperated: "For years and years now we have had a perfect riot of these 'Wild West' things. . . . In the homely phrase of the day, 'Too much of a good thing is bad.' "[16] How wrong they all were.

During the early 1910s, so many western subjects were released that to write about all of them is close to impossible. Because Chapter 1, through the lens of settler colonialism, analyzed early westerns in terms of a loose set of categories and tropes, the following section devoted to single-reel films will do likewise. The challenge, however, is to be much more selective in choosing representative titles.

Whites Confront "Alien" Others in Single-Reel Films, 1910–1912

Despite mounting trade press criticism, the popularity of western subjects for exhibitors and audiences makes them unusually relevant within the framework of settler colonialism. First of all, as before, that relevance depended on the depiction of the land or landscape over which settlers struggled for control. One characteristic image continued to closely associate or even equate the land with Indians. Notably that is evident in those films whose stories focused on the struggles and sufferings of pioneers attacked by hostile male warriors. Take Selig's *Across the Plains* (1910), which, unlike earlier westerns, has its pioneers set out supposedly from a small town in New England.[17] There, a destitute young farmer, Jack Mason (Hobart Bosworth), and a financially strapped blacksmith, Cyrus Ford, join a wagon train heading west. At some point, they soon meet others traveling in wagons, and Jack falls in love with another family's daughter, Mary Hooper. "Warlike Sioux" attack the wagons and are about to overcome the settlers, when the cavalry appears to drive off the warriors, but Mary is left an orphaned young woman and adopted by the Ford family. Later, a "half-breed" incites the Sioux to attack the cabin that the blacksmith has built for his family; after they kill him, his little daughter Jennie escapes to round up neighbors, joined by another troop

SINGLE-REEL WESTERNS, 1910–1913   41

of cavalry, who finally rout the Indians. Two years later, Jack and Mary are married with a baby boy, and the widow Ford "finds comfort in the happiness of her children." "A Mammoth and Colossal Picture of the Plains—on the Plains," this Selig film apparently was shot on location in Colorado, but it also emulated popular paintings of the conflict between pioneers and Indians, such as Carl Wimar's *Attack on an Emigrant Train* (1856).[18] *Across the Plains* also staged two other crucial tropes. One was the villainous acts of a dangerous "half-breed"; the other was the kind of white family that came to define an emerging pioneer settlement.[19] The latter, in Joanna Hearne's concise words, suffered the violent "familial disruption" that often forced a crucial reorganization of "family structures."[20]

Another image even more frequent now was that of a vast desert or an empty land that could be exploited for its "invisible" natural wealth. Especially noteworthy was Biograph's *The Last Drop of Water* (1911), partly because the company's publicity billed it as "A Story of the Great American Desert."[21] Somewhere in the Midwest, two friends, John (Joseph Graybill) and Jim (Charles West), are suitors for Mary (Blanche Sweet), who accepts the former in marriage. All three join a wagon train crossing the plains, and John turns into "a weakling given to drink." When the pioneers reach the Great Desert, hostile Indians rise up out of nowhere and attack. The whites hold off the "savages" but are running out of water, so John and Jim volunteer for a desperate search. John is about to drink the last drop in his canteen when Jim, who has drunk his and is close to collapsing, begs his former rival for water. His conscience pricked, John gives him that last drop of water, and Jim revives.[22] They eventually find a small pool and fill all of their empty canteens, but John perishes from the heat and thirst. As Jim returns alone to the other pioneers, a troop of cavalry conveniently arrives to drive off the Indians. In the final tableau, Jim and Mary cradle the body of the man who died so his friend could live. Here, as in *Across the Plains*, a less extreme form of familial disruption leads, if implicitly, to another reconstituted family. A review in *Moving Picture World* shared D. W. Griffith's intent, in adapting a Bret Harte story of ironic sacrifice, to shoot the film on location in order to ensure a sense of the desert's "barren solitudes and sandy wastes with their utter desolation."[23] Within this empty landscape, the film's "humble heroes" are pushed to the limits of endurance in an effort, Biograph claimed, to open "up a new and wonderful land"—whether for farming, ranching, or mining—and demonstrate the "heritage of the American character"—or so went the mythical claim.

A third equally frequent image of the western landscape drew attention to its scenic beauty. Griffith's westerns shot on location—that is, *Romance of the Western Hills* (1910), *Ramona* (1910), *Iola's Promise* (1912),[24] as well as *The Last Drop of Water*—all publicized different vistas in Southern California. But Selig's *The Sergeant* (1910) was especially revealing because its story was set in Yosemite Valley in the 1880s.[25] From an army outpost in the valley, Sergeant Adams is ordered to chaperone Colonel Wesley's daughter, who often likes to ride into the wilderness (Figure 2.2).[26] One day they reach a favorite spot above Nevada Falls, and, while they are enjoying the view, an "Indian renegade" steals their horses. Next morning the alarmed colonel sends out a search party that finds the missing couple—and he busts the sergeant back to a mere private. Later, the colonel and daughter lead a small troop into the valley, are separated from the soldiers, and, with no explanation other than "savage" resistance to the whites, are attacked by Indians. Now Adams braves the treacherous river and, though wounded, saves them. During his convalescence, the colonel promotes him and grants his engagement to his daughter. Unlike the cavalry in the previous films,[27] here a lone

Figure 2.2 Selig, *The Sergeant*, 1910 (Academy of Motion Picture Arts and Sciences, Los Angeles, California)

soldier comes to the rescue and restores his honor. By the 1880s, some Sierra Miwok Indians whom the California militia had expelled in the Mariposa Indian Wars (1850–1851) had returned to Yosemite and now served as tourist attractions.[28] So, in this rewriting of California history, not only is the military outpost anachronistic, but also the Indian attack is inexplicable.[29] Ignoring these inaccuracies, Selig publicized *The Sergeant* as the first story film shot in Yosemite, and the carefully selected views of its picturesque scenery, like earlier travel films, much impressed spectators.[30] In fact, at times, the story primarily served to promote this wilderness as a tourist attraction, and even the intertitles named specific locations. Those few "who have seen the valley will see much that is familiar," wrote one exhibitor, while others had a unique opportunity to immerse themselves in its spectacular grandeur.[31]

Indian warriors attacking wagon trains, military outposts, and pioneer settlements now had become a staple of many westerns. Much more interesting, however, was the wide range of what Michelle Raheja described as "sympathetic" Native American characters.[32] The "Noble Savage," for instance, continued to play a heroic role in Griffith's Indian pictures. *The Heart of a Savage* (1911) stages a counternarrative in which a gang of white miners attack an Indian village, from which two men escape.[33] One eventually falls wounded and exhausted by a spring; the other returns to the village and gathers a war party. A white prospector's wife finds the fallen Indian and tends his wound. When he too returns to his village, he realizes the white woman and her family are in danger. Unable to convince the wife of the threat, he seizes her little girl to force the woman to follow him. When the prospector tracks them down, he shoots the Indian who still cannot get the woman to comprehend the danger. Finding their cabin burned to the ground, the white family now realizes the selfless motive of their Indian benefactor. Returning to bury his body, "they pay him posthumous honor." Even if this film was based on the oft-repeated cliché that "an Indian always fulfills his moral obligations," exhibitors agreed that its story developed "into a situation of great dramatic power [and moving] pathos and irony."[34] Set instead entirely within an Indian community, *The Song of the Wildwood Flute* (1910) has Gray Cloud serenade Dove Eyes (Mary Pickford in redface) with a love flute, which leads to marriage.[35] On a hunting trip, he falls into a bear trap, where his rival finds and leaves him to his fate. As Dove Eyes sickens in grief, however, the rival relents and rescues Gray Cloud, whose return revives his wife. This overtly melodramatic tale opened with a ritual Corn Dance, in a

44   OUR COUNTRY/WHOSE COUNTRY?

far from successful bid to embody the myth of the Native American's timeless "authenticity." *Variety*'s reviewer even laughed at the pitiable "attempt of the principal characters to act as Indians."[36] As if anticipating Raheja, Sumiko Higashi's pithy remark summarized this and other such Indian pictures as simply "a construction of Amerindian culture for white consumption."[37]

In parallel with films such as *Across the Plains*, family disruptions also could mark Indian pictures, but without the outcome of a newly reconstructed family.[38] Take another Selig western, *A Daughter of the Sioux* (1910), which tells a complicated story set in "an open expanse of rolling prairie on the borderland of American civilization."[39] It begins with a US military attempt to disarm a band of Sioux that goes fatally awry, and a Colonel Webb orders a Gatling gun to open up, killing half of the Indians and forcing the others to surrender. A dying Indian mother asks the colonel, in a blatantly sentimental touch, to take her surviving boy and girl as his own. Fifteen years later, as wards, Philip has enlisted in the US Army and Lorna is in love with a West Point graduate, Beverly Graham. Webb is ordered to Fort Frayne to subdue an uprising by the same band of Sioux, accompanied by Philip and Lorna. Appalled that they are fighting their own people, Philip deserts and Lorna releases an Indian spy to report on the fort's weakness. Beverly has to arrest Lorna, but she escapes to join the uprising as "a daughter of the Sioux." After brother and sister are captured, Philip grabs a revolver to shoot Beverly, but Lorna shields him and takes the bullet instead. Dying, she tells Beverly that "the law of the white man would never have looked with favor on our union [but] there where dwells the great White Spirit we will be equal."[40] If whites and Indians could not marry in a "civilized" America, the White Spirit of Indigenous peoples (so wrote the white scenario writer) allowed such a union in the land of the dead. However implausible this sentiment may have been, Lorna did embody the long-accepted trope of the Indian maiden who sacrifices herself to save one or more white characters.[41]

Other films reenacted this kind of story with crucial costume changes that, as Hearne has argued, could problematize racial and gender identity.[42] Although surviving only in a trade press synopsis, Pathé's *The Red Girl and the Child* (1910) offers an intriguing example.[43] Dick Sutton leaves his wife and little daughter at their cabin to join a "jollification" at a local saloon and stops a cattle rustler, Bill Duggins, from "bullying an Indian squaw." Duggins chances to meet the daughter on her way to a spring, seizes her, and, in a note pinned to the cabin door, says he did it out of revenge. The grateful Indian (now called a girl) accompanies Sutton and a posse, disguises herself as a boy to crawl into the rustler's camp at night, and rescues the little girl. Pursued, she returns the daughter, but not until after a remarkable stunt. At the end of a thrilling chase, the Indian (now called a woman), with the child tied on her back, hauls herself, "hand over hand, over a rope stretched across a wide and deep gully"; once on the other side, "she turns and cuts the rope, felling her pursuers who had already started across." With James Young Deer probably directing, Red Wing plays the "grateful Indian" as an unusually active heroine, even if she acts to restore a white family.[44] Kalem's *The Blackfoot Half-Breed* (1911) even more defiantly countered the tragic fate of the Indian maiden who betrays her people.[45] Maude, an educated, mixed-race young woman (Alice Joyce in redface), signals her allegiance to white society by disdaining her Indian culture, refusing an expected marriage to the tribal chief, and wearing westernized garb in the tribal camp. Angry at her actions, the tribe forces her to be confined. Another Indian woman, however, leads a military regiment to rescue the young woman. Not only does the latter reject the matrilineal link to her Indigenous heritage, but she also chooses a white officer as a fiancé. By prescribing "a strict division of the two races enforced by white military might," Charlie Keil writes, the film "effectively nullified any vestiges of Indian identity suggested by its title."[46] Moreover, that title ignores the usual connotation of "half-breed."

A very different narrative arc involving an Indian changed by education among whites appeared in Selig's blatantly titled *Curse of the Red Man* (1911).[47] The film reworks a story like that of Redfeather in Biograph's earlier *Call of the Wild*, but with a bitter ending. Terapal is a Mariposa Apache sent on scholarship to an Indian school much like Carlisle, where he stars as a football player.[48] Returning to his native village, however, he finds himself ostracized by his family's tribe. Brokenhearted, he drowns his sorrow in drink and soon "becomes a degenerate vagabond." After a day of heavy drinking in a nearby town, he kills a brutal bartender and has to flee into the desert. With a sheriff's posse in pursuit, he cannot escape an ignominious death. A final emblematic shot has "two of the sheriff's posse hold up a scholarship prize and a bottle of rum and wag their heads knowingly as if to say— 'These did it.'"[49] In other words, the moral is one that could not be more provocative: why educate an Indian if "civilized" learning cannot eradicate his supposed thirst for liquor? Yet this stereotypical assumption about a totally "unsympathetic" savage masked the historical record of its very opposite. The real curse came from the whites who for centuries traded liquor to Native Americans, creating an addiction to drink because fermented beverages largely had been unknown to them. Although an 1802 congressional act prohibited the sale of "spiritous liquors and whiskey" to Indian tribes, enforcement was pitifully lax.[50] Consequently, throughout the 19th century, traders set up "whiskey stations" along the Oregon and Santa Fe Trails, and John Jacob Astor's company grew immensely rich cheating Indians of their furs.[51] Partly because its taxes were among the largest sources of government revenue, "the liquor trade," Mark Lawrence Schrad argues, "was foundational to the entire system of colonial domination" across North America.[52] As with other forms of suppression in settler colonialism, *Curse of the Red Man* simply reversed and rewrote American history.

By contrast, the figure of the dying Indian in a host of films—from *Daughter of the Sioux, The Heart of a Savage, The Broken Doll*, and *Isola's Promise*, to *Maya, Just an Indian*[53]—embodied an implicit sign of guilty nostalgia that G. Harrison Orians perhaps first named "the Vanishing American."[54] Especially distinctive among such figures was the main character in Pathé's *The Legend of Lake Desolation* (1911), which a trade press review uncharacteristically claimed made "a laudable effort to give us a true picture and not a caricature of the redman."[55] Finding a lost "golden-haired little white girl," an Indian takes her to his camp "where she is reared in the ways and traditions of the red race." After the girl grows up to become "the idol" of her adopted tribe, her brother by chance recognizes her and persuades her to leave the people with whom she has been raised. How that happens remains unclear; besides, it runs counter to historical evidence of what many white captives actually chose to do.[56] Instead of emphasizing the reunion of brother and sister, the film unexpectedly focuses on the suffering of the Indians (See Figure 2.3). According to legend, the old chief, "particularly attached to the white girl," reverently sets a fire in his canoe and "without paddle lets it drift upon the water until he and the frail bark of birch are consumed by fire." In the "weird, beautiful, and original" final scenes, "even nature showed her sorrow by suddenly changing from the vernal charms of spring into the barrenness and desolation of winter." Remarkably, *The Legend of Lake Desolation* offered one of the more stunningly nostalgic images of the "Vanishing American."

Equally bleak was American Film's *The Vanishing Race* (1912).[57] Making their way across a flat landscape of waist-high grass, a small Hopi family— father, mother, son, and daughter—camp near a white settlement. A possible impetus for this opening shot was Edward Sheriff Curtis's well-known photograph, *The Vanishing Race* (ca. 1900).[58] One settler, attracted by the daughter, persuades her to elope with him; but he soon tires of her and goes

Figure 2.3 Pathé, *The Legend of Lake Desolation*, 1911, *Moving Picture World* (July 29, 1911)

back to an impatient white woman. When the daughter returns to her family, the brother goes to confront and shoot the white man, but his fellow cowboys kill him. The father reluctantly seeks revenge, but he too is shot and falls beside his son. Only the mother and daughter now remain. Despite the conflation of Southwest Indians traversing the high grass of the Great Plains, the company's publicity turns the mother and daughter's condition as lone figures into an epitaph: "the line of Hopi warriors [is ended] forever."[59] Somberly bracketing the film, the closing scene poignantly reenacts the opening, but now the Hopi family crossing a similar landscape is reduced to a mother and daughter struggling to survive.

Westerns with major Mexican characters had them playing an equally wide range of roles, in stories that not always followed conventionally expected patterns. In those that seemed to do so, Mexican men frequently appeared as stereotypical thieves or other sorts of disreputable villains.[60] Vitagraph's *The End of the Trail* (1912), for instance, has a sheriff pursue a Mexican horse thief into another desert landscape and catch up with him.[61] As they struggle, the thief tries and fails to knife the sheriff but does knock him out, handcuffs him, takes his gun, and rides off on his horse. He reaches his small cabin, where his young daughter accuses him, pointing at a crucifix on the wall, and he nearly strangles her before stomping off. When the exhausted sheriff, his hands now freed, staggers into the cabin, the daughter tends to him and, hearing her father returning, has him hide in a back bedroom. Finding a revolver in some straw, the sheriff accidentally knocks over a pitcher and has to step out to face the thief. The daughter gets between the two as they fire at one another, and she falls dead, shot by her father. In the final tableau, the lawman stands solemnly with his posse at her gravesite, but the father remains unmoved by her death and refuses to join in honoring her sacrifice. Here, too, as in Indian pictures like *The Legend of Desolation Lake* or *The Vanishing Race*, a Mexican family suffered a disastrous loss. By killing his daughter, moreover, this unrepentant horse thief not only sealed his own fate, perhaps by hanging, but also closed off any future for what little remained of his family. *The End of the Trail*'s title signaled the implicit, perhaps wished-for, vanishing of yet another "race."

More often, however, Mexican men acted as "sympathetic" characters similar to their Indian counterparts.[62] Take several films that also played out different stories of California history. Biograph's *In Old California* (1910), for instance, set its story in the early 19th century.[63] Jose Manuella, a wealthy young Spaniard and recent immigrant, falls in love with Perdita Arguello, but she marries Pedro Cortes, a local troubadour. Twenty years later, because Pedro has become a worthless drunk (like Terapal in *Curse of the Red Man*), Perdita asks Jose, now governor of Alta California, to take responsibility for her grown son. But the boy angers Jose by turning to drink like his father and then thieving. For her dying wish, Perdita asks to see her son, whom she imagines has become a reputable man, and Jose dresses him with his own military medals to appear before her. Once she dies, Jose tears the medals from the son's chest, orders his arrest, and lingers behind to tenderly kiss her hand. Here, the masquerade of a costume change allows Jose to create a fictional story that the woman he has long loved so desperately needs to believe. In contrast to Indian pictures focused on generational relations, an allegedly innate despicable nature also links this drunken father and his son. Selig's *In Old California, When the Gringos Came* (1911) takes place in the period of Reconstruction after the US government had taken over Alta California.[64] A wealthy young grandee refuses to cede his extensive lands granted by the King of Spain, but this decision leaves him vulnerable to claims by whites "without honorable scruples." An "American adventurer" tries to possess the estate by pressuring the grandee and his sympathetic land agent—and is nearly successful. But the padre of the Santa Barbara mission learns that the white man "has shot an Indian boy in cold blood" and charges him with being a criminal. Together with a band of frontier outlaws, the adventurer threatens the grandee, but the land agent shoots and kills him. In a telling whitewash, this film exonerated the US government of its earlier seizure of Alta California and shifted guilt onto an unscrupulous land robber and other white outlaws.

Given the long history of stereotyping Mexican men as dangerously deceitful villains, Vitagraph's *The Better Man* (1912) surprisingly features a horse thief named Gomez who proves to have a conscience.[65] The mother of a settler family asks her husband to buy a prescription for their sick little girl, but he gambles away the money. Hoping to get a reward, he spots the thief but fails to capture him, and Gomez reaches the settler's cabin and asks for some food. Once her fear is allayed, the mother persuades him to find a doctor. In the end, after the doctor treats the girl, she humiliates her husband, who finally arrives with his gun drawn, and firmly directs Gomez, "the better man," to go in peace (Figure 2.4). Unlike the crucifix in *The End of the Trail*, here the lithograph of a Madonna and Child hung on the cabin

Figure 2.4 Vitagraph, *The Better Man*, 1912 (George Eastman Museum, Rochester, New York)

wall shocks Gomez into playing a "Good Samaritan" or even a stand-in "father" figure to the white family. The Grand Guignol on display in American Film's *The Ranchman's Vengeance* (1911) is even more unexpected.[66] Lorenz Pedro, a "Mexican half-breed," is a sheep rancher who rescues a transient white cowboy, Tom Flint, whom his wife Marie nurses back to health. While Lorenz has to be away each day, Tom convinces Marie of his love; when Lorenz finds out, he sacrifices his own love for her and sends the couple off, warning Tom not to treat her unkindly. After an elapse of five years, Lorenz hears that Tom has been abusing Marie and her daughter, and he discovers his wife so weakened that she collapses and dies (Figure 2.5). Seizing Tom, Lorenz marches him to a seaside cliff and, in the midst of a fight, throws him into the sea far below. Later, standing over Marie's grave, the grief-stricken man is about to shoot himself, when his daughter rushes in to save him. A stunning anomaly, this film makes a white cowboy its villain and a "racially inferior" figure its hero. Is this why the general lack of reviews in the American trade press—a very brief one in *Moving Picture World* that never names the characters—contrasts sharply with the British acceptance of *The Ranchman's Vengeance* as a "clean . . . popular" film with a strong plot and

Figure 2.5 American Film, *The Ranchman's Vengeance*, 1911 (EYE Museum, Amsterdam)

"excellent acting."[67] One has to wonder how widely this film circulated in the United States—and what audiences made of it.

At least several films from Kalem also featured Mexican women as "sympathetic" characters for white audiences. In *When California Was Won* (1911), for instance, a US Navy commander orders the region's Mexican governor to surrender his control.[68] At the same time, Lieutenant Tom Marston adopts the disguise of a Mexican in order to meet his lover Manuella, the governor's daughter, but is discovered and captured. To protect the young woman from harm, he confesses to being a spy. Manuella, in turn, takes a rowboat out to warn the Navy commander, and the American forces free Marston just as he is about to be shot. In miniature, this film turns a romantic melodrama, dependent on Manuella's betrayal of her people, into a story of the seizure by white soldiers of what will become the state of California. Much like *The Ranchman's Vengeance*, *The Mexican Joan of Arc* (1911) is equally surprising.[69] It tells an allegedly true story of the recent uprising in Mexico against President Diaz. Suspecting danger everywhere, a Diaz officer, Colonel Cephis, has the father and two sons of the Talamantes family arrested, tried by a drunken judge in a "cortel federal," and immediately put to death (Figure 2.6). The widow swears vengeance and becomes a leader of the insurrection against the tyrannical dictator, chiefly to get revenge. In a special review of the film, W. Stephen Bush praised the company for filming in "the very neighborhood in which the actual scenes in the tragedy . . . had taken place" and for employing "real Mexicans, real half-breeds and real Mexican Indians."[70] Yet most impressive for Bush was the scene in which the widow (Jane Wolfe in brownface) entered the cortel federal "as a half-broken, pleading woman and left a few minutes afterward like a very goddess of vengeance." Her revenge fulfilled, this Mexican heroine leaves the insurrection and, with her head held high, simply says in the final intertitle, "Now I will go back to my people." Unlike the famous French martyr, this female avenger lives on alone, unable to reconstitute her own family, but remaining a model heroine to her Mexican community—and perhaps to others.

Finally, westerns with interracial relations at their core appeared ever more frequently. Some, of course, sought to stave off the cultural and legal threat of miscegenation. Unlike the earlier *Pocahontas, Child of the Forest*, Thanhouser's *Pocahontas* (1910), for instance, has the heroine, after wedding Rolfe, follow her husband to England.[71] But an intertitle comments: "the foreign flower cannot stand transplanting . . . she soon sickens and dies, and in her last hours is visited by visions of the home in the wilderness that

Figure 2.6 *Mexican Joan of Arc*, 1911, *Moving Picture World* (July 15, 1911): 19

she would fly back to if she could."[72] Here, Pocahontas's illness and death, far from home, serves to warn that the marriage of an Indian woman to a white man is untenable. Although poorly executed, Champion's *The Indian Land Grab* (1910) follows a different arc. An unnamed young chief goes to Washington to oppose a pending "Indian Land Grab bill," but fails, and the president vetoes the bill.[73] After a legislator's daughter falls in love with him, however, she makes her way to the chief's tribe and is accepted as "one of your people"—and apparently becomes his wife. Here, the trade press blatantly invoked the fear of miscegenation, finding the film's story not only implausible but also reprehensible. "There is an inseparable racial gulf" between whites and Indians, an exhibitor asserted, "which is repugnant to see crossed."[74] A reviewer was even more outraged to see a "degenerate heroine, a white girl, a 'society' girl, chasing an Indian and begging for a kiss."[75] "When the object of her misguided passion is an Indian, a member of an alien and inferior race," he fulminated, "our feelings simply revolt at the idea. It takes such an example to make us realize that there is really a moral law, a sentiment, a prejudice—call it what you will—against a union between a white girl and a member of a colored race." This conflation of Native Americans and African Americans as "colored races" explicitly assumed the legal boundaries earlier set by the Dawes Act and Jim Crow laws—and, at the time, those boundaries were supposedly ironclad.

Despite such "sentiment," a startling number of westerns actually countered this prejudice. Kalem's *Jim Bridger's Indian Bride* (1910), for instance, retold a supposed historical incident in which the famous mountain man rescues an Indian maid who has fallen into one of his bear traps.[76] When they return to her village, her brother suspects foul play, and Jim has to kill him in self-defense. The US cavalry saves him from her father's wrath, and an army chaplain marries Jim and the young woman. Perhaps given the company's slightly later films in which Indian maidens are caught between two cultures, *Jim Bridger's Indian Bride* papers over the dissolution of this Indian family. Essanay's *The Cowboy and the Squaw* (1910) also allegedly drew on "a real happening."[77] In the Silver Dollar saloon, Tom Ripley defends an Indian woman named Lightfeather from the insults of Jim Simpson, a fellow cowpuncher. In revenge, Jim tracks Tom to a precipice and, during a struggle, throws him off the cliff. Lightfeather finds Tom badly wounded and nurses him back to health. When Jim now stalks Tom and is about to shoot him, she kills him with a timely shot. Doubly grateful to Lightfeather, Tom flees with her on horseback to the county line and leaves a note for the pursuing sheriff's posse: "The squaw only killed a cur and you know it." The sheriff agrees, and the posse turns back to town. Although Lightfeather is called a "squaw" throughout (the label appears in all but a few Indian pictures), there is little sense of the usual derogatory connotation attached to the stereotype.[78] Not only that, but in a resolution unique in the company's westerns, this ending strongly implies that she and her cowpuncher are now much more than good friends.

Most consistently countering the threat of miscegenation, however, were the Indian pictures released by Pathé. Many of these were written and directed by James Young Deer, with his partner Red Wing (Lillian St. Cyr) often performing the central roles. Although shot in the East, *White Fawn's Devotion* (1910), one of Young Deer's few films that survive, probably is the best known.[79] A white trapper or squawman named Combs lives in a Dakota cabin with his Indian wife, White Fawn, and their mixed-descent daughter. One day a letter from the East arrives with the news that he is the recipient of "an unexpected legacy." When he makes plans to claim this legacy, White Fawn mistakenly fears he is leaving her with their child and, thinking herself abandoned, stabs herself trying to commit suicide. The daughter is shocked to find Combs bent over her mother holding a bloody knife, and she believes, "deceived by appearances," that he has killed her and tells her mother's tribe. The tribe pursues Combs and is about to execute him when White Fawn appears to explain that the knife she used only wounded her. In the end, the restored family returns to their cabin, and Combs decides that he will "continue his happy life with his native wife in preference to going east to gain possession of his inheritance."[80] Despite being simply and rather roughly made, Young Deer's film is remarkable. Not only does it have a white man renounce whatever family relations he still has in the East, but it also refuses to accept the convention of an Indian woman who sacrifices herself for the good of a white community. Hearne aptly describes White Fawn's last-minute rescue of her white husband "as a repurposed 'Pocahontas moment'" that directs attention "to a different political vision—one of tribal allegiance."[81] The film also, she adds, privileges the perspectives of White Fawn and her daughter rather than that of the squawman Combs on this "cross-racial marriage."[82]

There is only one brief positive comment in the trade press, unfortunately, on *White Fawn's Devotion*. But that is not the case with the lost *Red Deer's Devotion* (1911), in which Red Deer and the white daughter of a station agent fall in love, flee from her enraged father, and then have to escape a "bunch of desperadoes."[83] A reviewer remarked that it "hits one of America's most adamantine prejudices" and an "audience was heard to mutter about it."[84] "There is a feeling of disgust which cannot be overcome when this sort of thing is depicted as plainly as it is here," an exhibitor complained, echoing that directed at *The Indian Land Grab*, "even to the point where the girl decides to run away and join her Indian lover."[85] Despite these objections, Pathé went ahead and added the threat of bigamy to that of interracial marriage in *For the Squaw* (1911).[86] There, a white prospector bargains for an Indian woman to become his "wife" (Red Wing plays this role) but a few years later tires of her and their child, who, in a stereotypical throwaway intertitle line, "are only Indians after all."[87] His former fiancée writes about joining him; when the Indian woman's father learns this, they rush to the railroad station to intercept the fiancée and reveal his interracial ties. The white woman convinces the prospector "to remain loyal to his family" and, in the company's rather contradictory publicity, "leaves him more or less cheerfully resigned to the situation." Did redface slightly darken Red Wing's Indian "wife," emphasizing her subordination to the prospector and his former fiancée as well as, Raheja argues, "the uneven power relationships inherent in the motion picture industry" itself?[88] In any case, a trade press reviewer found this final tableau "considerably far-fetched."[89] Indeed, how could the fiancée's sense of honor nullify what the prospector has done by abandoning "her red sister" as his common-law wife?[90] Besides, that reviewer added, "the tale is a sordid one involving a despicable white man for the hero, so it is not likely to be very popular."

Pathé's *For the Papoose* (1912) featured an even more despicable squawman who lives with his Indian wife and their "half-breed" young daughter in a native village.[91] (See Figure 2.7.) One day, "tired of his squaw," he drunkenly struggles with her over the child, and her brother sends him away. After he tries to seduce a settler's daughter and is rejected, he provokes the chief of the native tribe to attack the settler but to "save the girl for some brave." He himself then sneaks up on his squaw talking to the captured daughter, seizes his "half-breed" child, and ties up his squaw. Once freeing herself, she informs the chief who takes a small group of warriors off in search of the squawman. Meanwhile, the brother promises his sister that he will avenge her and "bring back your papoose." After a prolonged chase, the brother finds the squawman and kills him, wiping the blood from his knife. The extant print breaks off at this point, but presumably he returns the child to her mother.[92] Rather

Figure 2.7 Pathé, *For the Squaw*, 1911 (EYE Museum, Amsterdam), *Film Index* (June 17, 1911): 13

56 OUR COUNTRY/WHOSE COUNTRY?

awkwardly staged and melodramatically acted, *For the Papoose* may have been directed by someone other than Young Deer and did not have Red Wing play the victimized squaw.[93] Still, the film has the squawman not only break up his native family but also violently try to remake another family with a white woman and his stolen child. In the end, an Indian exacts vengeance on this white man for his immoral, even criminal behavior,[94] which implies that interracial marriage cannot but fail. Instead, the film reconstitutes a different family within the context of Native American relations, one defined by an alliance between brother and sister, who now act as a "father" and mother to her mixed-descent daughter.

Rather than summarize this chapter's major tropes, first invoked and analyzed in Chapter 1, it may be more useful to address the question broached earlier: why were so many Indian pictures produced and circulated during the early 1910s? Moreover, why did they so often feature "sympathetic" Indians, both men and women, and why were they also often concerned with miscegenation and interracial marriage? Definite answers may be elusive, but perhaps several historical markers by the turn of the century offer an informative context. One, of course, was the government's reduction of Indian lands to restricted reservations, accompanied by a continuing decline in the Native American population. The latter was enshrined in James Mooney's essay in the *Handbook of American Indians North of Mexico* (published in 1910), which clearly evidenced that decline and became influential, even popularized, in the emerging discipline of anthropology.[95] Another was the ongoing effort to assimilate the remaining Indians into white "civilization." For Francis E. Leupp, Commissioner of Indian Affairs, also in 1910, that assimilation took the form of an amalgamation of red and white peoples, even in interracial marriage.[96] Although such marriages were more often still taboo, the "white" Indian or squawman and the "half-breed," Brian Dippie argues, did function historically as pivotal figures in the persistent aim of "whitening the red race."[97] Given such a context, perhaps it was not surprising Indian pictures seem such significant cultural artifacts that reveal how complicated and contradictory were popular views of Native Americans, along with Mexicans, in the early 1910s. Those views ranged from an overwhelming fear of enduring "savage" threats to a guilty nostalgia for the "Vanishing American" that suffused so many "sympathetic" Indians in motion pictures (and elsewhere) and could make them acceptable to white audiences, if not always to trade press reviewers. In parallel with Indian pictures that depicted the contradictory changes in Native American way of life, so too did early travel pictures project an unconsciously ironic transformation of the wilderness.

Whites Confront One Another in Single-Reel Films, 1910–1912

The Wild West fiction films within this second group generally assumed, without question, the dominant progress narrative of the time. Overall, their stories unfolded in landscapes largely depopulated of Indians, Mexicans, and Chinamen. Settlers clustered in scattered ranches and small rough towns, where ordinary white men tended to be the main characters, confronting other whites as rivals or villains. Sometimes they also ventured into supposedly empty deserts to extract "hidden" riches, as in Essanay's *Way Out West* (1910).[98] There, two partners set out from a Nevada town to prospect for gold and chance on the cabin of a dying old man who tells them how to find his lucrative mine. One night in the middle of the desert, one partner (played by G. M. Anderson) steals away with their mules and tools, after emptying the other's canteen. The deceitful thief finds the mine, advances into the darkness, and, reaching a vein of gold, suddenly has a vision of his betrayed partner who has lost his way in the desert. His conscience awakened, the thief tracks down his collapsed partner, revives him, and takes him to the mine. Confessing his guilt, he is forgiven, and the two men agree to share their unexpected wealth. The company's publicity promoted not only the revelatory scene in the dimly lit mine but also the "awe-inspiring [scenery] in the very heart of the American desert."[99] Accepted once again was the right of white men, even if it embroiled them in conflict, to exploit any land they "discovered"—that is, by mining for gold.

Several Biograph films also told stories of deadly disputes among whites lured by the profits of prospecting.[100] In *The Gold-Seekers* (1910), a desperate miner accidentally finds gold, stakes a claim, and sends his wife and young boy on horseback to a filing agent while he guards the site.[101] Two scoundrels spot him, run to the agent's office, scheme to get the wife to help an old woman feigning illness, lock her and the boy in the latter's cabin, and take the wife's place in line. She cleverly has the boy escape to find some ranchers who release her, and they rush back to the agent's office in time to thwart the scoundrels. Particularly impressive, wrote Linda Arvidson, was the location shooting in "the wonderful mountains and deep canyons . . . in the west fork

58   OUR COUNTRY/WHOSE COUNTRY?

of the San Gabriel Canyon."[102] Like *The Last Drop of Water*, *The Female of the Species* (1912) sets its grim story in a hostile desert.[103] The last survivors to leave an abandoned mining camp, four whites—a weakened miner, his wife (Claire McDowell), her sister (Mary Pickford), and a younger woman—undertake a desperate trek. As the wife and sister search for water, the miner tries to force himself on the other woman; spying the struggle from a distance, the wife mistakenly believes the young woman is at fault. When she intervenes, the miner collapses and dies. Disbelieving the woman's pleas, the wife and sister are about to take revenge; suddenly hearing a cry, they find a baby in a dead Indian mother's arms. This discovery—and another inadvertent Indian sacrifice—leads the three women to resolve their conflict and take the infant with them. The title initially assumes that an inherent jealous distrust governs women's "nature," but in the end, Keil writes, the intertitle "Motherhood" transforms their nature into a homily.[104] Despite that homily, the final long shot of three white women and an Indian baby continuing to trek into the bleak desert seems no less ambiguous about their survival than the ending of *The Vanishing Race*.

In even more westerns, rival cowboys competed for the love of a young woman, with one rival sometimes having to be exonerated of being falsely accused.[105] The most prolific of these cowboy films, however, had as the central character a white "badman" who undergoes a transformation or fails to do so. Essanay produced many of these, often penned by its chief scenario writer, Josephine Rector, whose "virile Western stories" had first attracted Anderson.[106] Although some of her scenario work must have been original, she later claimed that "a good portion of our best scripts came from pulp magazines and the shelves of the Oakland Public Library."[107] Perhaps the most notable of the company's cowboy films were a mainstay of the *Broncho Billy* series, in which Anderson played the lead role. Even when he was not an outlaw, Billy was just an ordinary cowboy between jobs and rarely a settled rancher, entrepreneur, or property owner.[108]

In the first of the series, *Broncho Billy's Redemption* (1910), he is a cattle rustler and hold-up gunman, who easily eludes a sheriff's posse.[109] One day he comes upon a prairie schooner with Millie Merrill and her sick father and, after a grateful cup of coffee, continues on his way. Later, when Millie finds an empty shack where her father can be more comfortable, Billy rides by, and she begs him to fill a prescription for the old man. He finds a Mexican to fulfill the task, but this "small, deceitful alien" simply pockets the prescription money. Later, while stealing some cattle, Billy comes across the empty prairie schooner and returns to the shack to find both father and daughter unconscious. Putting the two in the wagon, he drives to town, expects to be arrested, and has the sheriff's men carry the father and daughter to a doctor. But the sheriff frees Billy as long as he promises to mend his ways. A handshake seals the deal. Characteristic of the series, there is no hint of a marriage at the end or even a possible romance. A sense of combined gratitude and guilt prodded Billy into an act of self-sacrifice, which earned the sheriff's reward—with that stipulation. A similar ending marked *A Westerner's Way* (1910).[110] Big Bill Hastings (Anderson again) robs a real estate agent's safe and easily eludes the sheriff of Navajo, Arizona. Leaving a gambling house in another town, he unexpectedly walks into the sheriff and good-naturedly accepts his arrest. After he takes Hastings to a hotel for the night, the sheriff tries his luck at gambling, despite being warned, and loses the stolen money and his own. Learning of this, Hastings leaves the sleeping sheriff, sneaks into the gambling house, and recovers the money. Grateful, the sheriff lets him go free, again with "the promise of reformation." Although absent in this film as real characters, the Navajos of Arizona instead, following standard practice for many settlements, are turned into a place name.

Several later Essanay films starring Anderson as a "badman" involved even more startling plot twists.[111] In *A Pal's Oath* (1911), Jack Manley and John French are "bunkies" on the XX ranch.[112] When John falls ill, Jack goes for a doctor, who wants to be paid in advance. Lacking funds, he pursues a passing pony express rider and steals a pouch of money. When he reveals the theft, John says, "Your secret is mine. You did it for me" (Figure 2.8). Later they both fall in love with a young woman; when she chooses to marry Jack, John in a rage betrays his oath and has him arrested. A few years later, no longer imprisoned, Jack sneaks up to the house where John, his wife, and little girl live. When he aims his revolver through an open window, John picks up and hugs the girl. Jack lowers his gun, then raises it again, but now the wife embraces John and the girl. In despair, Jack turns away from the scene of a happy family and slips off into the darkness. Not only is that climactic scene unusually suspenseful, it also offered a psychologically poignant form of self-sacrifice that still cannot erase the unacknowledged guilt of his former pal. *A Wife of the Hills* (1912) delivered an even more surprising shock.[113] An outlaw gang leader, Bart McGrew, lives with his wife in a shack in the hills, but she, unknown to him, loves his partner, Dan Trout, and the adulterous couple plan to run away. Trout chances to see a sheriff's notice that promises to free any gang member who turns himself in, and he uses the opportunity to lead the

Figure 2.8 Essanay, *A Pal's Oath*, 1911 (US Library of Congress, Washington, DC)

sheriff to the shack, where McGrew is arrested. Now realizing the two lovers' treachery, he vows vengeance. The next morning, McGrew escapes jail and heads for the shack, pursued by the sheriff's posse (Figure 2.9). Looking in the open window at the lovers, he is about to fire his gun, when the sheriff's bullet meant for him misses and hits Trout, who falls dead across a table. Smiling at his wife sobbing over her lover's body, McGrew turns and lets himself be captured and led away. This ending plot twist was grimly ironic and contrasted sharply with the suspenseful scene in the earlier *A Pal's Oath*, where Jack had to pause and reluctantly decide not to exact vengeance. Here, satisfied with this outcome, the outlaw willingly returns to jail, leaving his adulterous wife to suffer alone. Strangely, an exhibitor found this startling denouement merely "interesting."[114]

Other Essanay films featured a "badman" who does not or cannot change. In *The Bearded Bandit* (1910), Jim Connors, "a ranchman of good repute," "skillfully disguises himself" and turns into a notorious bandit without "a shadow of suspicion."[115] His daughter Nan becomes engaged to Curt Wilson, the country sheriff, and Jim asks him to "take good care of her if anything happens to me." Curt enlists Jim in a search for the outlaw, but Jim ventures on

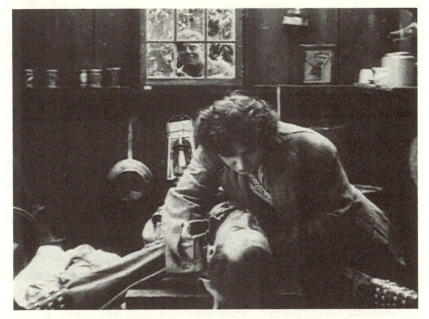

Figure 2.9 Essanay, *A Wife of the Hills*, 1912 (EYE Museum, Amsterdam)

one last holdup; afterward, he even joins the search, which comes up empty. Days later, engaged in a saloon card game, Jim is shot and asks that Nan come to him before he dies. He reveals the black beard and mask that will identify him and earn her the posted reward money, but she throws them into a stove fire. Curt and his cowboys find her weeping over her father's body, "little suspecting the double character of their longtime respected friend." Left hanging is whether Curt will ever discover the shared guilt Nan assumed in protecting her father. A unique variation on this lack of redemption occurred in *The Deputy's Love* (1910).[116] Bob Dean, a county sheriff, falls in love with Nance O'Brien, whose brother Walt, he believes, is a prospector. But Nance, in masculine disguise, actually partners with Walt as an outlaw. After successfully robbing a mail stagecoach, they split up to elude the sheriff's posse. Bob tracks down Walt and discovers a pile of men's clothes, along with a pair of gloves that he earlier gave Nance. Now seeking Nance, Bob empties his revolver before he confronts her. She wrests the revolver from his holster, aims at him, and pulls the trigger. Her perfidy revealed, the sheriff is forced to arrest her. Intriguingly, an exhibitor praised the film, stressing its moral lesson—crime doesn't pay—but strangely ignored the white woman's

62 OUR COUNTRY/WHOSE COUNTRY?

betrayal of her deceived lover.[117] More important, whereas the changes in costume in Indian pictures defined "in-between" figures unable to survive in the clash of cultures, in both films here costume changes allowed white men and women to thrive as deceptively double characters—at least until their masquerade was revealed.

As a number of films already attest, cowgirls and other white women often took on the roles of active heroines, with rarely an Indian or Mexican in sight. In Essanay's *Western Chivalry* (1910), a ranch owner's niece, a young Chicago girl, arrives for a visit and, in several comic scenes, rebuffs any attention from the "big rawboned" cowpunchers.[118] One day she mounts a temperamental mustang named Red Devil and clings to the saddle horn as it stampedes down the road with the cowpunchers in pursuit. One finally catches up and "swings her into his saddle," but, when they expect her to be frightened, she laughs, remounts the mustang, and races them back to the ranch. Now that she has shown herself to be an expert horsewoman, she agrees to be a masculinized "good fellow" as one of them.[119] In American Film's *The Outlaw's Trail* (1911), the heroine demonstrated a different "manly" kind of expertise.[120] The leader of an outlaw gang, Dad Winters, is "wanted in nearly every Western state for some crime, ranging from horse stealing to murder." Ordered to locate the gang, Jim Osborn, a Texas Ranger, stops by a mountain spring and meets Bonnie, a "mountain girl" who captivates him. She turns out to be Winters's daughter, and the next time she meets Osborn she spots his badge and realizes his mission. Warned by his daughter, Winters surprises Osborn and plans to hang him as an example to others. Afraid for Osborn's life, Bonnie rides to alert a sheriff and guides his posse to where the gang has just strung up Osborn. She shoulders her rifle, aims, and her shot cuts the rope, dropping Osborn to the ground.[121] A gunfight ensues, killing Winters, and Bonnie throws herself over his body, until Osborn "swears to love and protect her."[122] Yet would audiences at the time believe that this female gunslinger really needed protection?

An equally emphatic reversal of gender roles marked Essanay's *The Stage Driver's Daughter* (1911).[123] Old Lacey and his daughter Nell command a stagecoach that runs between mountain mining towns in the West. At one stop they meet Tom Percival, a young prospector from the East, who later has a gold strike and asks to ride with them so he can stake his claim. Several "wily miners" conspire to spike Old Lacey's drink during a lunch stop, and Nell finds him unconscious in a back room. Realizing what the "rascally Riley boys" are up to, she mounts the stage box and whips the horses into a gallop,

Figure 2.10 Essanay, *Broncho Billy's Christmas Dinner*, 1911 (EYE Museum, Amsterdam), *Moving Picture World* (December 30, 1911): 1082

with Tom perched at the rear, a revolver in his hand. Cowed by the gun, the pursuing miners fail to catch the stage; when they reach the claim office, Nell leaps off the box and yells at Tom, "Keep 'em off, while I file the claim." Finding Old Lacey recovered when they arrive home, Nell and Tom discover that "danger and sacrifice have awakened [their] love" (Figure 2.10). Some of the film's thrilling shots would be reprised in *Broncho Billy's Christmas Dinner* (1911), but there Billy would man the horses' reins.[124] Bison's *A Range Romance* (1911) told a very different story of the gendered upheavals of the settler frontier.[125] After quarreling with his wife Mary, Bob Adams heads west, taking along their young daughter Bessie, disguised in the clothes of a boy. Ten years pass. Bob gets work on a ranch; Bessie, still disguised, and the foreman become friends, until he discovers her secret. They fall in love, and she dons women's clothes. Coming west in search of her family, Mary gets hired as a cook at the same ranch, which leads to a surprise meeting over dinner and a reconciliation. Several years later, Bessie and the foreman, now married, show off their young child to her contented parents. A compact film full of melodramatic coincidence, *A Range Romance* "crystalizes fantasies of the West," Laura Horak writes, where not only a broken white family could be restored but also "a girl could spend her adolescence as a boy [and then] move smoothly into the role of wife and mother."[126] Surprisingly, Horak adds, the film alludes to "the homoerotic nature of the frontier" and to the untold stories of women who "lived their whole lives as men and even took wives."

Finally, two Vitagraph westerns offered conclusive evidence of such active white heroines. In *The Craven* (1912), Anne is the niece of a ranch owner who, like the local ranch hands, falls under the spell of Harvey Fiske, a boasting city slicker.[127] Once married, she discovers he is a coward when a bandit threatens them, and she has to grab a gun and chase him off. Elected sheriff, Harvey is asked to apprehend the outlaw Black Pete, but he admits to Anne that he cannot do it (Figure 2.11). In anger, she yanks off his pistol and ammunition belt, straps them to her waist, grabs her hat and rifle, and stomps out the door. She manages to track down the bandit and, after a suspenseful shootout among a stand of tall rushes, kills him. Returning home, she orders Harvey to recover the body and take credit for the killing. From a window, Anne watches silently as he rides into town with the body. "Only goes to show that the wife is sometimes the 'better man,'" a Vitagraph ad quipped, recasting as comic the outcome of the company's own *The Better*

Figure 2.11 Vitagraph, *The Craven*, 1912 (EYE Museum, Amsterdam)

Man.[128] If this heroine chooses to be silent about her own bravery, can she and her husband ever renegotiate their marriage? *How States Are Made* (1912), by contrast, dramatizes an epic story of the Cherokee Land Rush of 1893, but at the cost of silence about its violent history.[129] (See Figure 2.12.) A demoralized white family, learning of the land rush, joins hundreds of covered wagons in a long line extending to the horizon. An intruder harasses the wife and later shoots and wounds the husband. She has to take the reins of their wagon, race along with the others, and find an ideal plot to claim—but the intruder wants the same ground. After a struggle, they race back to the registration office, where he disputes her claim. Luckily, a witness identifies him as the shooter, and he is arrested. In the final scene, years later, exuberant children surround the couple on their fertile farm. Erased in this story's telling was the US government's infamous expulsion of Cherokees and other Indians from their verdant lands in the Southeast and onto what was named Indian Territory (later Oklahoma), where they found the region arid rather than, as promised, good for farming.[130] Much later, the government bought back a huge strip of the northwestern Territory and offered it to white homesteaders. Unlike the film's happy ending, the first winter following the

Figure 2.12 Vitagraph, *How States Are Made*, 1912 (EYE Museum, Amsterdam)

66 OUR COUNTRY/WHOSE COUNTRY?

land rush was bitter for white settlers: of those who filed claims, only 20 to 30 percent remained on their plots for the six months mandated to turn a claim into a deed.[131] As the historical record vanished before the "legend" of the land rush, an exhibitor claimed that audiences took to *How States Are Made* "with marked enthusiasm."[132]

In contrast to Indian pictures, these cowboy and cowgirl films assumed that the West already was settled, if not yet "civilized." Their stories still took place in "empty" lands, from which Indians and Mexicans were excluded, lands allegedly now open to exploitation such as prospecting for gold or staking a claim to individual plots of farmland. Settlements could be scattered farms and ranches or small and roughly built towns, and settlers of various kinds moved relatively easily between and beyond them on fast horses and stagecoaches. Some cowboys, always white despite the historical presence of numerous African Americans, faced off as rivals for the love of a white woman. More often, however, the threat to settlements came from white outlaws who adopted a different kind of exploitation that defied the still fragile rule of law. Most of these "badman" figures, notably Broncho Billy and others played by Anderson, underwent transformations that led them to be accepted into settled communities. The result was they served as models of redemption that supposedly defined American "civilization." Those that refused to be redeemed, even an occasional female bandit, suffered as betrayers of the tenets of that civilization—and had to be excluded in one way or another. Young women, whether or not as cowgirls, also could outperform men as skilled heroines who could take over for fathers or beaus and some-times save them from false charges and death. A remarkable context for their presence included the "sisters" who starred in the Miller Brothers 101 Ranch Wild West—as sharpshooters, champion ropers, and suffragettes—and who appeared as the title characters in contemporary juvenile series fiction such as *The Ranch Girls*.[133] In short, young white women in these westerns could be as active as men in settling the West, and equally adept, when needed, at taking violent measures to secure the rights to "empty land" as property.

Man.[128] If this heroine chooses to be silent about her own bravery, can she and her husband ever renegotiate their marriage? *How States Are Made* (1912), by contrast, dramatizes an epic story of the Cherokee Land Rush of 1893, but at the cost of silence about its violent history.[129] (See Figure 2.12.) A demoralized white family, learning of the land rush, joins hundreds of covered wagons in a long line extending to the horizon. An intruder harasses the wife and later shoots and wounds the husband. She has to take the reins of their wagon, race along with the others, and find an ideal plot to claim—but the intruder wants the same ground. After a struggle, they race back to the registration office, where he disputes her claim. Luckily, a witness identifies him as the shooter, and he is arrested. In the final scene, years later, exuberant children surround the couple on their fertile farm. Erased in this story's telling was the US government's infamous expulsion of Cherokees and other Indians from their verdant lands in the Southeast and onto what was named Indian Territory (later Oklahoma), where they found the region arid rather than, as promised, good for farming.[130] Much later, the government bought back a huge strip of the northwestern Territory and offered it to white homesteaders. Unlike the film's happy ending, the first winter following the

Figure 2.12 Vitagraph, *How States Are Made*, 1912 (EYE Museum, Amsterdam)

land rush was bitter for white settlers: of those who filed claims, only 20 to 30 percent remained on their plots for the six months mandated to turn a claim into a deed.[131] As the historical record vanished before the "legend" of the land rush, an exhibitor claimed that audiences took to *How States Are Made* "with marked enthusiasm."[132]

In contrast to Indian pictures, these cowboy and cowgirl films assumed that the West already was settled, if not yet "civilized." Their stories still took place in "empty" lands, from which Indians and Mexicans were excluded, lands allegedly now open to exploitation such as prospecting for gold or staking a claim to individual plots of farmland. Settlements could be scattered farms and ranches or small and roughly built towns, and settlers of various kinds moved relatively easily between and beyond them on fast horses and stagecoaches. Some cowboys, always white despite the historical presence of numerous African Americans, faced off as rivals for the love of a white woman. More often, however, the threat to settlements came from white outlaws who adopted a different kind of exploitation that defied the still fragile rule of law. Most of these "badman" figures, notably Broncho Billy and others played by Anderson, underwent transformations that led them to be accepted into settled communities. The result was they served as models of redemption that supposedly defined American "civilization." Those that refused to be redeemed, even an occasional female bandit, suffered as betrayers of the tenets of that civilization—and had to be excluded in one way or another. Young women, whether or not as cowgirls, also could outperform men as skilled heroines who could take over for fathers or beaus and sometimes save them from false charges and death. A remarkable context for their presence included the "sisters" who starred in the Miller Brothers 101 Ranch Wild West—as sharpshooters, champion ropers, and suffragettes—and who appeared as the title characters in contemporary juvenile series fiction such as *The Ranch Girls*.[133] In short, young white women in these westerns could be as active as men in settling the West, and equally adept, when needed, at taking violent measures to secure the rights to "empty land" as property.

Touring the West 2

By the early 20th century, the formation of national parks, together with a transcontinental railroad system and modern corporate marketing, encouraged "white, native-born middle- and upper-class Americans," writes Marguerite Shaffer, "to reaffirm their American-ness by following the footsteps of American history and seeing the nation firsthand."[1] "In the process," she adds, "they created and marketed tourist landscapes as quintessentially American spaces, consciously highlighting certain meanings and myths while ignoring others." The history invoked, of course, tacitly assumed the narrative of settler colonialism—that is, of westward expansion through a "virgin wilderness" that displaced the landscape inhabited by and often managed and sustained by Indigenous peoples.[2] In one instance, the Sierra Miwok Indians had for centuries cultivated black oaks for their food crop of acorns in Yosemite Valley, until the California state militia tried to starve them out and then displaced them in the mid-19th century.[3] Indeed, "the consumerist ideology of recreational tourism," in Jennifer Peterson's concise words, aligned closely with "the territorial ideology of Manifest Destiny."[4] The "mythic ideal of the West soon became the basis for a new national consciousness" that, Shaffer provocatively argues,[5] paralleled and perhaps superseded the concept of a nation-state reuniting North and South after the Civil War. Abetting this new national consciousness was the explicit goal of the See America First movement.

In January 1906, a See America First Conference opened in Salt Lake City, hosting "125 delegates representing boosters, businessmen, and politicians from across the West."[6] The delegates formed the See America First League, led by Fisher Sanford Harris, whose mission was to promote the scenic grandeur of the West. Its rally cry was "See Europe if you will, but See America First." Lack of funds, partly due to the 1907 financial panic, limited the League's success, and it disbanded after Harris's death in 1909. Yet that did not hinder the movie industry from exploiting both settled and unsettled landscapes in the West. Spectacular vistas made Yellowstone a favorite perennial subject, even luring Kalem's cameramen to shoot *A Trip to*

Our Country/Whose Country?. Richard Abel, Oxford University Press. © Oxford University Press 2023.
DOI: 10.1093/oso/9780197744048.003.0005

the *Wonderland of America, Yellowstone National Park* (1909), which Col. Edward Justus Parker could lecture in exhibition.[7] By then, however, Francis Boggs even complained that "crowded conditions" kept him from trekking in to make another film there for Selig.[8] Perhaps that was why Essanay moved farther west for *Wonders of Nature in the Twin Falls Country, Southern Idaho* (1909).[9] Many of these films now, either explicitly or implicitly, promoted further settlement in the West. Union Pacific, for instance, produced *Frontier Day at Laramie* (1909) and another film in Idaho "to show the resources" of the states to "the home-seeker."[10] For its part, Selig released *Outing Pastimes in Colorado* (1909), which featured very civilized sports rather than the rigors of ranch life.[11] In early 1909, the Alaska-Yukon Exposition in Seattle featured motion pictures that promoted the industries exploiting the resources of the Pacific coast from Alaska to California.[12] Singled out were whaling, seal hunting for furs, and salmon fishing and processing. As if juxtaposing the "Native" to the "Civilized," an Eskimo village exhibited films of "Siberian natives catching and killing seals," an ancient traditional practice.[13] Similarly, E. B. Thompson, who earlier had shot footage of Yellowstone for the US Department of the Interior, also produced films of the salmon industry located in Puget Sound, again set in stark contrast to scenes of "aborigines fishing with reef nets."[14] In his August 1909 letter to Selig, Boggs reported that he had joined others in the Northwest to make "some educational features of the Columbia River Salmon fishing" and then was heading to the "Hood River Valley to get a logging subject."[15] The second of those split-reel films was released at the end of the year.[16]

Tourist attraction films coinciding with these adventures invited audiences to experience cowboy life in the modern-day West. In Selig's *Ranch Life in the Great Southwest* (1910), for instance, a number of well-known cowboys— "Henry Grammar, Tom Mix, Chas. Fuqua, Johnny Mullens, Pat Long and others"—show off their skills in a series of rodeo events: lassoing and branding cattle, riding bucking bronchos, hanging on to running bulls, and other tricks of horsemanship.[17] In a fictionalized bit of Selig publicity, a recent migrant to the big city claimed the film lured him into a fantasy world of "limitless plains . . . the ranchman's life in the open air and his intimacy with nature, which is, after all, the proper way of living."[18] But a more realistic version of what Kevin Brownlow termed the "visual encyclopedia of Western life"[19] came in *Life on the Circle Ranch in California* (1912). Shot on a working ranch near Santa Monica, it depicted the basic cowboy tasks involved in cattle ranching, from dawn to dusk over two days.[20] On the first day, cowboys leave

Figure W2.1 *Life on the Circle Ranch in California*, 1912 (UCLA Film & Television Archive, Los Angeles, California)

a bunkhouse with their gear, saddle a "green horse," and ride off with surplus horses onto the open range to set up a camp. On the second, they awaken to wash hands, pour coffee into cups, and spoon sausages from a cooking pot. Then they ride out in pairs to create a circle, "bunching in" herds of cattle, and to brand the spring calves. (See Figure W2.1.) While some cowboys drive one herd to a "home range" in the hills, others trail a second herd to a railroad junction, load them into cattle cars, to be shipped to Chicago for slaughter. "Home again" after their work is finished, they join a few women for a meal and begin dancing to a fiddler and banjo player. While *Life on the Circle Ranch* "neatly compressed a full season of work and play into two days and one reel,"[21] it also celebrated contemporary ranch life that hardy white settlers had "civilized."

By 1911, a national publicity organization, the See America First Association, had replaced the original group. A booster named A. L. Sommers began publishing the *See America First* magazine, whose "patriotic" aim was to stimulate interest in America as a wilderness of unique scenery for tourists. Pacific Northwest businesses in particular supported the magazine with advertisements, and, in March 1912, among the first issue's pages, was an article on President Taft's automobile tour of Mount Rainier. The following year, the business members of the Trans-Mississippi Commercial Congress even advocated creation of a national See America First Day. And what did the movie industry make of this heightened promotional interest? As one more strategy for establishing its legitimacy, the industry saw an opportunity to produce a series of films that not only would capitalize on the See America First movement but also perhaps be of use to its boosters. Yet there was an even more important consequence. Although the largely white millions who comprised the audiences for these films could not afford train travel and expensive accommodations, they could gape in amazement even more at the "wonderland" of the national parks. Moreover, if the films' ultimate quest was a magnificent scenery, Peterson astutely argues, they were "equally invested in representing the *process* of getting to that scenery ... and the *experience* of viewing the scenery" once they reached it.[22]

From 1911 through 1914, one film after another sought to lure actual and virtual tourists to follow the way westward to take in remote, "uninhabited" natural sites. Rex, for instance, filmed *Picturesque Colorado* (1911), which opened with an industrial parade in Denver and then tracked tourists on

Figure W2.2 Northern Pacific Railroad map, 1885 (Norman B. Leventhal Map Center, Boston Public Library)

trips into the Rocky Mountains, including the Georgetown Loop railway, Cheyenne Canyon, and Garden of the Gods near Colorado Springs.[23] A year later, Edison focused exclusively on one industry in *Copper Mines at Bingham, Utah*, which, in showing Italian and Eastern European immigrants housed in ethnic enclaves, promoted the need for more non-white workers.[24] At the same time, in cooperation with the US Department of Interior, Kinemacolor planned a series of films that took viewers through national parks such as Grand Canyon, Yellowstone, Glacier, Rainer, Great Crater Lake, and Yosemite.[25] To promote better roads for travel by automobile, C. Francis Jenkins and William Rau made a film of their "ocean-to-ocean" tour that explicitly invoked the See America First movement.[26] Most tourist travel, however, still had to rely on railroads. (See Figure W2.2.) The Northern Pacific Railway Company, which first adopted "See America First" as its slogan in 1910, used films of Yellowstone National Park (likely shot by Watterson Rothacker, head of a Chicago firm specializing in advertising films) to publicize its transcontinental system for tourists, investors, and homesteaders.[27] Pathé distributed its own "See America First" series, beginning with *A Trip to Mount Rainer* (1912), followed by films of Glacier National Park, *The Waterfalls of Idaho* (1913) and *Blazing a New Trail through Glacier National Park* (1913).[28] Although some films did include scenes with Indigenous peoples, they typically appeared as props adorning the scenery: nostalgic, colorful, "primitive Americans," whose images could not completely hide the ruthless destructiveness of genocide that cleared a path for the past westward expansion.[29] For Pathé's Glacier Park film, the cameraman had members of a Blackfoot people take a stereotypical pose: "arrayed in their best blankets and feathers, [they were] grouped on a great crag, their arms extended to the sky."[30] This was one more sign of the now iconic "Vanishing American."

3

Multiple-Reel Westerns, 1912–1914

In 1912, American motion picture companies began to produce multiple-reel films to compete with European imports—from *Dante's Inferno* and *Temptations of a Great City* to *Notre Dame de Paris* and *Zigomar*—that had been circulating widely on the US market for at least a year.[1] Along with historical "features" such as Selig's *The Coming of Columbus* (1912), westerns quickly became a popular subject for these longer films. In parallel with the westerns analyzed in Chapter 2, the majority of these multiple-reel films were Indian pictures. Perhaps that was not surprising for several reasons. First, companies took advantage of shooting their stories on location in a range of scenic western landscapes. The valleys, deserts, foothills, and mountains of California in particular offered the illusion of "authenticity" to the continuing struggles that Indians had with settlers and the US military. Second, companies employed more and more Native Americans to perform as Indian characters, from major figures to hundreds or more warrior and village extras. The NYMP Company, reorganized with Thomas Ince at its head, for instance, sought to enhance that sense of authenticity by hiring a large number of Pine Ridge Sioux who, in an arrangement with the Miller Brothers 101 Ranch Wild West show, lived on and worked out of the extensive Inceville grounds.[2] Third, companies could amass and maintain a host of materials that could be reused, with slight changes, from one film to another. These ranged from town buildings (sometimes only fronts), cabins, stockades, and teepees to wagons, stagecoaches, herds of horses, and weapons of all kinds. In short, multiple-reel Indian pictures soon seemed to be supplanting all those popular one-reelers.

Ince's first Indian pictures, released as Bison-101 "special features," offer excellent examples of the multiple-reel westerns to examine through the lens of settler colonialism.[3] *War on the Plains* and *Blazing the Trail* (both 1912) used two reels each to tell stories of the violent encounters between Indians and whites during the latter's westward march across the continent. *New York Dramatic Mirror* praised *Blazing the Trail* for "the magnitude of

Our Country/Whose Country?. Richard Abel, Oxford University Press. © Oxford University Press 2023.
DOI: 10.1093/oso/9780197744048.003.0006

[its] backgrounds" and its "management of the exceedingly large numbers of players" that gave "an air of reality" to the familiar narrative of pioneers under threat as they crossed the open vistas of the Great Plains.[4] Striking scenes shot in the hills around Inceville exploited foreground/background contrasts: Indian warriors on a hilltop look down on a wagon train encampment far below; later, white men similarly eye a distant Indian village before mounting a bloody attack.[5] Equally striking were final images, as in the same film, where a young woman, her lover, and her brother are silhouetted on the distant horizon after leaving the foreground crosses marking their parents' graves.[6] The "large number of players" featured those Pine Ridge Sioux who performed many of the Indian roles, without being asked to indulge in melodramatic overacting.[7] As if surprised by such performances, Ernest A Dench, remarked with undisguised sarcasm that "to act as an Indian is the easiest thing possible, for the Redskin is practically motionless."[8] Assuming the "authenticity" of its Native American characters and landscapes, by contrast, *Moving Picture World* praised *War on the Plains*, for instance, as a worthy rival to the latest historical spectaculars from Italy.[9]

Especially noteworthy about several of these Bison-101 "special features" was their relatively balanced treatment of the conflict between Indians and whites. Take *The Lieutenant's Last Fight* (1912), which company ads described as a "military drama," in which a "troop of cavalry is entirely wiped out by Indians" and "the Lieutenant meets a heroic death."[10] Yet the surviving print, along with several trade press reports, makes the film's actual hero a Sioux chief's son, Great Bear, who is sent to a military school and graduates as a commissioned lieutenant.[11] Stationed at Fort Reno, under the command of Colonel Garvin, he is scorned by all but the colonel's daughter Ethel, who even greets the Sioux chief with respect when he visits to admire his son. Jealous of her attention, Captain Haines insults the lieutenant, provoking him into a fight; unfairly accused and court-martialed, Great Bear is sent back to his tribe in dishonor. Enraged, his father threatens war, and the colonel sends the fort's young women on a stagecoach to another fort for safety. The chief wants his son to join the war party, but Great Bear reads a letter taken from a dead courier that reveals the stagecoach bearing Ethel will be in danger. Instead, he finds and dons his old uniform, grabs his army revolver, and rides off to try to save the white woman who once trusted him. The Sioux warriors ambush the stagecoach halted in a gulch, and Ethel is wounded; Great Bear takes the bugle from the fallen courier and then positions himself on a shrubby hillside above the encircled whites and begins firing at the warriors. Seeing a soldier escape and go off toward the fort, he waits to sound the bugle until the cavalry approaches—and the Indians withdraw. (See Figure 3.1.) But a retreating warrior sneaks up, shoots Great Bear in the back, and leaves him for dead.

The Lieutenant's Last Fight recapitulates the familiar story of an "in-between" Native American who can neither assimilate into white society nor return to his tribal community, but with intriguing differences. As Great Bear, Francis Ford (who probably also directed the film), models his restrained body language after that of the uncredited Indian playing the Sioux Chief, his father. At the same time, Great Bear is forced into the role of a "shape-shifter" whose identity is unstable, marked by repeated changes in the costumes and props he adopts.[12] Despite being unjustly stripped of his stripes and sword, he recovers his uniform and revolver, now in disguise of an officer in order, not to rejoin the army that has dishonored him, but rather to rescue the only white person who has shown him respect. The colonel's misreading of the fight provoked by Haines explicitly undermines that

Figure 3.1 Bison-101, *The Lieutenant's Last Fight*, 1912 (EYE Museum, Amsterdam)

dishonorable discharge, and it implicitly critiques the fear of miscegenation. To revenge his son's dishonor, the Sioux chief goes on the warpath to ensure an even deeper divide between Indians and whites, one individualized in the killing of Great Bear, now in uniform, by one of his own tribe. As a result, the film ends with a grimly ironic final intertitle. A victim three times over, Great Bear's tragic sacrifice goes "unwept, unhonored, unsung," his heroism, implicitly supporting the white community that abandoned him, unknown even to the injured young woman for whom he gave his life.[13]

An even stronger sense of ambiguity marked *The Indian Massacre* (1912). The first scenes set up contrasting stories: in a Sioux Indian village on the plains, Ravenwing's baby has died, while at the Brown's settler cabin, another mother cradles her baby as the father goes off to plow. Then an Indian hunting party comes upon a white scout they have named "Bad Medicine," who has just shot a buffalo; when they attack him, three of their small band are killed. Together, these scenes quickly establish a narrative in which the struggle between Indians and whites is driven by parallel desires crucial to each's survival. One involves sustaining resources and escalates into a Sioux attack on the larger white settlement and the US Army's retaliatory massacre of the Indian village. The other involves the future in the form of offspring and, during the initial massacre, leads to the seizure of Mrs. Brown and her baby, in order to replace the dead Indian child. Yet just before the retaliatory massacre, Ravenwing takes pity on the white woman, secretly returns her child, and allows her to escape. After a lengthy siege of the army stockade, which evoked images like Charles Schreyvogel's recent painting *Defending the Stockade* (1905), the Sioux are driven off in defeat.

In an unusually long trade press article, Louis Reeves Harrison was greatly impressed by the battle scenes: "I have never seen action more vivid and realistic."[14] That action was heightened by camerawork. The Indians attack the white settlement in an unusual high angle/extreme long shot that stresses the choreography of the action, and they later descend on the Browns' cabin from over a distant hill. Yet the film's title creates the most surprise. There is not one massacre but two: the first in retaliation for the whites' destruction of the Indians' food supply (evoked in miniature by the buffalo hunter); the second, in the whites' counterattack laying waste to the Indian village. (See Figure 3.2.) The final long shot tableau focuses not on a trope of the victorious army and settlers, although the Brown family's own future may remain uncertain, but on that of the "Vanishing American." Ravenwing stands silhouetted on a bare hilltop, her arms raised high to the fragile pole platform

Figure 3.2 Bison-101, *The Indian Massacre*, 1912 (David Shepard, Film Preservation Associates)

on which her dead child rests. This makes a perfect match with the film's initial lengthy shot, where a band of Sioux Indians slowly move in a curving diagonal across the screen, to a new camp in the distance—a poignant emblem of the long arc of Indigenous peoples' tragic history.

Even less ambiguity marked Kay-Bee's three-reel *The Invaders* (1912).[15] Again, two interrelated storylines drive this narrative.[16] In one, Sky Star, a Sioux chief's daughter, rejects a suitor her father has approved and then is attracted to a white man in a railroad survey crew. In the other, the Sioux protest to the colonel at a nearby fort that the survey crew is violating a recently signed treaty and then persuade the Cheyenne to join in an uprising. In alternating sequences, Sky Star is injured in a fall, riding to warn the whites, but recovers just enough to reach the fort, while the Sioux attack and kill the surveyors. From then on, the combined Indian warriors ambush a cavalry detachment, cut the telegraph lines, and lay siege to the fort. Proving himself worthy to the colonel (and his daughter), a lieutenant escapes and returns with troops from another fort—who rout the Indians. The impressive camerawork in many scenes certainly parallels that of earlier films—that is, reverse-angle full shot/extreme long shots, some taken from a high-angle position. Yet more striking is the film's evenhandedness in depicting the Indians

Figure 3.3 Bison-101, *The Invaders*, 1912 (US Library of Congress, Washington, DC)

and whites: the surveyor's point-of-view shot of Sky Star through his scope is matched by the shots of the jealous Indian suitor viewing their later meeting and shared attraction from a distance.[17] Indeed, the film seems to neither approve nor criticize either conflicting party at the expense of the other. Most surprising, however, is the intertitle that confirms the Sioux's argument by actually naming the surveyors, who act like advance scouts for the railroad that will "civilize" the land, as the real "invaders."[18] (See Figure 3.3.) In the final long shot of a darkened room, lit only by shafts of moonlight falling through a background window and an open side door, the white characters pay their respects to Sky Star, who has died of her injuries shortly before the siege. The colonel's daughter kneels and weeps over the barely visible body and then moves to stand by the downcast lieutenant (who closes the door); the colonel himself pauses over the body and then closes the window shutters. This tableau strongly evokes a sense of white guilt and regret for yet one more sacrificial figure of the "Vanishing American."[19]

Produced in June but not released until October, Kay-Bee's three-reel *Custer's Last Fight* (1912) confirmed there was no more need for any sense

Figure 3.4 Kay-Bee, *Custer's Last Fight*, 1912, *Moving Picture World* (June 22, 1912): 1116

of ambiguity, already evident in the endings of *Blazing the Trail* and *The Deserter*.[20] The film begins quite differently from *The Indian Massacre*, with the warrior Rain-in-the Face killing two amateur naturalists—and not railroad surveyors as in *The Invaders*—who had wandered into the wilderness. Captain Custer overhears him bragging about the killing, arrests him, and gets him to confess. But before the trial he escapes and joins Sitting Bull, who ignores a government order in 1876 to move his people to a reservation and instead engages in a buffalo hunt. Pursuing the killer, Custer moves toward the tribal encampment, dividing his troops into two other columns flanking his own. The Sioux chief Gall, who realizes the dispersion of troops at Little Big Horn, now leads his large number of warriors, superbly equipped with Springfield rifles, into a frontal attack on Custer's forces, limited by short-range carbines. Ambushed and surrounded, with no help coming from the other troops in retreat, Custer and his soldiers are gradually overwhelmed and all die. (See Figure 3.4.) A photograph advertising the film evokes the commemoration of Frederic Remington's popular painting *The Last Stand* (1890).[21] Unfortunately, *Custer's Last Fight* does not survive, so any analysis has to depend on trade press reviews and the story's fictionalization in *Photoplay*.[22] Although several reviews laud "the most realistic battle . . . ever witnessed," Louis Reeves Harrison's is blatantly jingoistic.[23] Custer and his men are gallant heroes, and the Sioux are merciless, "destitute of nobility as other savage races." The ending even adds a "touch of pathos" more blatant than the romance subplot in the earlier Selig film: a little girl, a "tiny representative of the greatest civilization," lays flowers at the dedication of the Custer monument on the battlefield. Custer, writes Harrison, "gave his life to the preservation of what was best in this fair country of ours." If white settler colonialism had a hero in Buffalo Bill, it now had a "martyr" in Custer.

As New York Motion Picture and Universal fought over the Bison-101 brand, American Film saw an opportunity to release several multiple-reel Indian pictures. *The Fall of Black Hawk* (1912) opens in 1830 with Black Hawk reluctantly signing a treaty that removes the Fox and Sac tribes from east of the Mississippi River.[24] White settlers flood in to follow them west, and the Indians determine to resist until General Winfield Scott sends a large troop to confront them. When Black Hawk sends a small group of his warriors to Fort Crawford, Prairie de Chien, under a white flag, they are shot by drunken rangers; in retaliation, he stages a series of attacks and ambuscades before laying siege to the fort. After several attempts fail, he and his warriors are dispersed and eventually captured. The final scene, set in 1832, has the Indian chief in a hopeless situation and forced to sign yet another treaty. Not unexpectedly, what cannot be depicted were Black Hawk's efforts to disrupt the white's liquor traffic, which was the primary cause of his resistance in war.[25] Although promoted as an Indian picture shot on the grounds where the historical events took place, this two-reel film also gives at least equal attention to more famous historical white men.[26] Zachary Taylor, later a US president, is a major whose daughter is courted by private Jefferson Davis, later the president of the Confederacy. At one point, Taylor's daughter Sarah is abducted, escapes, cleverly hides submerged in a river, and is rescued by Davis, with help from her sister. A volunteer for Scott's army, young Abraham Lincoln meets Davis at a hospital camp, demonstrates his skill as a wrestler, and aids Davis in Sarah's rescue. (See Figure 3.5.) The company's publicity offered a conveniently financial reason for why the coincidental encounters of these white men loom so large in the film: "The great names . . . are always vital in their appeal, and mean money to exhibitors."[27] Despite its title, then, *The Fall of Black Hawk* assumes, in doubled terms, an overwhelming sense of white superiority and privilege.[28]

Figure 3.5 American Film, *The Fall of Black Hawk*, 1912, *Moving Picture World* (July 6, 1912)

The Indian pictures that continued to appear now came through Universal-Bison, many directed by Frank Montgomery and starring Mona Darkfeather. Some like *Star Eye's Strategy* (1912) featured Indian characters exclusively, but its story was hardly unfamiliar.[29] A Cheyenne warrior loves a Sioux chief's daughter (Darkfeather in redface), who has been promised to a rival, whom she refuses. They escape to the Cheyenne camp, but during the wedding celebration the Sioux attack, capture the warrior, and threaten to burn him at the stake. Star Eyes devises an unusual strategy to lure his Sioux rival away from the camp and out into the woods, where he falls into a pit that becomes his grave. She rescues her Cheyenne warrior; the Sioux are routed; and the marriage goes on. Here, an Indian maiden twice betrays her own tribe of Sioux to wed the young warrior of a rival tribe of Cheyenne. *The Massacre of the Fourth Cavalry* (1912), by contrast—supposedly the retelling of an 1885 historical event in Arizona—narrates a grim story of repeated violence between Indians and whites.[30] Apache chiefs are refused liquor at a military fort and resort to their native brew, which puts them in a warlike mood.[31] After a troop of cavalry threatens them, the Apaches burn down a

Figure 3.6 Universal-Bison, *The Massacre of the Fourth Cavalry*, 1912, *Moving Picture World* (November 23, 1912)

settler cabin; the cavalry, in retaliation, takes a number of "squaws" prisoner. One of the Apache chiefs breaches the fort and rescues his wife, one of the seized squaws, and the cavalry rides out to seek more revenge. Instead, the Apaches bury themselves in the desert sand (however implausibly), literally becoming one with the landscape, only their rifle barrels showing like weeds or stubble. (See Figure 3.6.) When the unsuspecting cavalry appears, the Apaches spring up and annihilate them: "All that is left the next day are the naked bodies of the dead troopers, left to bleach in the terrible heat of the Arizona sun."[32] This ending boldly counters the more frequent image of an empty landscape ripe for exploitation. Both the US military and the Apaches share blame for all the acts of vengeance that lead up eventually to the concluding massacre: the US cavalry repeatedly attempts to exert more and more control over the Indians, and the Apaches are unable to avoid the stereotypical "curse of the redman," the temptation to drink. Strangely, the trade press was remarkably nonplussed by the film's gruesome ending of dead white soldiers.

During the late 1912s, Broncho and Kay-Bee multiple-reel westerns continued to tell stories featuring white characters in their encounters with Indians. A fascinating anomaly among them was Broncho's *The Man They Scorned*.[33] The hero is a newly enlisted soldier named Stein—and explicitly Jewish. As a "raw recruit," he is "insulted, scorned, and derided" by his fellows at the fort, with any sympathy coming only from the colonel's daughter. One day, in a scene similar to that in *The Lieutenant's Last Fight*, he turns on his tormentors and holds them off in a fight, but they accuse him of being the aggressor, and the colonel has to order him to the guardhouse. An Indian uprising against emigrants and settlers frees him, and he joins the troop hunting the attackers. Overwhelmed, they retreat, and the colonel is pinned beneath his dead horse. Stein pulls him up onto his own horse, but the extra weight slows their flight as the Indians close in. Coming to a rocky hillside, Stein jumps off, and the Colonel rides on, after giving him his pistols. Hidden behind rocks in a narrow pass, Stein holds off the Indians who can't get to him. Before more troops finally rally and send the Indians fleeing, he is shot several times and has to be carried unconscious to the fort. A doctor and nurse bring him slowly out of danger, and his former tormentors recognize his heroism with loud cheers. In an ending ceremony, the colonel promotes him to sergeant, and all the men "join hands in a clasp that forever wipes out racial prejudice and makes them brothers." The company's publicity, however, insisted that Stein initially is scorned as a "raw recruit" and not as a Jew.

MULTIPLE-REEL WESTERNS, 1912-1914   83

So, the final sentence of racial harmony and implied assimilation, "under the same flag," comes as a surprise.[34] That assimilation, however, did not extend to marriage with the colonel's daughter.

Broncho's *The Vengeance of Fate* has an even more complicated plot.[35] After finding a gold mine, Evans bashes in the head of his partner Porter and leaves him unconscious. Reporting his partner's death, he gradually persuades Porter's wife Hazel to marry him, for the good of her baby girl. Indians revive Porter and help him recover, but he has lost his memory. When soldiers order the Indians, along with Porter, to move to a reservation, they are outraged and subdue the soldiers. Hit in the head, Porter suddenly regains his memory. The Indians attack settler cabins, but Porter cunningly secures Hazel and the girl in a safe place. Returning to Porter's former cabin, Evans is not so lucky, and the Indians ambush him. After more soldiers arrive to defeat the Indians, Hazel finally recognizes Porter as her lost husband. The last scene has Evans's body lying before the partially destroyed cabin, with coyotes sniffing around. While the Indians here have generously come to the aid of an injured white man, it was the US government's policy of removal that goaded them onto the warpath. As an in-between white man, Porter neither turned against his benefactors nor took revenge on his former partner Evans. The "vengeance of fate" was left to the Indians. A different fate awaited both whites and Indians in Kay-Bee's *The Altar of Death*.[36] Lieutenant Hart befriends a young Indian woman, Bright Star, who falls in love with him. Hart, however, courts the visiting niece of the fort's colonel (who later weds someone else), and Bright Star is crushed. Without an explanation, at least in the company's publicity, her tribe prepares to go to war, and Hart is ordered to take a supply of gunpowder to another fort. The Indians ambush the troop in a canyon, and, as the soldiers fall, Bright Star resolves to save Hart and takes him through a hidden passage into a cave. Desperate, Hart lights the gunpowder to stop the Indians closing in. But the unexpectedly heavy explosion destroys the mountainside, killing the Indians as well as the remaining soldiers. In the end, Bright Star dies with her arms around Hart's body. This ending leaves all the familiar conflicts between whites and Indians unresolved or simply erased in what, despite the film's title, can hardly be seen as a tribute.

Those conflicts may have been resolved in Biograph's *The Yaqui Cur* (1913), but in an unusually bizarre, contradictory way.[37] A Yaqui youth (Robert Herron in redface) is strangely drawn to the nearby camp of white prospectors, where an "evangelist" reads him passages from the Bible, including "Greater love hath no man than this, that a man lay down his life for his friends." But other prospectors show him how to make and smoke cigarettes and to dress and walk like a white man. His "civilized" ways do not impress his mother, and a young woman he tries to court becomes the wife of his friend Ocallo, a young chief. When a rival tribe attacks the Yaqui encampment, "the moans of men caught under falling horses" terrorize him, and he is banished as a coward into the desert. Later, starving and alone, he sees a drunken prospector attack his friend's wife; when Ocallo kills the white man, the youth remembers the biblical passage, takes his friend's knife, and sends the couple away. Before being executed for the killing, the youth asks to have one last cigarette, but an angry prospector shoots him in the back as he smokes. The final scene focuses on Ocallo and his wife backlit by the setting sun as they enter "their tepee in happiness and peace." This Yaqui youth seems an implausible figure of the familiar Indian caught between cultures. First of all, the biblical passage that leads to his "honorable" sacrifice is deeply compromised, not only by his comic parody of "civilized" behavior but also by the title that demonizes him as a "cur," an inferior dog or disreputable person.[38] Rightly describing the film "a deeply ambiguous tragedy of cross-cultural contamination," Tom Gunning notes that the youth's contradictions—matched, I would add, by the white prospectors'— make it difficult to take his "conversion to Christianity" seriously.[39] Yet the picturesque final scenes seek to honor that conversion by recalling an earlier backlit shot of the youth smoking against the setting sun, for now Ocallo and his wife are suffused with the memory of his sacrifice.[40] Second, this "Yaqui cur" evidences nothing of the actual experience of Yaqui Indians who had long resisted the Diaz regime in Mexico, even after many were driven across the border.[41] In league with the *magonistas*, they smuggled guns and ammunition in support of what became the Mexican Revolution. Suppressing that history, the film sets another Indian tribe against the Yaquis and has the youth sacrifice himself for the good of his tribe and the illusion of its stereotypically peaceful community.

A late anomaly among Indian pictures was Kay-Bee's *The Last of the Line* (December 1914).[42] Its story resembled Selig's earlier *Curse of the Red Man*, but with a bitterly ironic ending twist, similar to that of earlier Broncho and Kay-Bee films. The "last of a long line of Sioux chiefs," Gray Otter, awaits the return of his son Tiah from a "white man's school."[43] (See Figure 3.7.) The chief is sorely disappointed, however, when Tiah turns up drunk (again, like Terapal in *Curse of the Red Man*), refuses to shake his son's outstretched hand,

Figure 3.7 Kay-Bee, *The Last of the Line*, 1914 (Museum of Modern Art, New York)

and angrily denounces him inside his teepee. Tiah compounds that anger when he tries to assault a young Indian woman and refuses any blame. While the chief promises, in a peace pact with the nearby US Army commander, to ensure that no Indians "molest" any white man, Tiah continues drinking with several friends in a saloon. Later, with no motive given, he and a bunch of "renegades" rob the army paymaster in a stagecoach protected by horse soldiers. This leads to a fierce battle between the Indians and the soldiers trapped in a barricade behind their overturned stage. Having gone off alone to nurse his sorrow, the chief hears gunfire, climbs a hilltop overlooking the battle, and begins firing at the renegades. Stunned to see his uniformed son leading them, he slowly, sadly decides to shoot Tiah. Reaching the body, he places it alongside the dead paymaster, as if Tiah was defending the soldiers, thus creating a false sense of honor for his disreputable son. In the end, after a military burial, Gray Otter kneels by the grave, clutching Tiah's military uniform. Despite gaps in the narrative and extended scenes of riding horsemen, the film still comes to a startling climax.[44] Tiah is an unusual "in-between" figure, less a realistic than a symbolic product of a white-run Indian school

86   OUR COUNTRY/WHOSE COUNTRY?

(how he becomes a drunk is not given), and his father tragically becomes one as well, when he aligns himself with the US military to falsely honor his son. Consequently, the "Vanishing American" alluded to in the film's title is doubled. Not only does Gray Otter explicitly embody that icon, but so does Tiah, who will not replace him as the next hoped-for chief of the Sioux.

In so many of these multiple-reel features the relations between Indians and whites were sometimes even more complicated and contradictory than they were in the one-reel films. "Sympathetic" figures continued to be marked by a kind of nostalgic shame as "Vanishing Americans." Whether as an Indian maiden and mother such as Sky Star and Ravenwing or an Indian chief and son such as Gray Otter and Great Bear, they all endured degrees of suffering and sacrifice that guaranteed the future of settlement communities and their military protectors. Yet a surprising number of these features went beyond sympathy or empathy in representing their central Indian characters and actually claimed they had a rationale for resisting the advancing whites or they were being misled and corrupted by hypocritical settlers. Moreover, a few either implicitly or explicitly mounted an argument against that advancement, even to the point of admitting it was an invasion and illegal seizure of Indian lands. At the same time, however, just as many Indian pictures adhered to the opposite position, overtly celebrating the triumph of white "civilization." Although that triumph might include disastrous losses, it secured the future for whites, as in the restored settler family of Porter, Hazel, and their child and in the little girl who commemorates the myth of Custer's supposed martyrdom. That's why the massacre of an entire cavalry troop, in which the Apaches literally are equated with the desert landscape, seems even more of an anomaly than Custer's familiar "last stand." With the possible exception of the "lyrical postscript" that posed Ocallo and his wife backlit by the sun in *The Yaqui Cur*, Native Americans forever were denied a future. Not only that, unlike the acceptance and even promotion of mixed marriages in the Indian pictures of Young Deer and others, even the suggestion of interracial romance now seemed impossible.

Settlers and Other Whites in Multiple-Reel Features

Westerns with white heroes, of course, did not disappear or reach what Stephen W. Bush described as the "destined end" of the trail.[45] The Buffalo Bill and Pawnee Bill Film Company produced the most unusual and least successful of these, *The Life of Buffalo Bill* (1912) in three reels.[46] Essentially a biographical sketch of the famous celebrity, it opens with Colonel Cody on horseback in a wilderness, dismounting and taking a nap, as he dreams of several episodes from his past life. In the first, Buffalo Bill saves a wagon train from a Cheyenne Indian attack on the "Old Santa Fe Trail."[47] In the second, he learns that Buck McCandell's gang is going to rob a stagecoach and leads a posse to capture the bandits. In the third, dated 1876, after discovering that the Cheyenne are joining the Sioux in a war party, he duels and kills Yellow Hand to avenge Custer's death. In the end, Cody awakens from his dream, remounts, and slowly rides away. Many of the scenes in these episodes, Sandra Sagala writes, "came straight out of the Wild West show scenarios," which partly explains their awkward "staginess" at times.[48] As in the Wild West shows, hostile Plains Indians repeatedly threaten white settlers and army troops until Buffalo Bill kills them with ease or drives them off the land. By contrast, he has no need to dispatch white outlaws, even if later they may hang.

Most of these westerns, however, now focused exclusively on white cowboys and sheriffs, in settled territories devoid of Indians and Mexicans. As Essanay's *Bronco Billy* series remained popular, the company tried to expand some titles into two-reel films, beginning with *Broncho Billy Gets Square* (1913).[49] Yet other cowboy figures, notably from Selig, were threatening to replace him. An early example was the two-reel *Cowboy Millionaire* (1913), a remake of its popular 1909 one-reel film.[50] Here, "Bud" Noble, foreman of the Diamond S Ranch, suddenly inherits a fortune and moves to Chicago, where he acquires a mansion, a wife, and a wearying social life. He invites his former cowpunchers to visit and, in his auto, leads them on horseback through wide streets to his palatial home. One day he treats the boys to a performance of the popular melodrama, *Bertha, the Sewing Machine Girl*, and they stop the play by shooting at the villain. All of this rowdy, "uncivilized" behavior convinces him to send them packing and to remain in the city. With a good deal of snap and go, this film concisely mapped the historical subject of the western: a passage in space—from ranch life in the West to urban life in the Midwest and East (where most of the film's spectators lived)—and in time—from the end of one century to the beginning of another. It also recycled some of the images and stories out of which the western emerged: an opening *actualité* of rodeo stunts, a train ride, and a large Hoskins oil painting that recalled Frederick Remington's *Cowboy on Horseback*.[51] Moreover, Bud changed from participating in the "Wild West"

88   OUR COUNTRY/WHOSE COUNTRY?

to being a spectator himself, "shocked" at the increasingly comic antics of his uncouth buddies. In the final scene, he turned the painting to the wall, as if the mythic cowboy of the past no longer had a place in the present of his own story. The gesture and intertitle—"Never again"—would prove futile, at least in the continuing history of western films.

With *The Law and the Outlaw* (1913), Selig tested the appeal of Tom Mix in a multiple-reel western.[52] "Dakota" Wilson escapes from a penitentiary, and sometime later Buffalo Watson hires him at the Diamond S Ranch.[53] His daughter Ruth admires Dakota's horsemanship and follows the cowpunchers as they round up the ranch's cattle. Her red handkerchief attracts a charging bull, and Dakota, leaping from his horse, wrestles it to the ground. Just then a sheriff happens by, recognizes the escapee, and handcuffs him. Riding through the mountains on the way back to the penitentiary, Dakota escapes, leaps off a cliff, and then gets into a gunfight with the sheriff who thinks wrongly that he has taken "never-miss" aim. Dakota now steals a horse and revolver from a slumbering shepherd and uses a gunshot to free himself of the cuffs. A "long distance rifleman" spots him and stuns him with a "brain-bruise" that tumbles him out of the saddle. But his boot catches in a stirrup, and he is dragged along until the boot comes off. When he recovers consciousness, he finds himself once again a prisoner. Before he is led away, he tells Ruth he will return a changed man—and she promises to wait for him. Because Mix played Dakota, an audience could easily side with the outlaw and anticipate the possibility of his transformation. The real pleasure of the film, however, came from all the stunt work that Mix performed, from "bull dogging" to tumbling down a mountainside and getting bruised as he's dragged by the heels across the prairie. Months later, Mix reappeared in *The Escape of Jim Dolan* (1913), where he is a prospector falsely accused of cattle rustling and has to escape jail, exonerate himself, and win a woman's love.[54] Yet again, the real appeal came in his reprising the latter stunt as well as another when, submerged in a river, he breathes through his rifle barrel to elude a sheriff's posse.

One of the more unusual of these westerns was Lubin's *The Toll of Fear* (1913).[55] Written and directed by Romaine Fielding in Nogales, Arizona, this film was essentially a two-hander, with Fielding playing two sheriffs at different times. A young deputy, Dick McKnight, goes off alone to capture members of a gang of Mexican cattle rustlers, leaving a note for his brother Bill who is away. In the mountains he comes upon a note attached to a tree: "Go Back or You Will Die with the Sun." As he rides slowly on, Dick becomes

MULTIPLE-REEL WESTERNS, 1912–1914   89

more and more anxious; finally, terrified, he holes up in an abandoned adobe. His nerves worn raw, according to an intertitle, "he places his pistol to his head, the revolver explodes, [and then] darkness." Having returned home, Bill finds his brother gone and follows the trail to his dead body, the warning note still in his hand. He too now becomes so fearful that he tries to hide in an abandoned monastery. Sinking into a deep crevice, he fires his pistol wildly, and the old clay walls crumble, burying him in a tomb. In the end, the sun breaks through to reveal his hand sticking out of the rubble, still clutching that cursed note. Here, Fielding developed a strange psychological study of two white men who became equally traumatized by fear and, as a result, self-destruct. Although a Mexican gang set this plot in motion, they never appeared as characters; instead, they seemed to haunt a landscape that Mexicans and their forerunners inhabited in the past. Consequently, the film evoked their imagined presence as a continuing threat that could unsettle, unnerve, and "unman" supposedly white authority figures. Assuming the perspective of a "northern race," without alluding to such an "alien" threat, at least one exhibitor found his audiences deeply divided in their responses to this story and reported that it "affected us unpleasantly."[56]

Finally, three important, yet very different, western features released in 1914 demand attention. An unusual anomaly among them was *Salomy Jane* (1914), adapted from a popular stage play based on Bret Harte's "Salomy Jane's Kiss," with an adventurous young woman in the leading role.[57] Set in the "Days of '49" among the California redwoods, the film focuses as much on a host of settlers in Hangville as on the title character, and the plot is un-usually complicated.[58] Madison Clay and his daughter Salomy Jane arrive in the town from Kentucky, where they had been involved in a feud. A stranger called "The Man" also arrives and recognizes a man named Baldwin, who in the past had betrayed his sister. At least four men quickly court Salomy without success: gambler Jack Marbury; Starbottle, a bibulous lawyer and real estate agent; Larrabee; and Baldwin. Other "citizens" include Honest Yuba Bill; dishonest Rufe Waters; and lazy "Red Pete" Heath and a tramp named Gallagher, who rob a stagecoach and are pursued by a posse. When Red Pete is captured, so is The Man, whom the posse mistakes for his partner. After he escapes, The Man trades gunshots with Larrabee, who mistakes him for Clay, the feuding rival of his kin back home. Marbury now lets him escape the posse again, and Starbottle helps both Salomy and her father flee as well. After an exciting chase climaxing in the couple clinging to a log in a raging river, The Man, Salomy, and her father meet on a riverbank at the "Dawn of

90 OUR COUNTRY/WHOSE COUNTRY?

a New Day"—and Madison blesses their union. While managing this convoluted plot more or less well, the film often is most interested, much like travel films, in giving spectators a tour of the redwood groves in Marin County, nearby foothills, and a reconstructed pioneer mining town.[59] Salomy is introduced stepping out of a cleft in a giant redwood and then seated on a white horse dwarfed by that tree; in half a dozen scenes, the stagecoach races back to report the robbery, along winding roads amid scattered live oaks. Hangville supposedly is a gold mining town, but there is no evidence of that, nor are there any Indians or even a military presence. Eschewing the title's alleged historical period, the film seems to be located strangely in a much later period of settler colonialism.

The other two westerns introduced more conventional white heroes.[60] The first was Jesse L. Lasky and Oscar Apfel's six-reel production of Famous Players–Lasky's *The Squaw Man* (1914), an adaptation of Edwin Royle's 1905 stage play, directed by Cecil B. DeMille and "playing to enormous crowds throughout the country."[61] An English aristocrat, Jim Wyngate (Dustin Farnum), ships out to America to escape the authorities, who think he, rather than his brother, has embezzled funds to pay a gambling debt. Jim drifts to ranch life in the far West and rescues Nat-U-Rich (Red Wing), daughter of a Ute chief, from a cattle rustler, Cash Hawkins, in a railroad train station, and they begin living together.[62] Realizing she is pregnant, he finds a pastor, who refuses to wed a white man and an Indian. His ranch hands, however, force the pastor at gunpoint to marry them. (See Figure 3.8.) When Hawkins seeks revenge in the same train station, Nat-U-Rich saves Jim by shooting and killing the outlaw.[63] Later, a sheriff discovers what she has done, and they have to escape into the mountains. At one point, Jim goes snow-blind and falls into a crevice, where Nat-U-Rich struggles to rescue him and returns him to their cabin. Diana, an English countess secretly in love with Jim, soon arrives with news that his brother, dying from an accident in the Alps, has confessed to the earlier crime.[64] Although Jim refuses to return to England, he allows his mixed-race son to go in his place and become the "future Earl of Kerhill."[65] Nat-U-Rich, in turn, refuses to abandon the boy and Jim has to take him away from her. As Diana and her retinue prepare to depart, Nat-U-Rich takes a gun, goes behind the cabin, and shoots herself. While the play concludes with the Indian chief, her father, standing stoically with her corpse in his arms, the film is strikingly different. In the final tableau, as Diana shields the boy, it is Jim who cradles the prone body of Nat-U-Rich, who has followed the long tradition of self-sacrifice as a "Vanishing American."

Figure 3.8 Famous Players–Lasky, *The Squaw Man*, 1914, *Moving Picture World* (February 28, 1914)

Joanna Hearne claims that *The Squaw Man* "offers the defining example of the early Indian drama's mixed-race narrative pattern."[66] The numerous earlier westerns that established the trope suggest rather that the 1914 feature was a kind of culmination of this narrative. That said, Hearne's lengthy analysis of the film is remarkably insightful and persuasive. For one thing, Nat-U-Rich's name, in English, could mean "naturally rich," which would connote her connection to the land's natural resources and her "function as the source of her husband's wealth."[67] For another, Haskins's and Nat-U-Rich's deaths also supposedly rid "the taint of lawless violence" from this settler community. Hearne is especially astute in focusing on the couple's "half-breed" son. Initially, he is associated with a pair of moccasins that recur at several key moments, lastly when his mother holds them in her hands before she goes off to commit suicide. Signaling the boy's transformation into a future English gentleman is the trope of a costume change, in which he abandons his Indian garb, including the moccasins, for the Western-style clothes adopted for the departure. Nat-U-Rich's death also then serves to further "cleanse her son of his Native identity."[68] Moreover, he "will inherit western American land as well as an English estate and title, uniting Europe and America," as Owen Wister would appreciate, through a double sense of inheritance.[69] In

92 OUR COUNTRY/WHOSE COUNTRY?

the context of earlier Wild West subjects, however, at least two more points are salient. Unlike those prior films, in which the "half-breed" could act as a threatening villain or an assimilated figure shoring up a settler community, here the boy has his "half-breed" nature simply erased. Perhaps even more significant, the possible union of an Indian woman and a white man or squawman that was accepted or even promoted in earlier films now is undermined in the breakdown of *The Squaw Man*'s interracial marriage.

Also directed by DeMille was Famous Players–Lasky's five-reel *The Virginian* (1914).[70] "The Virginian" (Dustin Farnum) arrives in Wyoming a stranger who, after a saloon confrontation with Trampas, a local bully, hires out as a cowpuncher on Judge Henry's ranch.[71] He quickly meets his old friend Steve, and the two enjoy lots of practical jokes. But Trampas gets Steve to join his gang of rustlers, including a Mexican, Spanish Ed; when the rustlers are caught after a chase, the Virginian has to witness Steve's hanging, which, given their emotional bond, weighs heavily on him.[72] Trampas, who has escaped, now prods a band of Indians to attack and badly wound the Virginian, but Molly Wood, a schoolteacher who has emigrated from New England, finds him and helps him recover. In the end, the Virginian finally kills Trampas in a shoot-out, weds Molly, and becomes a partner in the judge's ranch. Much like *The Squaw Man*, *The Virginian* was a prestigious feature, drawn from Owen Wister's famous 1902 novel and Kirke La Shelle's successful 1904 stage play.[73] Again, it starred the same highly respected movie actor, who also had played the lead in the stage production, as a "daring and free man of the early West."[74] Several reviewers praised the "great expanse of uncultivated land" where many of the sepia-tinted scenes were shot on location at "the Johnson ranch in Lower California."[75] The film's story seemed to extend that of earlier westerns centered on the conflict between white rivals, where one was a "badman" who resorted to partnering with a Mexican outlaw and Indian warriors. But it also allied the Virginian with the "civilizing" figure of a schoolteacher, resulting in a sanctioned marriage and future family. Moreover, in moving westward from what likely was the defeated Confederacy, the Virginian helped clear the land of outlaws, Indians, and Mexicans, with an expansive ranch property as his reward. In short, the film arguably staged and fulfilled the myth of Manifest Destiny, implicitly defining *our country* through a union of the East (both North and South) with the West.

In the midst of these westerns, a decided shift already was underway. Universal-Bison was releasing fewer Indian pictures, and the trade press dismissed the company's *The Flaming Arrow* (1913), written by the melodrama playwright Lincoln J. Carter.[76] Not only were its Indians light-skinned, but also it was full of "trite," "well-worn action."[77] Even more important, in the context of the current Golden Jubilee celebrations, Broncho, Kay-Bee, and Universal-Bison were embracing the subject of the Civil War.[78] From Broncho's *Sundered Ties* (1912) and Kay-Bee's *Blood Will Tell* (1912) to Universal-Bison's *The Light in the Window* (1913) and Broncho's *The Pride of the South* (1913), all exploited the spectacle of large-scale battle scenes and white masculine heroics. The culmination, prior to *The Birth of a Nation*, came in Ince's *The Battle of Gettysburg* (June 1913), a five-reel extravaganza now lost. Of crucial interest in many of these was the now dominant ideology of "The Lost Cause," which sought to reunite North and South by honoring a revisionist idea of the Confederacy.[79] Lubin's two-reel *Reunited at Gettysburg* (1913) served as a perfect example for its focus on the reunion of former Civil War combatants and especially for its startling flashback story in which two fathers share a drink and a smoke during a momentary truce, but then the Northerner shoots the Southerner in the back just before he returns to his post.[80] Universal-Bison even produced multiple-reel films of the Spanish-American War, such as *The Stars and Stripes Forever*, *The Grand Old Flag*, and *The Battle of Manila* (all 1913). Exploiting the emergence of a cult of flag worship, these films, in the words of the formerly abolitionist *Independent*, celebrated the more recent war as "a splendid outburst of Americanism in which the South equaled the North."[81]

By 1914, as Indigenous peoples and Mexicans, whether depicted as villainous or sympathetic characters, at least from a white perspective, tended to disappear—African Americans remained largely invisible—and Indian pictures became a rarity.[82] Instead, westerns now increasingly privileged the ideology of not only white supremacy but also superior white masculinity. In Chapters 4 and 5 that follow, such privileging took on a guise very different from that of only a few years before. This was especially the case with the "badman" figure who underwent a transformation, if not always willingly. From now on, in both shorts and features, William S. Hart would epitomize a masculinized figure quite unlike Broncho Billy, for instance, and one a little closer to the Virginian.

Touring the West 3

During the early 1910s, American movie audiences also could tour wild lands in a number of longer films. The most well known of these tracked large-scale hunting expeditions to Africa, such as the much ballyhooed, *Roosevelt in Africa* (1910), which enjoyed high-level official sanction.[1] The naturalist-photographer Cherry Kearton, assisted by James L. Clark, a taxidermist at the National Museum (Washington), shot footage of the expedition that eventually was edited into 36 scenes making up the two-reel film.[2] Only the final 17 scenes were devoted to the actual hunt; with the exception of a rhinoceros kill, however, they focused on large and small animals in their habitats. For all of its advance publicity, *Roosevelt in Africa* disappointed audiences (the list of scenes suggests its lack of coherence), especially in contrast to Selig's *Hunting Big Game in Africa* (1909), ironically filmed "in the jungles" of its Chicago studio grounds.[3] Whatever their popularity and merits, both films assumed that American white men would lord it over black Africans as well as all kinds of African animals.

The most successful of these expedition features was the five-reel *Paul Rainey's African Pictures* (1912).[4] According to a synopsis of the reels, Rainey's film created a relatively coherent storyline that tracked the expedition and its encounters with a great variety of animals and occasional meetings with the chiefs of Somali and Marsai peoples.[5] Nearly every trade press article and newspaper review singled out one specific desert scene as especially notable. All kinds of animals gathered at a water hole, in unexpected groupings or at different hours of the day, leading one writer to say that it reminded him of Noah's Ark.[6] That said, some scenes did exploit common stereotypes that anthropomorphized and sentimentalized the images of wild animals in "laughable scenes" that endowed them "with a sense of humor."[7] During the film's run in Washington, DC, a lecturer, Reginald Carrington, not only helpfully introduced "the men as they appeared on the screen as well as the animals" but also added to the humor.[8] Although *Paul Rainey's African Pictures* enjoyed record bookings—16 weeks at the Lyceum in New York and three months in Boston and Chicago—and

Our Country/Whose Country?. Richard Abel, Oxford University Press. © Oxford University Press 2023.
DOI: 10.1093/oso/9780197744048.003.0007

five "state right" companies toured the country with prints,[9] a second series two years later did not do well.[10]

Against this background of African tours, *Wild Animal Life in America* (1915) stood out as a notable tour of American wild lands. This feature was made under the direction of Edward A. Salisbury, another millionaire filmmaker, writer, and world explorer, whose articles frequently appeared in *National Geographic*. For three years, assisted by the government, trappers, cameramen, and trained dogs, Salisbury traveled through the West, from Alaska to the Mexican border, compiling 250,000 feet of film.[11] "I hunt with the camera," not with a gun, Salisbury told Kitty Kelly in an interview, admitting that initially he wanted "to secure material for scientific study" (without "a bit of staging"), especially for schools and colleges, and "never expected to show these pictures for public exhibition."[12] In early 1915, all that footage was edited into six or seven reels, depending on where and when it was shown.[13] In March, the Studebaker Theater in downtown Chicago hosted one of the film's first screenings outside of California, with Salisbury himself lecturing the film.[14] The wild life captured on film ranged from mountain lions, bears, lynx, and trout (from spawn in hatcheries to adults hooked by fishermen) to birds of prey, game birds, and others "in the rookeries of the U.S. Biological Survey Reservations."[15] A trade press ad in October 1915 boasted that these were "the only pictures ever produced of Wild Animal Life in Our Own Great Country" and specifically invoked the logo of "See America First."[16] No complete print of Salisbury's film seems to survive, so the organization of its six or seven reels is difficult to determine. According to Kelly, the first reel focused on trout life, which she found "too biologic" for a general audience, but W. Stephen Bush found it fascinating, suggesting perhaps his interest as an avid fisherman. Both, however, were appalled by the scenes of hunters shooting wild geese. (See Figure W3.1.)

Intriguingly, a fragment of *Wild Animal Life in America* turned up nearly a decade ago in the New Zealand film archive, and half of its 12 minutes are devoted to the goose hunt in California.[17] After a series of long-held shots of various waterfowl, including a closeup of 11 speckled eggs in a coot's nest, comes "Hunting Wild Geese for Market." This sequence begins with a group of hunters taking a train from San Francisco to the Sacramento Delta, where they use injured birds as decoys and conceal themselves in deep holes dug into the ground. A camera operator also hides in one of those holes with a Bell and Howell camera as evidence of the subsequent footage's authenticity. The hunt is grisly in its detail. Shooting repeatedly into the air, the hunters

Figure W3.1 Edward A. Salisbury, *Wild Animal Life in America*, 1915 (Academy of Motion Picture Arts and Sciences, Los Angeles, California)

take down dozens of geese; soon the ground is littered with carcasses, much like a battleground in the raging European war. One hunter even chases a wounded bird into a small pond and kills it. The sequence ends with hunters corralling the flightless, injured "decoys" into trucks, and an intertitle says that as many as 800 geese have been shot dead. This is a "cruel waste" by "so-called hunters," Kelly writes. Bush is even more emphatic, describing the geese as "wantonly and willfully exterminated by men who are utterly devoid of every instinct of sportsmanship." Known as an ardent conservationist, Salisbury inserted an intertitle after the shot of littered carcasses: "Proper legislative measures must be passed to eliminate this work of destruction and conserve our wild life."[18] Most of the film admittedly celebrates the "romance" of roaming the open country of the West and finding unusual animals and masses of birds perhaps not seen before in motion pictures by virtual tourists in picture theater seats.[19] But this sequence refuses to ignore the destruction, the threatened extermination, that results from marketing the progress allegedly made in a century of westward expansion.

4

William S. Hart, "The Man with the Face That Talks"

In October 2019, Diane and Richard Koszarski and I curated seven programs devoted to the early two-reel films and features of William S. Hart (1865–1946) for the Giornate del cinema muto (Pordenone, Italy).[1] Eleven films on these programs showcased Hart's busiest and most creative period (1914–1918), ending just as he separated from Thomas Ince and Triangle Films, finally coming into his own as one of Paramount-Artcraft's best players. A 1918 poll in *Motion Picture Magazine* even put Hart among the country's top five stars, which suggests how popular he was with most adult moviegoers. No other westerner came close, not even Tom Mix. The festival catalogue entries offered detailed information on the films' production and distribution. They also highlighted Hart's persona and his relations with other characters, stylistic patterns in the camerawork, and key moments of tension and poignancy in the stories. All perfectly fine film analyses. But Hart's westerns deserve a different look. What happens when his films, including those recently rediscovered, restored, or reconstructed, are re-viewed through the lens of settler colonialism, especially as they become more and more distinct from earlier westerns?

Because this chapter, unlike the previous three, focuses on a single movie star, a brief sketch of Hart's background would be useful. Growing up in the upper Midwest, he learned the skills of farming and ranching, especially riding horses and handling guns, but his family moved to New York City when he was a teenager. To escape a cramped world of illness and poverty, he abandoned schooling and ventured to try his hand at stage acting. So, he came to filmmaking rather late, after what became a long career as a well-known theater actor. On stage from 1888 as an interpreter of Shakespeare and Dumas plays, he initially won attention as a "muscular and insolent" Messala in *Ben-Hur* (1899). The figure of the "Westerner" was not part of his professional persona until he took on the small role of villain Cash Hawkins in Edwin Milton Royle's *The Squaw Man* (1905). Other western roles followed,

Our Country/Whose Country?. Richard Abel, Oxford University Press. © Oxford University Press 2023.
DOI: 10.1093/oso/9780197744048.003.0008

98   OUR COUNTRY/WHOSE COUNTRY?

and the "authenticity" of his characterizations, he thought, helped forge the theatrical successes of *The Virginian* (adapted from Owen Wister's novel and stage play), Rex Beach's *The Barrier*, and *The Trail of the Lonesome Pine*. By 1914, the collapse of the traveling roadshow economy led him, in collaboration with Thomas Ince, to introduce his branded western persona and skills as a horseman and gunman into the movies.[2] The timing was fortuitous.

Ince began producing the first of Hart's westerns, both features, in the summer of 1914. *The Bargain* was released through Paramount in November, just months after *The Virginian*, but *On the Night Stage*, for debatable reasons, was delayed by Mutual until April 1915. Perhaps as a cautious strategy, *The Bargain*'s plot bore similarities to titles from the early 1910s, notably Essanay's *A Westerner's Way*.[3] W. Stephen Bush even called it "nothing more than an old-fashioned 'Western,'" not even "one inch above the average of such pictures."[4] Known as the "Two-Gun Man," Jim Stokes is a feared outlaw who robs a stagecoach, is pursued and wounded, loses his way in the Badlands, and falls unconscious near a spring. Stokes is found by the father of Nell Brant, and she nurses him back to health, falls in love, and marries him, unaware of his past. Before he can return the stolen money, Jim is recognized and pursued; after he pins a note to his saddle and sends his horse home, he reaches a large casino where a sheriff arrests him. The sheriff, however, gambles away the stolen money, and Jim promises to recover it if he is allowed to go free. He holds up the gambling room cashier and escapes a posse, plunging over a precipice, but reaches the sheriff and is handcuffed again before the posse arrives. The next day, once they leave town together, the sheriff loosens the cuffs and Jim returns to Nell; after explaining what has happened, they cross the border into another state. Three things are worth noting in this "old-fashioned western." One is Hart's performance, as "fine and polished bit of artistic creation as a Frederick Remington sketch." [5] Another is the unusually large interior set of the casino, seen in the high-angle long shot of a production photo.[6] This is the all-male space of a settled frontier town full of cowboys, miners, and entrepreneurs—except for a couple Mexicans on the right frame edge, marked by their sombreros. The third is the initial stagecoach robbery, which was shot in and around the Grand Canyon, highlighted in a trade press ad that posed Jim and Nell together against a "magnificent" view of the national park, which, for those who could afford it, now was a favorite tourist destination.[7] (See Figure 4.1.) Choosing the Grand Canyon heightened the myth of the desert wilderness as a supposedly empty landscape where a white outlaw could undergo a redemption.

Figure 4.1 Paramount-Artcraft, *The Silent Man*, 1917 (US Library of Congress, Washington, DC)

Beginning in December 1914, the half dozen two-reel Broncho and Kay-Bee films starring Hart introduced a series of tropes in terms of spaces, characters, and stories that would prove characteristic. First of all, in the context of the North American continent, Hart's westerns were set in the last stages of settler colonialism. The landscapes were defined by sage brush and mountains, gulches or canyons, and deserts, otherwise empty except for scattered cattle ranches, mining companies, stagecoach waystations, and small, roughly built frontier towns with crowded saloons and dance halls. For the most extreme expression of those landscapes, see the intertitles that open *The Silent Man* (November 1917): "Primordial desolation, a huge waste.... A trackless solitude ..."[8] Hart's character often was an outlaw, and of a kind very different from Broncho Billy, but he also appeared several times as a sheriff or sheriff's deputy or miner and once each as a casino owner, cattle rancher, and lumberjack. In the latter cases, if not always respectable, he was a figure of authority controlling the inhabitants and resources of an emerging, predominately white male community. His rivals were white men, from gamblers and womanizers to other outlaws, and, in certain films, thieving Mexicans. Most women also were white, like the intrepid mine owner's daughter in *In Sage Brush Country* or the pioneering mother in *The Sheriff's Yellow Streak*. Although usually restricted to secondary roles, they served as the prime agents of Hart's transformation into a "good badman." With two brief exceptions analyzed later, despite his earlier nostalgic sympathy for Native Americans as "Vanishing Americans," Indigenous peoples were nowhere to be found.[9]

The first of these short westerns—*The Passing of Two-Gun Hicks* and *In the Sage Brush Country* (both December 1914)—are exemplary. Another "Two-Gun Man," Hicks is a feared gunfighter who drifts into the Red Eye saloon in Moose Gulch, coldly refuses a drink with the local bully, and calmly shoots him in the wrist when he angrily goes for his gun.[10] Stepping outside, he meets May Jenks, wife of the town drunkard, who rebuffs him; realizing that the woman inexplicably loves Jenks, he decides not to challenge her husband. Hayes, a local gambler, bent on getting May for himself, now incites Jenks to confront Hicks, expecting his demise in a gunfight. Liquored up, Jenks orders Hicks to get out of town by sundown or else. But May begs the gunfighter, "If you love me as you say, spare him." At sundown, Jenks and his fellow drinkers wait outside the saloon, while Hicks, true to his word, rides away over the hills, passing out of the frontier town forever. Promoted as a "bad man's sacrifice for a good woman," this film is less notable for its rather meager, conventional plot than for Hart's stone face, betraying hardly a flicker of emotion beyond insolence, and his fierce gaze in closeups: "the effect they create," one reviewer wrote, "is clear and forcible."[11] Unlike *The Bargain*, it also ends, as several later films will, with him riding slowly off on horseback, leaving behind the woman he briefly loved. While the people of Moose Gulch celebrate what they imagine is the gunfighter's cowardice, only Hicks and May know the real reason why he has left a town that remains far from "civilized"—once more a figure, as in the opening, "alone and silent."

In the Sage Brush Country, by contrast, is far less conventional.[12] It begins with Jim Brandon, in a rough-hewn cabin, looking through the Lost Hope Mine payroll he has robbed from the Wolf Creek stagecoach.[13] Confident of his concealed identity, Brandon later enters the frontier town's saloon to down shots of whiskey, evidence of Janet Flanner's tongue-in-cheek depiction of Hart as "the hardest drinker on screen."[14] He overhears other drinkers say it is "payday," soon realizes that the mine owner Frank Wilding has entrusted his daughter Edith with the payroll, and follows her onto the stage. When it stops at a mountainside "restaurant," with a wooden Indian and two lolling Native Americans by the door,[15] he forges an unacknowledged bond

WILLIAM S. HART, "THE MAN WITH THE FACE THAT TALKS" 101

with Edith by protecting her from the advances of a "lady's man." He does that with a quick sure gunshot that corrects a sign on the wall, followed by a witty quip: "My teacher told me to always dot my 'i's." A Mexican thief (so says an intertitle)[16] later stops the stage, tosses Brandon's revolver over an embankment, pockets his watch, and steals a kiss from Edith, who slaps him. Insulted, he takes her off to a deserted shack in the brushy hills and forces her into a bedroom, where she barricades the door. With some skillful stunt work, Brandon retrieves his gun, follows on foot, and finds the thief trying to break down the door and attack Edith. In an exchange of gunshots, he not only kills the Mexican but recovers his watch. Edith then entrusts Brandon with the payroll for safekeeping, and he leads her, seated on his horse, until they reach a ridge overlooking the mine far below. Abandoning his own robbery plans, he returns the payroll, kisses Edith's hand, and watches her ride slowly down toward the waiting miners. In the final shot, he turns and walks off alone on the barren road.

In this tightly condensed film, a few remarkable moments stand out. The interior of Brandon's cabin exemplifies Hart's concern for "authentic detail" in the overturned barrel he uses for a table, the pouch of stolen gold he hides in the fireplace, and the can used to brew coffee. He also begins to set the characters he plays apart from other white men, with his knee-length black coat and embroidered vest as well as the "stone face" he adopts as a mask throughout. There also are the gestures that begin to define his persona, admired in this snippet of parodic gossip: "William S. Hart, who can roll a cigarette with one hand and light a match in the other without scratching it on anything, is now learning to take off his hat with his left ear."[17] Before joining Edith in the stagecoach, his steely looks and stilled stance outside Wilding's office slowly register his growing awareness of how the payroll will be delivered. An unusual series of shots mark the climactic gunfight, as Brandon stealthily cracks open the cabin door and spots the Mexican reflected in a window, which lets him fire before the thief can. Finally, the ending establishes what was becoming a familiar trope in Hart's westerns: a lone white male figure, having disavowed love, walking into the empty background of an unknown future. If he doesn't return to his outlaw ways and the gold pieces hidden in his cabin's chimney, can he ever find acceptance in a settler community?

The Sheriff's Streak of Yellow (February 1915) differs from other Hart westerns in that there is no potential romantic partner to transform his "badman" figure through love.[18] Instead, here Sheriff Hale, much admired in the frontier mining town of Gold Bar, rides out alone to find the wanted outlaw Bill Todd, who has just buried his mother. Getting the drop on Todd, Hale is startled to recognize him as the son of a woman who once saved him from dying in the desert—and a flashback reveals his indebtedness. Threatening to kill him if they meet again, he lets Todd go free; but he refuses to explain why he failed to arrest the outlaw, and the townspeople demand and accept his resignation. Later, when Todd and his gang raid the local bank, Hale awakens in his room across the street and begins shooting the gang members standing guard outside the bank. Sneaking inside, he finds Todd and another man trying to break into the vault; in the fight that ensues, Hale kills the other man, and Todd, accepting his own debt to the lawman, shoots himself. The grateful townspeople now realize that Hale is not the coward they thought and return his sheriff's badge. This story turns on a misrecognition of Hart's character (a trope of melodrama), the singular conflict between Hale and Todd, and the redemptive power of a mother figure. Tellingly, the film opens with a relatively long scene of Todd's loving care for his deathly ill mother and then for her gravesite, giving the outlaw a past (Hale has none other than his rescue by that mother) and a conscience. The reciprocal caregiving of mother and son then heightens the doubled sense of indebtedness that eventually binds and redeems the two white male antagonists.

For the next six months following the April release of *On the Night Stage*, which one critic dismissed as a short western drawn out to five reels,[19] Mutual exploited Hart's increasing popularity by producing more than half a dozen more two-reel westerns.[20] The first of these, *The Taking of Luke McVane* (April 1915), works a somewhat surprising variation and reversal of certain typical tropes.[21] In a spacious saloon, Luke is either a miner or a "range rider" playing cards with "Crooked Jim" Ashley, while Mercedes, the "Belle of Chuckawalla Valley," dances for a crowd of white and Mexican patrons. After she approaches Luke and hands him a rose, he protects her from being menaced by Garcia, a local bully who covets her. Soon she reciprocates, silently alerting him to the gambler's cheating. After a brief struggle, Luke shoots the gambler, flees the saloon, and rides into a sandy desert landscape. The town sheriff pursues him, and Mercedes follows with an extra horse she has stolen and misleads a posse onto a false trail. The sheriff catches up with Luke, who wounds the lawman with a rifle shot, carries him to his bare cabin, cares for his head wound, and explains why he fled the saloon—rightly fearing he could be lynched. The sheriff now convinces Luke to return to town and promises to use his influence to exonerate him. On the journey, however, they are waylaid by a band of Apaches who have jumped a reservation (according to an intertitle). They try to fight off the circling Indians; in the end, a search posse finds both men dead.[22] Here, the Apaches first appear in what was becoming a visual trope of early westerns: in a striking low-angle extreme long shot, they ride single file, as if one with the landscape, along the crest of a distant sand dune. In an unexpected twist, Luke's possible love interest is the Mexican dancer (played by Edith Markey, in slightly darkened makeup) who aids him twice in exchange for his rescue of her. Moreover, alternating with the "Circle of Death" gunfight near the end is a bedroom scene with Mercedes looking at herself in a dresser mirror, turning slowly toward the camera, closing her eyes, and bowing her head—as if she knows Luke will not be returning. In the last somewhat sentimental close shot of Luke, his hand is clutching the rose she gave him earlier in the saloon. But the last shot of Mercedes, by contrast, is poignant, for she now is the one left alone with an uncertain future, as a non-white "alien" in a settler community dominated by men and easily provoked to violence.

The Man from Nowhere (May 1915) begins with Buck Farley on horseback looking down from a ridge on the town of Snake River, Arizona, a stranger "from nowhere" and without a past, much like Clint Eastwood's loner in *High Plains Drifter* (1973).[23] In the Chicago Saloon, the owner Johnson jokingly gets his customers to name a drunk, Jake Frazer, as sheriff and then is rebuffed by Emma, Frazer's daughter.[24] Entering the saloon, Buck breaks up a fight in which Frazer is being beaten but fails to realize that Johnson pretends to have saved him, when he actually was about to shoot him. Buck becomes Frazer's deputy, begins to fall in love with Emma, and is surprised to find Johnson courting her. Johnson then uses a ruse to get Buck searching for some allegedly stolen horses in the desert but is forced to accompany him. Surreptitiously, Johnson hides their waterskins, one after another, and one night shoos Buck's horse away. Invoking Buck's earlier promise to save him in return, Johnson tries to retrace his steps in the desert, fails to find any of the buried waterskins, and dies drinking from an alkaline-poisoned water hole. Meanwhile, Buck also backtracks, finds one buried waterskin, which gives him the strength to struggle back to Frazier's cabin, where he learns about Johnson's "true character" and "wins Emma for his wife."[25] While Buck becomes an integral part of a pioneering settler community, how much of his desert ordeal he shares with Emma and the townspeople is unclear. He may still remain a stranger, a bit of a cypher. As in the previous film, one point of

104   OUR COUNTRY/WHOSE COUNTRY?

interest comes as the two white men wander in the trackless desert, and at least one review praised the film's atmosphere, sometimes "realistic to the extreme," especially in the "engrossing" desert scenes.[26] In fact, they strikingly foreshadow the marvelous ending in *Greed* (1924).

A similarly bleak, unforgiving desert landscape marks *"Bad Buck" of Santa Ynez* (May 1915).[27] "Bad Buck" Peters is a hard-drinking cowboy who clatters on horseback into a frontier town of clapboard buildings, takes over The Red Dog Saloon, and dares the local sheriff to a duel of whiskey shots. The sheriff proves a sore loser and threatens Buck who has to escape the sheriff's posse that is eager to lynch him. In a semiarid desert, he comes upon a lone grieving pioneer family, a mother and her young daughter, who beg him to help bury the dead father. He refuses until the little girl arouses his pity, and he drives them and their covered wagon to his isolated shack. At one point, from a mountain vista, Buck tracks his pursuers on a trail far below while he whittles a doll for the girl. When she is bitten by a rattlesnake, Buck rides back into town to fetch a doctor, but the sheriff's posse follows, plots an ambush, and badly wounds him. Buck gets the doctor to the shack in time and, while the mother stops the sheriff and his men at the door, drags himself to the girl's bedside and expires next to her. This is the second film in which Hart's "good badman" has to die in the end. In contrast to the scene of Apaches filing across a ridge line in *The Taking of Luke McVane*, here it is Bad Buck, in crisp silhouette on the horizon, who tops a rugged landscape as he is returning to town for the doctor. A trade press review called attention to how popular these short westerns were becoming for audiences of all kinds, chiefly because "the personal magnetism of William S. Hart is almost immeasurable."[28]

Mutual released the last of these two-reel westerns in August 1915. Among them were *Pinto Ben* and the tongue-in-cheek titled *A Knight of the Trails*.[29] The most interesting, however, was *Keno Bates, Liar*.[30] Joint proprietors of the "Double Stamp" casino and dance hall, Keno reigns over the faro table while Wind River handles the bar.[31] A Mexican dancer, Anita, is in love with Keno, but he carelessly dismisses her.[32] As the casino is closing and the partners are alone, a man robs them and escapes with the night's winnings. In pursuit (the town has no sheriff), Keno kills the robber and finds a locket with a miniature portrait and a letter from Doris Maitland, calling him her brother and saying she will soon arrive from the Northeast. The two saloon owners report the circumstances of the killing and warn the townspeople to say nothing about that to the young woman. Instead, Keno tells Doris that her brother died in

WILLIAM S. HART, "THE MAN WITH THE FACE THAT TALKS" 105

a mining accident, and, as his "partner," gives her his well-built cabin, horse, casino winnings, and even his gun belt. But she does not respond to his gesture of courtship—in an atypical scene he gathers creekside flowers for her. In a fit of jealousy, Anita tells Doris that Keno killed her brother; horrified, she takes his revolver and shoots him in the shoulder. Luckily, Wind River intervenes and reveals the truth about her brother before the wounded Keno can ride off in stoic silence. Doubly horrified now, Doris nurses him back to health, and, in the end, Wind River plays chaperone to the couple on horseback. Here, the film's villainous rival is both Mexican and female, the very opposite of Mercedes in *The Taking of Luke McVane*. Intriguingly, the final shots of this romantic couple mask the guilt they share, the one for lying and the other for not only accepting a half lie but also trying to kill her presumed lover. In that masking, the film refuses to draw attention to the compromised love of this "happy ending."

While the last of the two-reel westerns were in production, Ince and Hart began turning to feature-length films that would be distributed through Triangle. Given the limited number of features that survive, the following analyses focus largely on those screened at the 2019 Giornate del cinema muto and/or are available on DVD. The first of these, *The Darkening Trail* (May 1915), merits only a brief mention because its story was set in a white mining town in Alaska, a story later worked out more fully in *Blue Blazes Rawden*.[33] The second feature, in five reels, was *The Disciple* (November 1915), and this film is somewhat of an anomaly among Hart's westerns.[34] He plays Jim Houston, a parson with a wife named Mary and a little girl, who arrives in Barren Gulch intending to "reform" the frontier town.[35] When Mary is seduced by "Doc" Hardy, a saloon owner and gambler, and elopes with him, Jim abandons his ministry and takes his child to a log cabin in the mountains. There, as melodramatic coincidences pile up, the child falls ill, Mary turns up at the cabin, and Hardy (the only doctor in the area) is called to treat the girl. Forced to choose between the two men, Mary goes to her child; unexpectedly sharing Mary's humbled contrition, Jim forgives her and sends Hardy off unharmed. Where they will live now seems uncertain because he clearly will not return to his ministry. One sign of Hart's stature as an actor and star by this time comes in a glowing review by Louis Reeves Harrison, the very opposite of his earlier dismissal of *The Bargain*. Now he praises Hart's "manly physique and face peculiarly suited to that highly expressive suppression of emotion so effective in screen portrayals."[36] (See Figure 4.2.) Put simply, Hart's stoic strength and "steely-eyed" gaze was

Figure 4.2 "In the Frame of Public Favor," *Chicago Sunday Tribune* (December 12, 1915): 5.3

creating a model of "cowboy tough" self-reliance for the performance of white American masculinity.[37]

A much-admired treasure among these features is the five-reel *Hell's Hinges* (February 1916).[38] The title comes from a town called Place Center, Oklahoma, known in the region as "Hell's Hinges," so "everyone who could gave it wide berth."[39] The setting, somewhere in the Southwest and "patterned after Virginia City in the early seventies," is a rough, uncivilized frontier town in a bleak, desert landscape.[40] Into what an intertitle warns is a "gun-fighting, man-killin' den of iniquity" comes an Eastern preacher, Robert Henley, and his sister Faith, to the consternation of Silk Miller who runs this lawless place, lording over his saloon and dance hall, the pretentiously named Palace of Joy. When Blaze Tracy, a known "badman" and resigned loner rides into town, Miller tries to get him to neutralize the preacher's reformist ambitions. Meeting Faith, Blaze hesitates and eventually stands aside as the preacher erects a new church. Routing a bunch of saloon drinkers bent on disrupting the first sermon, Blaze listens to Faith but not to her brother and, undergoing a transformation, becomes their protector. Miller now sets Dolly, one of his dancers, to prey on Henley, who ends up drunk in her room. Plied with liquor, Henley joins the saloon drinkers in planning to burn down his own church. While Blaze has gone away to bring back a doctor to treat Henley, a gunfight erupts between the congregation members and the saloon drinkers; Henley is shot dead, and the church is set afire. Returning to find chaos, Blaze strides into the saloon, backs the crowd into another room, killing some of the men, and sets the building on fire. As the whole town is destroyed, the survivors scatter into the desert, Blaze and Faith go off alone, burying her brother along a trail and hoping to begin "a new life."

The staging of the climactic inferno undoubtedly produces some of the more amazing moments in the film. (See Figure 4.3.) Interspersed with closer shots of Blaze dragging away Henley's body and his rampage in the Palace of Joy, most scenes of the spectacular fire that engulfs the entire town "are taken from considerable distances, immense in their sweep of atmosphere and realism."[41] They also reveal, as the raging fire engulfs it, how strangely

Figure 4.3 Triangle, *Hell's Hinges*, 1916 (EYE Museum, Amsterdam)

108   OUR COUNTRY/WHOSE COUNTRY?

isolated the town is in such a desolate landscape. At the same time, the names given to Blaze and Faith suggest the extreme dichotomy of forces at work in that nightmarish climax. On the one hand, his name evokes a sense of Old Testament damnation that turns the town into a literal Hell; on the other, hers gestures toward a faint sense of hope. Yet where, "beyond the mountains," can this reformed badman and good woman find a new life in such a bleak landscape?[42] In the end, as Scott Simmon writes, *Hell's Hinges* "hasn't the slightest interest in the Western's standard theme of civilization's advance via America's westward progress."[43] In fact, despite a publicity claim that "no one will find 'Hell's Hinges' objectionable," one can argue that it mounts a stark critique of any progress assumed by a white community—free of Indigenous peoples, Mexicans, and African Americans—built through the Manifest Destiny of settler colonialism.[44]

The Return of Draw Egan, in five reels (October 1916), reverts to a more conventional narrative and to less complexity in Hart's "badman" character, but with a surprising twist.[45] (See Figure 4.4.) The leader of a large gang of outlaws, "Draw" Egan first appears in a wanted poster, offering a high reward of $1,000 dead or alive. Pursued by a posse through hills and canyons, the gang holes up in a cabin and, though surrounded, cleverly escapes through a hidden tunnel; but his friend, Arizona Joe, is captured and jailed. As a lone "stranger," he now enters a saloon in Broken Hope, shows off his fast draw against a bully, and Mat Buckton hires him as sheriff of nearby Yellow Dog. At first, now named William Blake and supported by the town's Reform League, he plans to use his position as a cover. He quickly rejects the advances of Poppy, "Queen of the Dance Hall," then falls for Buckton's daughter Myrtle, and begins to establish "law and order" by singlehandedly holding off a crowd of rowdy cowboys in the town saloon. Meanwhile, having escaped jail, Joe reappears and teams with Poppy to undermine Blake by threatening to reveal his "badman" past. Seeming a coward, Blake agrees not to confront Joe, who takes over the saloon, but when Joe orders the Bucktons and half of the townspeople to leave, Blake finally intervenes. Accepting the revelation of his past as Egan, he promises Buckton to give himself up, but only after he has it out with Joe in a gunfight at sundown.[46] Using a window reflection to spot Joe hiding behind some barrels (repeating a tactic from *In the Sage Brush Country*), Egan aims a sure shot that kills Joe and then tries to fulfill his promise. Now it is Myrtle who overcomes her sense of betrayal and persuades him to stay. In a relatively unusual scene for a Hart film, Blake and Myrtle's courting is framed by flowers and trees, creating an explicitly

Figure 4.4 Triangle ad, *Moving Picture World*, October 21, 1916

domestic space both within and outside the increasingly lawless town.[47] When they later ride together, he embraces his pinto before embracing her! With no Mexicans or Indigenous people menacing Yellow Dog and the surrounding landscape, the film pits whites against whites, even pairing Blake and Myrtle against Joe and Poppy, for control of this settler community. On the one hand, Hart's character seems to embody the "Vanishing American" of other westerns, described by one reviewer as having an "Indian-like composure [of] surprising alertness."[48] On the other, he has to confront and resolve his own inner conflict, whether to continue as a lawman of authority, under the name of Blake, or return to his former outlaw ways, as Draw Egan.

In the five-reel *Truthful Tulliver* (January 1917), Hart takes the role of "a good man straight through from beginning to end."[49] Tulliver is an "itinerant editor" from Texas who arrives in Glory Hole, Arizona, hoping to start a newspaper with his printer, "Silver Lode" Thompson.[50] In the Forty-Rod saloon they find "plenty going on"—dancing to a Mexican band, gambling, a shooting—and Tulliver announces his aim of publishing "all news fit to print." This rankles "Deacon" Doyle, the saloon owner, and York Cantrell, whose mining properties make him a force in the frontier town. During a brawl outside the saloon one day, a crowd accosts two sisters, Grace and Daisy Barton, and Tulliver stops Doyle from threatening them. Tulliver prints a notice calling for Doyle's banishment, and he is chosen as the leader of vigilantes. That night he mounts up, bursts through the saloon's back door, lassos Doyle and a henchman, and drags them across the floor and right through a window into the street. Doyle and his fellows are banished, and the saloon closes. When York courts Daisy, Tulliver mistakes her dark silhouette for Grace, whom he is beginning to love. Now Doyle sneaks back into town at night and, from York's room window across the street, tries to shoot Tulliver in his office but hits Thompson instead. Tulliver confronts the two men, and in a struggle over his gun, Doyle is killed; York is then ordered out of town. After talking with the sisters around Thompson in bed, Tulliver rides after York, stops the train he is on, and brings him back. To his surprise, York goes to Daisy, and Grace puts a fond hand on Tulliver's shoulder. Hart's promotion of "authenticity" or the "enactment of authenticity," led to the use of rare old photographs to construct a realistic newspaper office of the period, locating a hand press and type racks in a Los Angeles antique shop.[51] Besides the spectacle of dragging the lassoed villains through the saloon and crashing through a window, singled out by several newspapers, Hart also devised another in which he leaped from his racing horse onto the back of a train.[52]

Although Mexicans appear briefly as musicians, they already have been integrated into this lawless frontier town, well before Tulliver and his vigilantes turn it, somewhat ambiguously, into a "civilized" white community.

No complete copy of the five-reel *The Gun Fighter* (February 1917) has been found, but three very different fragments do survive. The Giornate del cinema muto arranged for the film's reconstruction, using those fragments, which was screened in 2019.[53] Kevin Brownlow donated his much condensed 9.5mm Pathescope print (1926) for the film's opening. The Cinémathèque Suisse contributed a tinted 35mm nitrate print, surviving in two reels (a European export version with Dutch intertitles), which covered the middle of the film. A different 9.5 Pathex version provided much of the film's climax, a nighttime shootout. Production photos and inserted explanatory intertitles filled in gaps in the plot. Although this reconstruction still could not match *The Gun Fighter*'s original five reels, it proved more than Louis Reeves Harrison's dismissal of yet another Hart western that simply "follows copy."[54]

Hart begins as an unusually ruthless "badman," Cliff Hudspeth, feared for killing the bullies who challenge him. Nicknamed "Killer," he tallies their names in a notebook.[55] While he and his band of outlaws, from their hideout in the Gila Mountains, threaten the border region around Desert Pass, Arizona, he has a rival in El Salvador, a half breed, who has his own gang of desperadoes. After "Cactus" Fuller, El Salvador's henchman, takes the gang to town and robs some miners of their gold, he boasts, in the Golden Fleece saloon, of how he could handle Hudspeth. When Hudspeth appears, he throws the braggart out of the saloon, waves a milliner back inside her shop, and quickly shoots "Cactus" in a gunfight. The milliner, Norma Wright, denounces him as a cold-blooded murderer; stung by the accusation, he seizes her, returns to his mountain cabin, and locks her in a room. Hudspeth tries to drown her words with whiskey, but in a nightmare (like Richard III"s) his earlier victims reproach him, and the next morning Norma, improbably, persuades him to pledge no more killing. "The government" offers Hudspeth a pardon if he will rid the territory of El Salvador. Enraged, the rival sets fire to the frontier town and drags Norma away into the mountains. After rescuing her, Hudspeth kills El Salvador in an exchange of gunshots in the dark of night, but he himself is mortally wounded.[56] Sending Norma off on his horse to safety, the gunfighter dies, consoled in knowing that he has killed only in her defense. Desert Pass is a strangely divided town. Hudspeth's white outlaws fight for its control with a gang of Mexicans led by a half breed, whose attack on the town echoes that

112   OUR COUNTRY/WHOSE COUNTRY?

of a raid one year earlier "on Columbus, N.M, which took American troops to the Mexican border."[57] In miniature, their rivalry reenacts the story of white encroachment on land formerly governed by Mexico (Indians seem absent). Yet Norma's milliner shop gives it a veneer of "civilization." Aiming to extend that veneer, government authorities in the Arizona territory then hire one killer to get rid of another, a compromised bargain that aims implicitly to ensure a safe place for more settlers like her. Hardly unique among Hart's characters, Hudspeth ends up sacrificing himself for a more lawful white community, one in which he cannot be part.

Another five-reel feature, *Wolf Lowry* (June 1917), has Hart in the surly role of Tom "Wolf" Lowry, a cattle baron who is owner of the Bar Z ranch.[58] A grim, hardened man—one reviewer strikingly described him as a "frontier bully, who has a German-like faith in the rule of force"[59]—Lowry is quick with a gun and lords it over his rowdy band of cowboys. He runs off anyone who dares to try living in a distant cabin on the ranch and prepares to threaten the latest squatter. But he is stunned to find Mary Davis there, a young woman searching for her fiancé, Owen Thorpe, who has gone West to recover his health. Surprised by his attraction to her, he even goes so far as to hang around the cabin at night, a silent stalker watching her shadow on the window shade. She slowly begins to "civilize" Lowry, especially after he saves her from the advances of Buck Fanning, the real estate agent who sold her a claim on the cabin and who then shoots and wounds Lowry in retaliation. Forced to nurse him back to health, she feels more and more alone—and finally agrees to marry him. Later Lowry finds Thorpe and brings him to Mary, mistakenly assuming he is her half-brother; discovering the deception and the couple's plan to run off together, Lowry demands she keep her promise. On the wedding day, however, he suddenly announces that the preacher will be marrying her to Owen. After deeding the ranch to her, he goes off alone, supposedly to his "holdings" in Alaska. Again, no Indigenous peoples or Mexicans lurk in this wild country; instead, the "alien" is a stereotypical Chinese cook, the butt of cowboy jokes and a mock lynching. Lowry's rivals also are other white men for the love of a young white woman. In a gesture of self-sacrifice, Lowry gives up both the ranch and woman he has come to love. In the surviving print, he looks down from a distant hilltop on the celebrations of a domesticated settler community, from which—like a lone character in several Shakespeare comedies—he is excluded. A recently discovered fragment, however, includes scenes from five years later, with the couple reading a letter from Lowry, whose words conceal the truth: in a final shot, he has no "holdings" and sits freezing and alone in a rough, snowbound cabin.[60]

Ince and Hart's distribution contract with Triangle grew acrimonious, and soon W.H. Productions was reissuing retitled versions of Hart's earlier two-reelers as "new features."[61] To counter any damage to Hart's brand, they arranged for Paramount-Artcraft to take over the distribution of his features, and the first to be produced was *The Narrow Trail* (December 1917). Although shot and edited by October 1917, New York Motion Picture (part of Triangle) sued to get an injunction against the film (the writer and director were still under its contract), which allegedly delayed its release for several months.[62] Uncertain of a legal resolution, Hart quickly produced *The Silent Man* for exhibition in November.[63] This haste led to a more conventional story than usual, in a script written by the playwright Charles Kenyon, and some confusion in the film's continuity.[64] Unlike his previous characters, Hart's "Silent" Bud Marr is a hardworking, honest, even naïve miner who is swindled out of his claim, forced to become a hunted "badman" in an effort to recover it, and then, vaguely motivated, turns himself into a kind of "sacrificial lamb." Another strange dichotomy, rather different from previous films, separates the family of good white people who befriend Marr and are building a church in the mountains (but for whom?) far from the lawless town of Bakeoven, run by the conniving saloon owner "Handsome Jack" Pressley. Whether the town undergoes a "civilized" transformation in the end, after Pressley is unmasked and arrested, remains unclear.

The Narrow Trail, arguably one of Hart's best westerns, tells a surprising story written by Hart himself—based on tales told to him by a friend of his father in the Dakotas[65]—that moves from the frontier town of Saddle City in the California mountains to the big city of San Francisco and back.[66] As "Ice" Harding, Hart is the leader of an outlaw gang and owner of a prize pinto he has lassoed and tamed. (See Figure 4.5.) When he holds up a stagecoach, Ice is stunned to find among its passengers Betty Werdin, a niece of the vacationing "Admiral" Bates. Later, forced to abandon the gang who believe his pinto is too well known, Ice rides alone into the settled white town of Saddle City. There he meets Bates, posing as a San Francisco businessman ironically named Washington, and he reciprocates, calling himself Jefferson and pretending to own a distant ranch. Taken with Jefferson, Betty refuses for once to join Bates's scheme to rob him of the fictional ranch. Both Ice and Betty conceal their pasts from one another, and she gives him a false address in San Francisco. When he decides to go there, he can't find her; thugs try

Figure 4.5 Paramount-Artcraft, *The Narrow Trail*, 1917 (George Eastman Museum, Rochester, New York)

to shanghai him and take him to Bates's saloon, where Betty ("Queen of the Barbary Coast") is ordered to seduce him in a back room. Horrified, they recognize one another, and, belying his name, Ice angrily threatens her. After an especially brutal fight with the thugs (Hart was "severely bruised"),[67] Ice escapes and returns in shame to Saddle City; later, Betty follows. After Ice enters a horse race, he and Betty meet by chance, warily apologize to one another, and realize that "we need each other real bad." Fearing he will be arrested after he wins the race, Ice seizes the $1,000 prize and pulls Betty up onto his horse, and, escaping a posse again, they ride off into the mountains.

By now, audiences would expect many characteristic scenes and moments in a Hart western: the extremely deep space of Bates's saloon, high-angle extreme long shots of horsemen racing through canyons, Hart's lone figure slowly riding into town. Yet one was particularly striking. As he leads a vigilante group away from his gang, Ice crosses over a chasm on a fallen tree trunk. What is not shown, however, is that in one take the tree trunk broke, seriously bruising Hart and his pinto Fritz when they plunged into the chasm.[68] More relevant for this analysis, by locating part of this story in San Francisco, *The Narrow Trail* invokes a later stage of settler colonialism

Figure 4.6 Paramount-Artcraft, *The Narrow Trail*, 1917 (George Eastman Museum, Rochester, New York)

than in most other Hart films. Moreover, the white community there is thoroughly disreputable and far from "civilized." (See Figure 4.6.) The story also is unique in having Ice and Betty bond through a mutual deception that they have to overcome by revealing and accepting not only their equally troubling pasts but also the kind of shared guilt that would later define a number of Hitchcock's paired lovers. That bonding, however, excludes them from the more "civilized" community of Saddle City and sends them into what they believe, in an intertitle, are the "clean, cool mountains." The couple may not be banished into a desert or waste land as in *Hell's Hinges*, but those mountains likely are little more than the illusion of a "free land" or even a lost paradise—that is, simply one more delusion.

The mountains are far from "clean" in *Blue Blazes Rawden* (February 1918).[69] Leaving the sagebrush hills and deserts of the Southwest behind, Hart takes on the role of a crew boss for a team of lumberjacks in the forested frontier of the Canadian Northwest in the 1880s.[70] A rough, virile, "primal" character (some reviewers likened him to Jack London's *Smoke Bellew*)[71], Rawden and his comrades tromp into the hamlet of Timber Cove and take over the saloon and dance hall owned by "Ladyfingers" Hilgard, a crooked Englishman. Hilgard resents Rawden's attention to his mistress, Babette Dufresne, and challenges him to a card game, staking his saloon against Rawden's earlier winnings. When Rawden wins again, they get into a fight, and Hilgard is shot. Before dying, the renegade Englishman begs Rawden to keep the story of his life from his mother, who is coming to visit him. Mother Hilgard arrives with her younger son Eric, and Rawden, struck by her kindly nature, says her son died a natural death, loved and honored by all. Mother now stays to settle her son's affairs, and Rawden finds himself changed. Provoked by jealousy after he rejects her, Babette tells Eric that his brother really died from Rawden's gunshot. In a rage, Eric shoots Rawden as he is trying to leave. Badly wounded, he keeps his comrades from hanging the boy, who learns the full story of the conflict leading up to the gunfight. As for Rawden, he sets out in a blinding snowstorm, taking the "long trail" back into the mountain wilderness alone, apparently to die.[72]

Blue Blazes Rawden is surprising in several ways.[73] The people inhabiting Ladyfinger's Saloon are a diverse bunch: the "black sheep" émigré Englishman, a half breed woman (French Canadian and Indian), and even a few Indian men playing cards in the background—little more than part of the décor. Familiar tropes mark the central characters: like many of Hart's earlier westerners, Rawden's own past and origins are unknown; Babette is an "alien" figure, even if rather different, whose revenge results from a perceived betrayal. Rawden's transformation comes from his lengthy encounter with the gentle nature of a white woman, but this time, more explicitly than usual, that woman is a respected mother figure. Yet the only way for this mother to continue as an "innocent" is to live on in ignorance because everyone remains silent about the dissolute nature of her eldest son. In the end, as happens in several earlier films, Rawden is excluded from a settler community, however "uncivilized" and hardly all-white, not only departing alone but also apparently choosing his own death.[74]

Trade press reviews increasingly faulted Hart's westerns released after *Blue Blazes Rawden* for not varying his badman figure and plots of action and romance or for sending his re-costumed character off to the big city, as in *Bucking Broadway* (December 1918) and *The Poppy Girl's Husband* (March 1919).[75] But at least two films stood out. "For keenness of conception, and fidelity to truth," one reviewer wrote, Hart's performances now were "becoming a standard" for the cinematic depiction of white male westerners.[76] The first film was *The Tiger Man* (April 1918), whose story, uncommon for

WILLIAM S. HART, "THE MAN WITH THE FACE THAT TALKS" 117

Hart, reverts to the early 1850s.[77] It begins in a small town in New Mexico with Hawk Parsons (the name proves ironic) and his outlaw pals, after escaping from jail and a sheriff's posse, riding off into the desert. There they encounter a small wagon train of missionaries lost and desperate for water; attracted to Ruth Ingram, the wife of a sickened man, Hawk disperses his gang and leads the wagon train out of the desert.[78] When Apaches attack, a cavalry troop, led by the sheriff, approaches searching for Hawk. The missionaries set a signal fire for them, but only after he forces Ruth to go off with him. Secluded in a mountain cabin, she tries to kill herself, and Hawk is conscience-stricken. Now he goes back to the small town, where her husband is pastor of a church threatened by gamblers. Hawk bargains with the sheriff and his men at gunpoint, agreeing to give himself up if they protect the pastor, his wife, and the church. True to his word, when he returns Ruth to her husband, Hawk is arrested and taken back to his cell. This story seems to be set somewhere along the old Santa Fe Trail, in land inhabited by Apaches hostile to settlers whom the US Army has to protect. The Apaches apparently are no match for white men in authority, especially when the cavalry and sheriff band together as figures of the white man's law. Perhaps most startling are the last scenes. Instead of having Hart's reformed outlaw leave the woman he has come to love and ride off alone, here Hawk accepts his fate, which one trade press review implied will end with a noose around his neck.[79]

The second very different standout was *Selfish Yates* (May 1918). Owner of the notorious Devil's Own saloon and dance hall in the mining camp of Thirsty Centre, Arizona, Yates is a brutal, egotistical man whose motto is "You can do as you please . . . so long as you don't get in my way, and I shall do as I please anyway."[80] After their prospecting father dies, Mary Adams and her younger sister struggle out of the desert and, desperate for money, Mary takes a job as the saloon's scrubwoman, and they are given shelter in a rude shack. Through a series of small gestures and ordinary events, Yates gradually starts to change. He reluctantly refuses to sell liquor to an old man's dissipated son; one morning he angrily upbraids Mary for playing "Nearer My God to Thee" on an organ; after a Mexican kills the young drunkard, Yates gives him a decent funeral, with Mary allowed to play an organ hymn; he lets her sister teach lessons to a tough orphan boy; and he finally resolves to close the saloon. One night "Rocking Chair" Riley, Yates's dance hall manager, uses a ruse to get Mary out of the shack; when Yates discovers the ruse, he finds Riley striking the struggling woman, beats him up, and would have killed him except for her pleas. After carrying the badly wounded Mary to

118   OUR COUNTRY/WHOSE COUNTRY?

the shack, he gets a doctor to care for her. Hearing of Riley's actions, a group of miners at the saloon are ready to lynch him, but Yates stops them and orders the villain out of town. While Riley rides off in a storm, only to die in a remote canyon, Yates returns to the shack and finds Mary recovering from her delirium and assuring him of her love. Again, one trade press reviewer praised the film's lighting effects, especially in scenes that have "all the somber gray of real night."[81] Although the mining camp saloon has a Chinese cook and a Mexican who, trying to rob the drunkard, kills him, these "alien" characters are marginal to the conflict between Yates and Riley. What particularly arrested Louis Reeves Harrison, however, was the unusual psychological study of a subtle process of change in Yates's character rather than the sudden transformation that marked most Hart bad men in earlier films.[82] That change leads to a slowly dawning awareness of some hidden inner goodness and unexpected love.

Within the framework of settler colonialism, it is perfectly apt to end this chapter with *The Aryan* (April 1916), the most striking and controversial of the Hart films shown at the Giornate del cinema muto in 2019.[83] Long thought to be lost, the newly rediscovered fragments of *The Aryan* prove more intriguing than those of *The Gun Fighter*. First, most of what survives comes from an Argentinian 35mm print (probably released in 1923), transferred to a 16mm internegative, and held in the Museo del Cine Pablo C. Ducrós Hicken in Buenos Aires.[84] Second, this surviving material differed from the initial Argentinian import in 1917, and the latter, as an export version retitled *La fiera domada: Il bandito della miniera d'oro*, also was not the same as the original print released in the United States. Third, the print reconstructed for the Giornate includes two fragments from the US Library of Congress and another from a compilation film, *The Saga of William S. Hart* (1959), at the Academy Film Archive. Analyzing this version of *The Aryan*, consequently, has to come with a large caveat.

Here, Hart plays another especially cruel, unsavory character.[85] A miner named Steve Denton, he first appears in the distance, coming out of an empty desert, planning to return to his mother and old home.[86] Stopping in a border town, he enters a saloon, where the owner, "Ivory" Wells, and a dance hall woman, Trixie "The Firefly," trick him out of his mining wealth— as in *The Silent Man*. What is worse, he learns that they keep back a telegram from his dying mother, which leads Denton to kill Wells and drag Trixie off into the desert. (See Figure 4.7.) Swearing vengeance on women—"Women! God, how he hated them!"—he settles in a remote desert outpost, becomes

Figure 4.7 Triangle, *The Aryan*, 1916 (Museo dei Cine Pablo C. Ducrós Hicken, Buenos Aires, Argentina)

head of a gang of half breeds and Mexicans, and forces Trixie into a kind of slavery. A wagon train of Mississippi farmers loses its way in the desert and wanders near Denton's town. Finding there are women among the pioneers, he angrily refuses their appeal for help. A young girl, Mary Jane Garth (Bessie Love), steals away from the thirst-stricken camp and calmly, fearlessly pleads with him. Her steadfast belief in human goodness and his persistent refusal lead her to accuse him of not being a member of the white race. That finally shocks Denton, who saves the girl and the other pioneering women from the threatening Mexicans and half breeds and then abandons his gang to lead the pioneers to safety. In the end, while the wagon train goes on its way, Denton returns to the empty desert in an apt reversal of his first appearance.

According to Richard Koszarski, Hart claimed that he drafted the scenario for the first half of *The Aryan* and C. Gardner Sullivan wrote the second half.[87] Hart's contribution, then, makes Denton, once his mother has died, a figure of deep misogyny and hatred of women.[88] And a trace of that misogyny remains because the film seems to forget Trixie, the only white woman left behind to continue serving his criminal gang. Sullivan was responsible for the

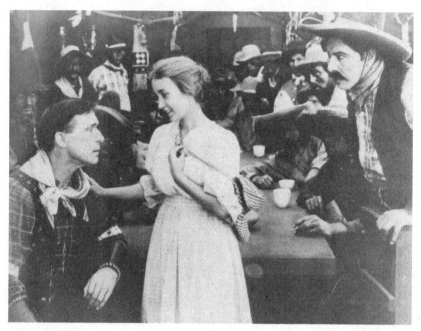

Figure 4.8 Triangle, *The Aryan*, 1916 (Museo dei Cine Pablo C. Ducrós Hicken, Buenos Aires, Argentina)

film's title and its emphasis on Aryanism and the supremacy, along with the obligation, of white men.[89] Clearly spelled out in an epigram is this "code of the Aryan race": "'Our women shall be guarded'; and a man of the white race may forget much—friends, duty, honor—but this he cannot forget."[90] A host of the film's characters challenge that code. They range from the border town whites to the gang of Mexicans and half-breeds and, of course, Denton himself, after his vow of vengeance. That Denton brutally lords it over a gang of "alien" non-white men surprisingly condenses the violent hierarchy of settler colonialism. Good white people are few: Denton's dying mother, the pioneer farmers, and he himself briefly in his initial chivalry toward Trixie. Yet those pioneers, tellingly, are Southern migrants lured west by a promise of finding gold; Denton too begins as a miner plundering the earth's resources. (See Figure 4.8.) Mary Jane proves a startling anomaly.[91] Not only is she depicted as an innocent girl among the pioneers, but she is clothed completely in white, a virginal figure of ethereal transcendence. Whether intended or not, she is reminiscent of the white-robed figure of Columbia, in John Gast's iconic painting, *American Progress* (1872), hovering over and guiding the country's westward expansion. But how can she remain a stereotypical symbol of transformative power after she reenters the community of white pioneers who are still searching for gold? As for Denton, he becomes one more Hart hero excluded from any settler community, despite his "redemption," going off alone into an uncertain future.

Replacing the popular cowboy, cowgirl, and Indian pictures of the early 1910s, Hart's films revised the ideological framework of settler colonialism in the emerging genre of the western. While they established what would become stereotypes of western frontier towns—that is, saloons, dance halls, and churches—they also tended to exclude Hart's "badman" figure from those towns, after he transformed them into more or less peaceful settler communities. What accounts for this arguably radical change, this break from the very recent past? First, the industry was beginning to more openly distinguish genres in terms of gender roles. This differentiation could have curtailed productions with central female characters so prominent in the earlier cowgirl films and Indian pictures. Second, and more important, the advent of World War I continued the refashioning of American masculinity into a more robust ideal of manhood just beginning to emerge a decade or two earlier. Richard Slotkin described this as a "masculinized" aesthetic of "authenticity" that created a new and influential form of "virile realism" in American culture.[92] Hart's resolute persona, his quiet authority, his steely gaze, and his skill with a gun certainly offered a striking model. Indeed, this persona may have implicitly supported the policy and practice of training male soldiers for eventual combat. Would the uncertain future that awaited Hart's characters, whether alone or coupled, also have indirectly expressed an audience's anxiety about their own future, once the United States entered the war in April 1917?

Third, the extraordinary impact of *The Birth of a Nation* (1915) also may have played a role. If that notorious film resolved the conflict between the North and South and allegedly reunified the country within the ideology of the "Lost Cause," Hart's westerns, somewhat like *The Virginian*, shifted the conflict westward. They unfolded in a relatively bleak yet resource-rich landscape sometimes still threatened by inferior Mexicans and half-breeds and usually emptied of Indigenous peoples—although, according to one reviewer, in *The Return of Draw Egan* Hart appropriated as his own the stoic composure of an Indian, almost as if this was his inalienable right. Instead, they mostly either pitted Hart's character against one or more white male rivals and villains or else involved an interior struggle within his "good

122   OUR COUNTRY/WHOSE COUNTRY?

badman" figure, in conflicts that would implicitly define the conditions of a settler community. These dramatic even violent conflicts seemed to fore-shadow later reenactments that, as in Tombstone, Arizona, began to emerge in the late 1920s, events that mythologized the recent past of the West much as did the Civil War reenactments that already had gained such popularity. Indeed, those later reenactments would serve as celebrations of the nation's successful expansion driven by the interminable forces of settler colonialism and its triumphant white male supremacy.

Touring the West 4

In August 1914, the declaration of war in Europe, Marguerite Shaffer writes, "marked a pivotal moment for the promotion and status of the national parks."[1] Coinciding with the Great War, the Panama-Pacific International Exposition set to open in 1915 "publicized a grand tour of western America with the exposition as the grand finale."[2] For its part, the National Park Service published a promotional portfolio, in which borax millionaire Stephen Tyng Mather claimed, in an "Introduction," that "this nation is richer in natural scenery of the first order than any other nation . . . but it does not know it."[3] Touring the parks, Shaffer contends, would promote "an ideal of America as 'nature's nation,'" and "a ritual of citizenship"—specifically, of course, for middle- and upper-class whites.[4] The movie industry congratulated itself on the films of scenic wonders exhibited during the past few years and now urged the production of more to advance the "See America First" slogan.[5] Even the US Interior Department sent H. T. Cowling, photographer of the US Reclamation Service, on "a four-month tour of the national parks" to take "between 30,000 and 40,000 feet of motion pictures" for use in its own "See America First" campaign.[6] This footage included the ceremonies that opened a new park, the Rocky Mountain National Park in Colorado. But the industry again seized the opportunity as well. As early as November 1914, Mutual Film's vice president, J. R. Freuler, noted that "the demand for the scenic pictures is but a forerunner to a wholesale western emigration of tourists next summer."[7]

In late 1915, Mutual began releasing a long-running *See America First* series of short films produced by Gaumont cameramen.[8] The aim, however, was to cover the entire country, not just the parks, and one of the first films was a tour of historical Boston.[9] Some of these initially had a "pretty Mutual traveler" as a tourist guide. Although she probably was an added attraction for men, she also served as a model to induce women to travel and stand in for the women in picture theaters. One film took spectators to historic Lake Mohonk, New York, with its "fantastic" environs of glens and hills, the site of numerous international peace conferences.[10] The Mutual series ran

Our Country/Whose Country?. Richard Abel, Oxford University Press. © Oxford University Press 2023.
DOI: 10.1093/oso/9780197744048.003.0009

124   OUR COUNTRY/WHOSE COUNTRY?

through early 1917, gradually moving westward and to more natural wonders. In January 1917, *The Heart of the Blue Ridge* toured Lexington (with Confederate monuments) and the surrounding Virginia countryside, notably the "famous Natural Bridge: 215 feet high, 100 feet in width, with a span of 90 feet."[11] One of the last films apparently explored the coast of Oregon in the vicinity of Tillamook Rock Lighthouse and nearby unique rock formations.[12] Soon the Rothacker Film Company of Chicago began to supplement its advertising and industrial films with a related series promoting tourism. Harry Birch led a camera crew to Glacier Park; W. B. Klingensmith led another in "a comprehensive tour of the Rocky Mountains" that would result in "five complete scenic reels."[13] Pathé commissioned Ralph Radnor Earle, who had shot its earlier films, to motor through the West and return with footage for its *Our National Parks* series. Earle's route took him through familiar parks and some less well known: General Grant, Sequoia, Mount Lassen, and Mesa Verde, the latter "set aside to preserve one of the finest ruins of the ancient cliff dwellers."[14] Intriguingly, Peterson writes, *Glacier National Park* (1917) segregates tourists admiring the park's natural grandeur in the first half from "Indian types," shown separately, performing "Indian-ness" in the second.[15] Together, all of these *See America First* films aligned with the movement to celebrate, as Shaffer concisely puts it, "the best of both worlds: the virtues of nature combined with the benefits of commerce."[16]

According to trade press articles, hardly any of these films celebrating American natural grandeur paid much attention to the wildlife inhabiting the wild lands—and Indigenous peoples had vanished. Rothacker's footage of Yellowstone, in 1912 and again in 1917, was an exception. Along with images of wonderful geysers, splendid falls, and "fishermen's heavens" were scenes of "animal and bird life as it exists among the crowning peaks and fir-hidden canyons."[17] So was Edward S. Curtis's film of Yosemite, *Seeing America*, released in early 1916. W. Stephen Bush wrote in awe: "One picture of undreamed beauty follows another in bewildering succession and every scene is a climax."[18] Among those scenes were a "noble herd of buffalo fording the stream" and hundreds of "graceful birds now soaring in swift flight." From 1916 to 1918, the curator of the Bronx Zoo in New York, Raymond L. Ditmar, produced animal pictures of wildlife in a regular series of split-reel "fillers" for theater programs. These zoological films he branded *The Living Book of Nature*.[19] Although some were shot in Africa and elsewhere, many featured animals on the North American continent such as *The Beaver* and *Tree Animals*.[20] But Ditmar often indulged in comic stereotypes as in *Life in the Insect World*, where the "antics" of caterpillars and worms in disguise fooled their predators.[21] In June 1917, Mutual began releasing an *Outing-Chester* series of single-reel travel films produced by C. L. Chester.[22] Apparently with support from *Outing Magazine* (for outdoorsmen), they ranged from the South Seas and Africa to North America. Yet some did make wild animals the main attraction, as in *Pines Up and Palms Down*, which first "starred" moose, elk, and other wild game in a French-Canadian habitat and then alligators in the Florida Everglades.[23] The most prized of these travel films, according to the trade press, were the "Scenics Beautiful produced by Robert C. Bruce."[24] North America was the initial subject of most *Bruce Scenics*, as in *Alaskan Wonders*.[25] But they too erased Indigenous peoples as well as wild animals to highlight untrammeled natural scenery. Instead, in *The Valley of the Hoh* (1917), for instance, two Great Dane dogs led Bruce on an expedition into the "big tree district" of the Olympic mountains off the coast of Washington state.[26]

Figure W4.1 Essanay, *Lake Tahoe, Land of the Sky*, 1916 (US Library of Congress, Washington, DC)

126   OUR COUNTRY/WHOSE COUNTRY?

At least half a dozen films during these few years promote transportation advances that encourage further tourism. Perhaps the most unusual was Robert Bruce's *Deschutes Driftwood* (1916), produced by Educational Films.[27] It offers views of the Deschutes and Columbia Rivers region from a train running on the new Oregon Truck Railway.[28] The vantage point comes from a hobo riding the rails and apparently seeking work in Oregon, a strange choice until the film echoes Chaplin's *The Tramp* (1915) in its final image. Most of these films, however, tout the building of roads to stimulate touring by automobile. Essanay's *Lake Tahoe, Land of the Sky* (1916) makes a telling shift from an opening shot of a snowy train station at Donner Pass to the sudden experience of Emerald Bay, a kind of Shangri-la nestled on the lake.[29] (See Figure W4.1.) A recent road over Emigrant Gap and along the Truckee River in the Sierras now let monied tourists indulge in fishing, water skiing, horseback riding, and steamship trips on the deep, cold lake. *Seeing Yosemite with David A. Curry* (1916) was no less than an advertising film. Curry managed Camp Curry within the park, recently accessible by automobile, and the film shows some of its 40,000 annual visitors, among them athletic women, hiking and climbing up steep mountainsides and through glaciers.[30] Automobiles, however, could not hold up on all roads in the national parks. One of a series of western travelogues from the famous lecturer Burton Holmes, *Among the Geysers of the Yellowstone* (1917), for instance, follows tourists packed into stagecoaches that sometimes got snarled in traffic jams.[31] Even the US Department of Agriculture joined the efforts to attract tourists to the West. *Trails That Lure* (1920) takes viewers along the recently opened Columbia River Highway but also into the Eagle Creek campground and onto a "wonder trail" blasted into the rock leading to Punch Bowl Falls.[32] *Little Journeys in the National Forest of Colorado* (1920) returns to some of the areas explored in the earlier *Picturesque Colorado*. But now automobiles race around the Garden of the Gods and up the "WORLD'S HIGHEST MOTOR DRIVE" to the very top of Pike's Peak.[33]

Depopulated of both Indigenous peoples and wildlife, these travel films transformed the western wildlands into spectacular consumables for the pleasure of white American settlers, whether reconfigured as real or virtual tourists.

5

Harry Carey, Tom Mix, and Douglas Fairbanks

During the latter half of the 1910s, most of William S. Hart's westerns were popular and profitable, but they did face competition. This competition came from both short films and features in which three other male movie stars played the central roles.[1] One was Harry Carey who appeared in dozens of short films, many of them westerns, until he too moved into feature-length films directed by Jack Ford for Universal. Another was Tom Mix who also performed in numerous one-reel and two-reel westerns for Selig before moving into feature-length films, eventually for Fox. A third was Douglas Fairbanks who starred in five westerns among his increasingly popular early features for Triangle, Fine Arts, and Artcraft. Strikingly, the films of all three deepened the break with earlier westerns. Unlike Hart, they often played cowboys of one kind or another, sometimes even outlaws. Whether a "regular chap," a tough guy willing to endure physical injury in dangerous stunts, or an unusually athletic type, with an irrepressibly self-confident smile, all embodied American forms of white masculinity more contemporary than Hart's strong silent type. These characteristics made them apt models for young men and any other admirers as the United States prepared for its entry into the Great War. Their stories, also for the most part, were set in more "civilized" white communities than Hart's, which, with a few key exceptions, neither Indians nor Mexicans threatened and where African Americans remained absent. Most crucially, many of those stories now were overtly comic or tongue-in-cheek, implying that the centuries of westward expansion and exploitation not only were settled but also no longer, whether nostalgic or not, need be taken, as Hart did, so seriously. In short, although the ideology of settler colonialism may have seemed to fade into near invisibility, it continued to have an impact, if only sometimes as a structuring absence.

Our Country/Whose Country?. Richard Abel, Oxford University Press. © Oxford University Press 2023.
DOI: 10.1093/oso/9780197744048.003.0010

Harry Carey, "A Regular Chap"

Because all of these competing westerns also were constructed around a leading movie star, some brief biographical information is helpful as a means of introducing their films. The first was Harry Carey (1878–1947), whose popularity with fans took longer to achieve than either that of Hart or Mix. His life before the movies also differed from theirs. The son of a prominent lawyer and director of a sewing machine company in the Bronx, Carey graduated from a military academy, enrolled in New York University to study law, but contracted pneumonia from a boating accident. While recuperating, he wrote a play titled *Montana* that told "in vivid colors of pulsating life a romance of the great Northwest."[2] He then headed a stock company to tour productions, with himself as the lead, that for three years in the mid-1900s netted a good profit. A second play set in the Klondyke, *Two Women and That Man*, flopped badly,[3] however, and, with the help of Henry Walthall, he joined Biograph in 1911. During the next three years, he played many secondary character roles in D. W. Griffith films and became well enough known to sign with Universal in 1915. Working with producer-director Francis Ford, Carey initially starred as a cowboy, outlaw, or lawman in a series of two-reel westerns with titles like *The Sheriff's Dilemma*, *The Canceled Mortgage*, and *As It Happened* (all 1915). When Universal let him set up his own production unit, he began to develop the outlaw character of "Cheyenne Harry" (initially one of *Montana*'s secondary characters) in a dozen or more two- and three-reel westerns, sometimes from his own scenarios: *The Outlaw and the Lady*, *The Drifter*, *Goin' Straight*, and *Six-Shooter Justice* (all 1917).[4] Beginning with *Straight Shooting* (1917),[5] all were features directed by Jack Ford, often with Hoot Gibson as a sidekick and Olive Golden as a love interest, who eventually became his second wife. As befits a "regular chap," Carey wore the clothes of a working cowboy or ranch owner. He usually dressed in either a large-checked or dark shirt, denim trousers tucked into calf-length boots, and either a dark, high-crowned Stetson or a light-colored one with a medium crown, a dark band, and curled brim, often the worse for wear. Although an excellent horseman and crack shot, Carey rarely relied on stunts, unlike Mix and Fairbanks, and left those to his companion rough riders. By 1919, intent on depicting "the cowboy as he really is," Carey was one of the highest-salaried western stars.[6]

The earliest surviving western starring Carey, *The Heart of a Bandit* (February 1915), must be one of the last he made at Biograph before signing with Universal.[7] Although it "recalls innumerable other westerns" of a "good bad man," according to an exhibitor, the film packs a lot of action into a single reel.[8] The cast of characters includes the Johnson family, settlers "in the Far West"; the bandit "Texas Pete"; the passengers in a stagecoach he robs on little more than a whim; a sheriff and his posse that pursue him; and a Mexican named Mendoza who twice attacks Johnson's wife. The fat old man whose "bulging wallet" Pete snatches later angrily offers a $1,000 reward for the bandit, dead or alive. Pete tricks the posse into tracking his riderless horse and then takes shelter, hiding in the straw of the Johnson's barn. The second time Mendoza attacks the wife, he grabs her daughter as a hostage, backs into the barn, and the wife desperately follows. When the husband returns home, he picks up his wife's dropped rifle and hears her struggling with Mendoza. Hidden in the straw, Pete shoots the Mexican, but Johnson also fires, hitting Pete. After his wife explains that Pete saved her, he is carried into the house and laid on a bed. Finding the rifle and Mendoza dead, the sheriff arrests Johnson, but Pete confesses and asks that the reward go to the wife, before he dies. This story is located somewhere in the Southwest, with a villainous Mexican intent on raping a white woman. A moment in the robbery already reveals the bandit's hidden "heart": after taking an old woman's "gold chain," he returns it as "a present." As if to further insult the wealthy robbed man, in the end Pete, playing Robin Hood, presents the reward money to the Johnsons. Particularly surprising in the film's otherwise flat dusty landscape is a narrow, steep-walled canyon through which horsemen ride in silhouette, a feature that would return in several later Harry Carey westerns.[9]

One year later, the first film to feature Carey as Cheyenne Harry was Universal's five-reel *A Knight of the Range* (February 1916). Carey's own scenario opens with a "Whop-e-e-e-e! Bang!"—as cowboys gather after a roundup, each "rides to the center of the screen from a distance at breakneck speed, salutes, and takes his position with the company."[10] From then on, the story works variations on a series of coincidences stitched together by a circulating token of love. Harry and his younger brother, a weakling Bob Graham, are both in love with Bess Dawson, the postmistress in a small town on the plains. Bob has sent her a ring, but she has another admirer in the gambler Gentleman Dick. When he tries to embrace her, she drops the ring and hurries into her house, and Dick slips it on his finger. After Bob fails to win the ring back in a game of cards, Dick returns it, hoping later to blackmail the loser. Bob's story of how the gambler got the ring does not persuade Bess, and he drowns his sorrow in drink. Dick and several pals induce Bob to join them in robbing a stagecoach, and now Bob drops the ring; at some point a Mexican loosens a shoe on Bob's horse, and it goes lame. While a sheriff's posse, with the help of an Indian trailer, follows the signs of the lame horse, Harry finds Bob, hears his tale of woe, helps him escape, and mounts the lame horse. A "ridin' fool" badly wounded during a dangerous chase, Harry shelters in Bess's house.[11] Finding the ring, the sheriff goes searching for Bob, who guessing that Dick has played him false, shoots the gambler, but a deck of cards in his coat pocket stops the bullet. Finally, the sheriff finds and shoots Bob down, and Bess is left to care for Harry and accept his love. "A real old fashioned rip-roaring melodrama," wrote one reviewer, "with fast riding by a bunch of dust covered cowboys" and other bits of action.[12] As with most of Hart's and Mix's westerns, this film's setting of plains and hills, ranches, and a small town comes in a late stage of settler colonialism, but one in which a stray Indian can serve a sheriff's posse and a Mexican, inexplicably, can pop up to enable another coincidental plot turn. In alluding to an Anglo-Saxon heroic figure, the title, unlike Hart's slightly earlier film, reads as wryly tongue-in-cheek.

Figure 5.1 Fox, *Straight Shooting*, 1917 (Kino Lorber/Universal)

HARRY CAREY, TOM MIX, DOUGLAS FAIRBANKS   131

Found and restored decades ago, the five-reel *Straight Shooting* (September 1917) is Ford's first feature-length western starring Carey.[13] Ruling over a vast, lawless grazing land, cattleman "Thunder" Flint orders any settlers off or else suffer the consequences. His chief opponent is "Sweetwater" Sims, whose daughter Joan has a beau in Danny Morgan, one of Flint's cowpunchers. The cattleman wants to hire the notorious gun slinger "Cheyenne" Harry to get rid of those who refuse or are slow to act, and he sends Danny to Buckhorn, where Harry is sleeping drunk in a saloon. After Harry accepts, he "stops for refreshments" in Diabolo, meets Black Eyed Pete, who tells him where he has hidden his pal's share of some loot nearby, and then tosses back drinks with "Placer" Fremont, "a killer of another sort," also summoned by Flint.[14] When Sims's son Ted goes for water at a spring that Flint has fenced off against the settlers, Fremont shoots him. Seeing Sims, Joan, and Danny at the boy's gravesite, his eyes growing misty,[15] Harry realizes he is "sick of the job" and decides to quit: "there's some jobs too dirty even for me." Flint orders Fremont to put him out of the way, but in a dueling face-off Harry is clever enough to gun him down. Danny reports that Flint and his cowboys plan to attack the settlers that night, and, as the raiders grow in number, Joan rides off to gather other settlers in defense. Holed up in their cabin, the Sims, Danny, and other settlers desperately try to fend off the marauders who circle them as Indians had done in earlier films. But Harry gets Pete and his gang to help beat off the attacking cattlemen. The next day, Sims asks Harry to stay and take his son's place, but he has noticed Joan being tender to the wounded Danny. As Harry ponders his decision and then starts to go off by himself, Joan surprises him and changes his mind.

What thrilled trade press reviewers, unsurprisingly, were the scenes of immense cattle herds (Figure 5.1) (sometimes in high-angle, extreme long shots), furious horseback riding (including Joan's) over hills and across streams, the duel pitting Harry against Fremont on an empty street (an early "classic" face-off), the climactic gun battle between bitterly opposed whites, and the gang's stunts as they pursued the fleeing raiders.[16] Yet initially, some of these also were precisely what provoked the Chicago censors initially to refuse the film's exhibition because it "consists of detailed portrayals of murder and outlawry."[17] The rough building exterior in Diabolo fronted a series of adjacent spaces: a large gambling hall, second-floor hotel rooms, and a saloon with swinging doors. Besides the hills, plains, wooded glens, and stream, the most striking feature of the landscape was the deep narrow canyon (Figure 5.2), earlier seen just briefly in *The Heart of a Bandit*, that

Figure 5.2 Fox, *Straight Shooting*, 1917 (Kino Lorber/Universal)

served to guard the hangout of Pete's gang. Small details accumulated as well: Joan putting Ted's unused plate into a shelf drawer (later it's smashed in the gun battle); a lone Mexican in Pete's gang, ever a thief, who tastes and then steals a jar of Sims's jam after the gun battle[18]; silhouetted doorway shots that frame riders coming to the cabin, Harry slouching there, and Joan posed in thought or sadness. Many details define Harry and become familiar Carey gestures: a gloved finger scratching his chin, a hand mussing his hair, a cigarette butt in a corner of his mouth, a tight quarter smile, a hooded cool stare, one crossed arm holding the other at the elbow. The straightforward conflict between cattlemen and homesteaders situates this story clearly in the late stages of settler colonialism. The film may take the side of the settlers, but their survival depends on gunslinger Harry and Black Eyed Pete's gang. Although Harry, like many of Hart's characters, undergoes a change of heart due to a woman, his and Joan's love story remains subordinate to the central conflict, until the end. What's particularly remarkable is the opening intertitle: "There was a time when the western plains belonged to no man." What a stark assertion of the myth of the West, a landscape empty of Indigenous peoples, free to be possessed by whites, especially those with the most power to enrich themselves. A notably "bloody chapter," as one newspaper put it, "in the history of the development of our country."[19]

The Secret Man (October 1917), Ford's next feature, survives only in parts of two reels, so the story has to be pieced together from five very different synopses in the trade press, along with several newspaper articles.[20] A "likeable road agent," Cheyenne Harry hides in a refuse wagon to escape from an Arizona penitentiary, hops on a transcontinental train, and meets Henry Beaufort, a young Easterner traveling to his uncle's ranch on the Mexican border. After hearing his tale of unjust jailing, Beaufort gives him a change of clothes, and, before a sheriff's posse can find him, Harry drops out the train compartment's window. Luckily, he is hired by the cowboys of a neighboring ranch to help round up a herd of cattle. Meanwhile, given his disapproving uncle, Beaufort has secretly married Molly, the local sheriff's daughter. In order to preserve his inheritance, she, in turn, has secreted the couple's young daughter with a Mexican couple, Pedro and his wife, living near the ranch.[21] Beaufort mistakenly asks Bill, his foreman, to take the little girl into hiding, but Bill gives that task to Pedro, who tells Molly her daughter is dead—which drives her mad, then catatonic. Exposed and pursued by the sheriff again, Harry chances on the girl, who has been injured falling from Pedro's runaway horse. They travel together until his own horse falls down a cliff. Beaten up, exhausted, and dying of thirst, he gives himself up to the sheriff so a doctor can tend to the unconscious girl. Later at a church bazaar, the sheriff and uncle decide to hold an auction for the girl (so she is no longer orphaned), but Molly is stunned to recognize her and becomes lucid again. Through further complications, including the uncle's death, Molly and Beaufort are reunited, and the governor pardons Harry.

A slightly later interview reprinted from the *Cleveland News*, has Ford claiming that, "It's the 'Little Things' That Count"—that is, details that create a sense of realism.[22] One example is what's shaken out of a horse blanket once Harry is hired: rough clothes that suit him as a cowboy, along with a harmonica that he later plays to serenade the little girl. Another, near the end, is the repeated shot of Harry standing in the darkness of a jail cell and watching through the window bars that isolate him from the church bazaar and auction. Others are comic, as when a cowboy quips, eyeing Harry dressed in Beaufort's sporting outfit and white shoes: "What Christmas tree did you drop out of?" A telling difference marks the Mexican couple, who apparently are assimilated yet remain non-white "aliens." While Pedro greedily takes the money Bill offers for harboring the girl and flees with her on horseback

134   OUR COUNTRY/WHOSE COUNTRY?

(apparently only to be thrown and killed),[23] his wife seems to have grown fond of her. When she tries to embrace the girl in the street, after mother and daughter are reunited, Molly pushes her away. What might an audience have made of this Mexican woman, who may be unlike Harry but also is left out of an otherwise happy ending?[24]

Although *A Marked Man* (October 1917), like *A Knight of the Range*, does not survive, it does confirm, according to the trade press, the main tropes of Carey's westerns, with a few tricks of its own.[25] Here, Harry is hiding in a dugout to elude a sheriff and reading a letter from his mother, who has been deceived into believing he is a successful ranch owner. Feeling some remorse, he ventures out in a storm and stops at a ranch house owned by Grant Young and his daughter Molly. Aiming to rob them, he relents because of Molly, confesses his outlaw ways in the past, and promises to reform. Young gives him a second chance and hires him as a cowboy to work the ranch. At a rodeo, where he is just about to ride, Harry meets a former pal, Ben Kent, who convinces him to join up in one last stagecoach robbery. Ben shoots the driver, however, and the sheriff arrests both outlaws and condemns them to be hanged. Another letter comes revealing that Harry's mother will arrive soon, and the sheriff, reading it, postpones the execution for a week. Molly and her father offer Harry their home to entertain his mother, who again believes the lie he has told her. After she leaves, Harry goes back to jail and awaits the noose. In the nick of time, a passenger on the stagecoach now comes forward to tell the sheriff that it was Ben who shot the driver. Exonerated, Harry returns hopefully to the Young ranch where Molly is waiting. Given this melodramatic story, the film does have several unexpected moments. The robbery, for instance, is staged in a novel way, according to production photos: midstream in a relatively shallow river.[26] As in several Hart westerns, Harry's mother plays a crucial role in his redemption, and Molly does her part by pretending to be his wife.[27] Harry may be moving closer to the fantasy of success he has lied about, but, in the end, his mother remains blissfully ignorant of his outlaw ways.[28] And the law conspires to turn a blind eye to that ignorance and to mask Harry's disreputable past.

By late 1917, Universal was promoting Carey as Cheyenne Harry in a series of special features directed by Ford.[29] Each film's production supposedly involved extra time to work out scenario details and find the best locations for "the cavalcade of horsemen and actors" required.[30] One of the earliest of these, *The Phantom Riders* (January 1918), may be lost, but the trade press suggests the scenario, based on an original story by Henry MacRae, turned a familiar plot into something unique and perhaps controversial.[31] Again, a cattleman, Dave Bland, lords over Paradise Creek, a vast territory reserved by the government (the federal is implied) for grazing by any and all. That doesn't faze Bland, who exerts a right to the entire valley by gathering a band of masked, white-clothed riders led by the "Unknown"—that is Bland himself. He soon makes an intruder, Pebble Grant, his reluctant foreman, and plans to wed his daughter Molly. Onto this land comes Cheyenne Harry with a small herd and, when warned to leave, decides to fight Bland single-handedly. At one point he disarms Bland and slaps him, earning a sentence of death. One night, expecting to meet Grant, who has given him his support, Harry instead finds him hanging from a tree. Harry bests the "Unknown" (how is unclear) and in a barroom fight routs the drunken phantoms celebrating Bland's coming marriage to the unwilling Molly. But Bland's phantoms soon catch and besiege him until he signals Molly with a heliograph, and, riding to a nearby canyon, she gets a troop of "United States rangers" to rescue him.[32] This film is more specific than *Straight Shooting* in assigning possession of Paradise Valley as a grazing land to the US government, but it ignores the fact that the territory undoubtedly was seized, in one way or another, from one or more Native American tribes. Most startling, however, are the white costumes of the phantom riders, which the usually astute Genevieve Harris did not link explicitly to the triumphant Ku Klux Klan riders in the climactic scenes of *A Birth of a Nation*.[33] Their lynching of Grant also underlines the connection, despite an advertising aid that tries to sever the link by falsifying what happens in the film: "Lynching was not a punishment. It was a threat of the phantom rider."[34] Here, the terrorizing violence of the phantom riders, rather than directed at African Americans, is deflected to target the "regular chap" of an ordinary white cowboy. At the time, was the subtext of actual, widely reported lynchings ignored by moviegoers? It certainly was by trade press reviewers as well as by newspapers.[35]

Whereas *Hell Bent* (July 1918) stuck to a relatively familiar plot, it also introduced a bunch of novel ideas.[36] The opening has a publisher asking a novelist to make the hero of his next story "a more ordinary man, as bad as he is good."[37] As he looks at a Frederic Remington painting, *A Misdeal*, it dissolves into a saloon interior where a sheriff who has rushed in is told, "The stranger says there was cheating." The stranger is Harry, of course, and he escapes a posse, crossing a river to "freedom" in a neighboring county. A pal's note says a gold shipment is on its way by stagecoach to Rawhide, "if you want it," implying he has an outlaw past. A gang led by Beau Ross plans

Figure 5.3 Fox, *Hell Bent*, 1918 (Kino Lorber/Universal)

to stop the stage and steal the gold, but a small buckboard instead rushes the strongbox into town. Harry arrives half-drunk in Rawhide, clatters on horseback through the town's "center of life," a dance hall, and then upstairs to persuade "Cimmaron" Bill, at length, to share his hotel room—and they become fast friends. Meanwhile, Dave and Bess Thurston need to send money to their sick mother; Dave is fired from his Wells Fargo job; and Bess reluctantly has to get work at the dance hall. (See Figure 5.3.) Hired as a bouncer there, Harry defends Bess from a crowd of men, invites her for a drink, but she spurns him, which leads him to apologize. Ross persuades Dave to join his gang in robbing the Wells Fargo safe, but Harry discovers them and then lets them go because he doesn't want to accuse her brother. Unaware of Dave's culpability, Bess calls Harry a coward. The next day, in revenge, Ross and his gang race into town in a stolen stagecoach, abduct Bess, and head to their mountain hideout. Harry follows but is caught, tied to a wild horse that falls down a steep hill, loosening his bonds. While Ross goes off with Bess toward the Rio Grande, a posse led by Bill attacks the gang's cabin, but they escape in the stagecoach, until the driver is shot and the stage plunges into a canyon. Harry pursues Ross and catches up with him in the desert; in an exchange of gunfire, they wound one another. With their horses also shot, Harry sends Bess off on the remaining horse. As the two men stagger through the desert, a sandstorm blows up, and Harry is the one to know how to shelter. Aided by another Indian trailer serving white men, Bill eventually finds Ross dead and Harry barely alive. In the end, a still recovering Harry embraces Mary.

This "old-fashioned western melodrama" pitting rival white men against one another provides the scaffolding for all kinds of thrills and surprises, besides the opening painting that comes to life. When he stops for a sip of water at the river, Harry pulls card after card from his pockets, revealing he was the cheater in that card game. He stays half-drunk throughout until Bess spurns him and, after he apologizes, invites him to her cabin. There, for the first time in his life, he has to learn how to drink tea and conceal his distaste. Ross turns out to be a cultured badman, telling Harry that, when he is sent off tied to the wild horse, he will learn what happened to the legendary Tartar chieftain Mazeppa.[38] As expected, the film is full of horseback riders posed on hilltops, racing wildly through plains and barren hills, with stunts like Harry's horse plunging down a steep hillside and Harry using a rope to climb the sheer cliff of the same narrow deep canyon from *Straight Shooting*.[39] The most amazing scenes, according to one reviewer, were those shot in the desert, especially of "the terrific sandstorm . . . snatching the spectator from his chair and setting him down in the midst of the great wastes of the West."[40] Once again, in the fictions of westward expansion—"before the smooth batter of civilization was poured into the waffle iron of the west"[41]—a bleak, empty landscape became a testing ground for white men's endurance. Perhaps most novel, however, were the many comic moments in the first half of the film, most notably in the scenes in which Harry and Bill struggle for possession of the hotel room: one forces the other to tumble out a window (then vice versa), Harry's horse keeps eating bits of the straw bed, and the two men become friends by loudly singing "O Genevieve." As stock figures in the background, several Indians and Mexicans in the dance hall are sorely displeased when Harry and Bill drunkenly again begin singing at the bar, probably off-key. As long as white men did the drinking, now drunkenness became a comic act, ironically annoying a sober Indian and Mexican. One newspaper warned: "Are there drinking fountains in your town, . . . Then take a long, deep drink before you see Harry Carey."[42] The attraction of comedy, even if much of it is at Harry's expense, here aligned Carey with both Mix and Fairbanks in some of their westerns. Here, comedy redefined the myth of the West, which Hart

138   OUR COUNTRY/WHOSE COUNTRY?

took seriously as did Carey in earlier films, into a fashionable subject for off-beat shenanigans.

Although Carey's "regular chap" enjoyed a wide appeal with audiences, supposedly he was a special favorite of schoolboys. In Des Moines (Iowa), in early 1919, Dorothy Day alerted teachers not to expect they would show up for classes when Carey made a personal appearance at the Royal Theater one afternoon.[43] He is "no dude," she wrote, admiring his ordinary cowboy outfit, "chews gum and talks just exactly like you 'knowed' he would. . . . His face is tanned and his light brown hair is just as likely to be slightly mussed as not and he caresses his chin with his thumb when he's puzzled—just like he does on screen." The "little fellows who see him will not be disappointed in their idol, because he's human and understands boys." The tone of her column suggests that Day herself understands both Carey and his fans as well.

Tom Mix, "Master Cowboy"

The early years of Tom Mix (1880–1940) are not easy to pin down because he often embellished his experiences with tall tales, cribbed from others like his friend Will Rogers, or even lied.[44] His father taught him to ride horses as a boy, and he quickly became a skilled horseman and expert shot. But that didn't always come in handy during a peripatetic series of jobs: US Army enlistee, bartender, drum major for the Oklahoma Cavalry Band at the St. Louis World's Fair. In 1905, he was hired as a cowboy for the Miller Brothers 101 Ranch and soon was performing as a bronco buster and trick roper for its Wild West show and later winning national riding and roping contests. In the offseason, Mix often served as a sheriff or deputy sheriff in a number of small towns. In 1912, he and Guy Weadick organized the first Calgary Stampede in Canada. Eventually his expertise and charisma led to appearances in scores of short films for Selig that showed off his well-known skills as a horseman and stuntman. By 1913, Selig had Mix starring in several multiple-reel westerns, in which he did his own stunts, frequently was injured, and often played heroes named Tom—erasing any gap between star and character (see Chapter 3). That year he also seems to have bought the Bar Circle A Ranch near Prescott, Arizona, where he could recuperate when not filming and join in rodeo contests during the Prescott Frontier Days. Once Mix became head of his own production unit, he sometimes would write scenarios and direct them. In January 1914, along with director Colin Campbell and scriptwriter

Gilson Willets, he began preparing what, after unknown production delays, became a five-reel feature, *In the Days of the Thundering Herd* (November 1914).[45]

The film was shot in Oklahoma, on Pawnee Bill's huge ranch, where a big herd of buffalo and a large band of Pawnee Indians lived. In the beginning, Mix reprises his earlier role as a pony express rider, this time in "the days of '49," when riders were the sole means of communication "throughout the wilderness they traversed." Tom is in love with Sally Madison who, with her lazy brother Dick, lives in Two Forks, somewhere on the Great Plains. One day while Sally is wandering alone, Tom has to rescue her from a stampeding herd of buffalo. Soon after, a letter arrives from her father, who has struck gold in California. Sally, unlike her brother, accepts his proposal of finding a wagon train to join him, and Tom decides to accompany her. Following the southern Santa Fe Trail, their wagon train is attacked by a large band of Indians, led by Chief Swift Wind. After a ferocious fight, all of the gold-seeking pioneers are killed, except for Tom and Sally, who are led off to a camp of teepees. While the chief decides what to do with the captives, Sally has to help his sister Starlight, who asks her to care for her papoose. Sally and Tom escape on horseback, but the Indians pursue and recapture them. When the chief has Tom tied to a stake and brush around it set on fire, Starlight releases him and pleads with her brother to spare him because Sally had saved her papoose from another buffalo stampede. Again, Tom and Sally escape and find a nearby camp of pioneers and buffalo hunters. The Indians attack the camp and the whites flee in their wagons, but they are trapped against some foothills. Having warned the whites, Starlight joins the whites, telling them of another pioneer camp over the ridge. Sally volunteers to search and, after suffering a fall, stumbles into the camp and then leads the pioneers to the rescue. Tom fights in hand-to-hand combat with Swift Wind, who is shot dead. In the end, Tom and Sally become a conventionally happy couple.

The surviving print of *In the Days of the Thundering Herd* comes from an unknown source that is incomplete and cut down from the original release.[46] Scenes described in trade press reviews have disappeared: contrasting buffalo hunts by the whites and Indians and Sally's escape from another buffalo stampede by climbing a tree.[47] An intertitle alludes to yet another missing scene in which Sally saves Starlight's papoose from a third stampede, which explains why the latter joins the whites and betrays her tribe. Although the surviving print does not suggest that Starlight hopelessly loves Tom, one review describes Tom, Sally, and Starlight, in the closing scene, setting out "for

140 OUR COUNTRY/WHOSE COUNTRY?

the land of promise [in] the saffron west." Despite these problems, the film not only recapitulates but also piles on so many features of earlier westerns. A pony express rider, as in *Saved by the Pony Express* (1911), Mix performs several stunts in which he skillfully dismounts a horse on the run and quickly mounts another. He also twice pulls Sally onto his racing horse. At least two wagon trains of pioneers, leaving settled communities, are bound for California to mine for gold. On the southern plains, marauding Indians always are ready to attack and kill whites, but not the hero and heroine. Starlight is one more "Indian maiden" who abandons her people to partner with white pioneers. Yet the film engages in an equally relevant recapitulation: the spectacle of Wild West shows, from Buffalo Bill to the Miller Brothers, which showcased cowboy horse-riding stunts and reenactments of the long deadly conflict between whites and Plains Indians. Not shown, of course, were the Indians' extermination or removal that created the myth of an empty wilderness where pioneers could establish more and more settlements. In this film a potential family and community would be based on extracting gold, but what could the "Indian maiden" play other than a subservient role?

From January 1915 well into 1916, Selig produced many one- and two-reel westerns starring Mix as "the man who never fakes."[48] Several of those westerns survive, and a few others received some attention in the trade press. Mix played a range of characters: a cowboy or ranch foreman, rancher, sheriff, newspaperman, and once even a sheep herder. Especially as a cowboy, he wore a relatively consistent costume marking his difference from others: a high-crowned dark hat with a narrow white band, dark shirt and/or vest, white bandana knotted in front, and chaps with half a dozen or more bosses lining each leg. Whatever the film and its apparent setting in the Southwest, the story highlighted the performance of one daredevil stunt or another, one or more dangerous situations, and usually a gunfight. In *The Stagecoach Driver and the Girl*, for instance, Mix plays the stage driver whose sister invites a girl from the East to visit.[49] A gambler leads a band of Mexican bandits who rob his stage of a shipment of money, chase him and the Eastern girl passenger through a scrubby landscape, only to have one horse shot, a wheel come off, and a gun battle erupt until the stage guard rousts a posse to disperse the Mexicans.[50]

Nearly all engage Mix romantically with a young woman that ends with them coupled. The playfully tongue-in-cheek *Starring in Western Stuff* has a film company shooting a western near the ranch where Mix is the head cowpuncher.[51] Falling in love with the lead actress and disgusted by the

Figure 5.4 Selig, *Legal Advice*, 1916 (US Library of Congress, Washington, DC)

second-rate leading man, he and his fellow cowboys pretend to kidnap the actress so that Mix can take over as the rescuing hero—and "get the girl." No such luck occurs in *Legal Advice*, which looks like a throwback to Keystone comedies, with cowboys dragging Mix several times behind a horse and making him the butt of other jokes.[52] (See Figure 5.4.) After a young woman from the East sets up a law office in an all-male frontier town, Mix steals the sheriff's horse and shoots up the saloon so she can represent him, but his hopes of romance are dashed when her husband, a foppish caricature, suddenly arrives as the trial begins.[53] Like comic versions of Hart's short westerns, these films also are set in a late stage of settler colonialism. Although the exact period is ambiguous, Mexicans often play disreputable villains in several films, yet without any sense of the recent Mexican Revolution. But what about the threat of Indians?

They finally appear in the two-reel *Ma's Girls*, where unexpectedly Mix himself takes on the role of a devious gambler.[54] Madge and Rose live with their parents outside a small western town. The gambler engages an assayer in a card game, wins his money, and offers a loan, with a stipulation. The loser comes upon the girls' father working a mine and finds a piece of quartz

142 OUR COUNTRY/WHOSE COUNTRY?

to assay, but so does the father, and both ride toward town. After the sheriff warns the gambler to stop harassing the girls in a store, the assayer alerts the gambler that his quartz really is gold and then tells the father his ore is worthless. One day the gambler attacks Rose out riding, but Madge hears her screams, lassos the gambler, and drags him across a river, up the steep opposite bank, and releases him. Swearing revenge, the gambler tries to buy the father's mine and is refused. Even angrier, the gambler induces a few renegade Indians to help him abduct the girls and imprison them in their camp. Ma is alarmed at her daughters' absence and persuades the sheriff to collect a posse and search for them. When Rose and Madge escape before the posse reaches the camp and the renegades flee, the gambler spots the girls and follows on horseback. But Ma overtakes him and kills him in a running gunfight. Meanwhile, the posse pursues the renegades, badly wounding two and capturing two others. Now a hero, the sheriff asks to marry Rose, and the parents give their blessing. Here, Mix wears a more formal Stetson, a dark sports jacket, a white shirt, and light trousers—as befits a gambler. Yet he still cannot resist performing another dangerous stunt, lassoed and dragged roughly for a great distance by one of the women the gambler had assaulted. Although the gambler enlists a few Indians in his nefarious plot, where they have come from and how they can live not far from the white settlement is unclear. Because the setting and time period are ambiguous, they may have "jumped" a reservation or simply live on one of the Oklahoma allotments for the tribes once forced to move west on the Trail of Tears.

By July 1915, in trade press ads, Selig was promoting Mix as one of its biggest stars. One announced the opening of the Selig Jungle Zoo, with not only Kathlyn Williams and Bessie Eyton welcoming touring visitors but Mix also performing "dare-devil feats of horsemanship for their entertainment."[55] At the same time, two other full-page ads ballyhooed the "magic name" of "dashin' Tom Mix": "It gets 'em![56] Every week he pulls a new stunt which makes all th' folks rise right up in their seats an' hold their breath." Each of these ads has a large photo of Mix, yet not in the same cowboy regalia. (See Figure 5.5.) In one, he stands with arms folded, wearing his high-crowned dark hat, a light large-checked shirt, a bandana looped over one shoulder, the embossed chaps, and spurred boots. In the other, he stands, arms spread on hips, in the same costume except for a dark, horizontally striped shirt emblazoned with the diamond-shaped S of the Selig logo. That shirt never appeared in any of the films, of course, but he may have worn it during the daredevil feats he performed for audiences at the Jungle Zoo. Both photos of

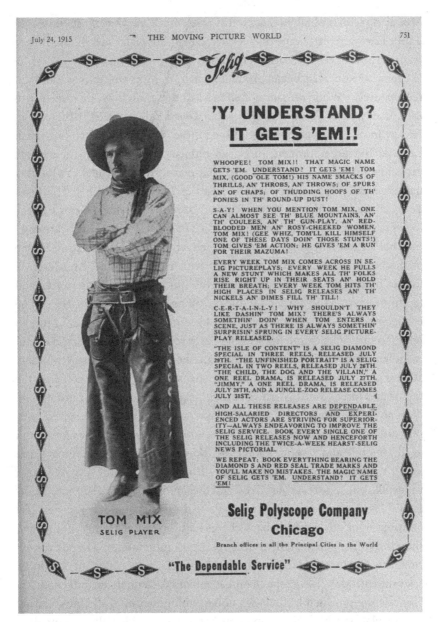

Figure 5.5 Selig ad, *Moving Picture World*, July 24, 1915

144   OUR COUNTRY/WHOSE COUNTRY?

Mix, along with the ballyhoo, served as a new model of white masculinity, (so unlike Hart) a skilled figure of inventive, dangerous feats of horsemanship or trials of endurance as well as a male action hero or romantic lead.

From 1915 on, Selig began producing many of Mix's westerns as multiple-reel features.[57] While romance often marked these westerns, increasingly so did comedy, as in *The Auction of the Run-Down Ranch* (1915).[58] There, Tom Hickey fools a prospector into thinking there is oil on the worthless ranch he buys. The target, however, is Isaac Goldplate, which renders the comedy explicitly anti-Semitic. At least one hilarious scene interrupts the looping narrative arc of Selig's five-reel *The Heart of Texas Ryan* (1917).[59] Set on a Texas borderland, the story has Texas Ryan returning from Vassar College to her father's prosperous ranch where Jack Parker is "a devil-may-care cow-puncher" who easily gets into scrapes fueled by too much whiskey.[60] In one of those scrapes, Jack gets into a fight with marshal "Dice" McAllister, a former road agent now in league with Antonio Moreno, a cattle rustler, and has to flee across the border. On his return he discovers Ryan is the girl he has long admired in a photo and now becomes a "changed man." Moreno hopes to marry Ryan and her fortune but is rejected; so, he kidnaps her, demanding a ransom, and Jack has to secure her release. McAllister, Moreno, and his gang then rustle some of the rancher's herd; again, Jack comes to the rescue and forces McAllister to flee and the gang to return the cattle. When Moreno escapes, Jack pursues him across the border, only to be seized himself. Just as he is about to be shot, Ryan and her father race into Mexico in an automobile and ransom his release. Now Jack discovers Ryan loves him rather than a supposed Eastern suitor. This film "has more variety than a vaudeville bill," one reviewer wrote, and the familiar plot, like Fairbanks's *The Lamb* (1915), seems concocted to stage one thrill after another: a suspenseful barroom fight, several horseback chases with "excellent riding, roping, and shooting stunts," then a last-minute-rescue by automobile.[61] Despite the excitement, Genevieve Harris admitted the plot was "occasionally lost in irrelevant episodes."[62] Perhaps the most egregious came in an Independence Day celebration when Jack, "laden down with fireworks of all kinds," climbs up to a platform high above an open water tank, accidentally sets off all of them, plunges into the tank, and "is almost blown out of the water" by exploding firecrackers.[63] Although the film has to partner a villainous marshal with the usual devious Mexicans, the huge Texas ranch, Vassar College, the Independence Day fireworks, and the automobile rescue all locate this story in a more or less "modern" settled white community.

By 1917, Selig was making fewer and fewer films at its studios in Los Angeles and Chicago as well as on location. This change prompted Mix to sign a contract with Fox Film, which initially confined him to two-reel comedies with titles such as *Six-Cylinder Love* and *A Soft Tenderfoot*.[64] Within months, however, he had the go-ahead to return to western subjects at feature length. Unfortunately, most of these early Fox releases are lost, among them the first, *Cupid's Round Up* (January 1918).[65] Two fathers agree to have their children, Helen Chadwick and Henry Kelly, marry, although neither knows the other. Both agree as long as they can enjoy a month of freedom, and Henry first sees and becomes interested in Helen on a train as she heads for her father's ranch. Helen pretends to be a maid in a hotel, and Henry courts her under an assumed name. Hired at a ranch near Chadwick's, Henry confronts a band of cattle rustlers in a shoot-out and has to flee when he is accused of murder. Racing after a train, he leaps in through an open window and lands at Helen's feet. They now reveal their real identities and head off "to their approaching wedding with joy." Again, this story is set in scattered ranches and a small frontier town, threatened only by apparently white cattle rustlers (according to the cast list of names).[66] Near the end, as if to one-up Hart's chase after a train in *Truthful Tulliver*, Mix concocts a new stunt, in which he not only springs from his galloping horse onto the moving train but also plunges through the window of a passenger car.[67] The most interesting thing about the film's publicity, however, is the production photo of Mix with a high-crowned, wide-brimmed white Stetson and a matching light-colored jacket or coat.[68] This is perhaps the first evidence of his new star turn as a rather flamboyant figure, famous for his fashionable costumes as well as his stunts and horsemanship—for the latter he wore more suitable garb. Unlike Hart or Carey, Mix now increasingly posed as a male model of American consumer culture.[69]

Intriguingly, a Fox ad for *Ace High* (June 1918) sported a photo of Mix in that white Stetson, although it's hardly part of his costume in a story set in the northwestern mountains.[70] (See Figure 5.6.) The same photo appeared with a far more characteristic Fox feature, *Treat 'Em Rough* (January 1919).[71] Adapted from Charles Alden Seltzer's 1911 novel, *The Two-Gun Man*, it was shot near Mix's ranch in Prescott, Arizona.[72] Here, Mix plays a daredevil cowboy, Ned Ferguson, hired by ranch owner John Stafford to hunt down a gang of cattle rustlers. On the way to the ranch, Ned is bitten by a rattlesnake and nursed by Mary Radford, "living in a shack getting 'atmosphere'" for writing a western novel.[73] Ranch foreman Dave Leviatt is jealous of Mary's

Figure 5.6 Tom Mix in Fox, *Treat 'Em Rough*, 1919 (*Illinois State Journal* [January 12, 1919])

interest in Ned and convinces Stafford that Mary's brother Ben is the head of the rustlers. In a deceptive move, Dave shoots Ben in the back, which leads the latter to think Ned has double-crossed him and is the culprit. Mary now will have nothing to do with Ned, even after he saves her life in a cattle stampede. After Ned runs down the rustlers, Dave is captured and confesses the truth; finally, Mary accepts Ned as her real, rather than fictional, hero. Although the film stages a familiar story of ranches and cattle rustlers in the usual settled white community, it gives the story a uniquely "modern" touch of self-reflectivity with the heroine (a young woman from where is unclear) writing a novel about the West. Mix gets to indulge in his expected stunts as a skilled horseman, but he also adds several more feats. In order to save Mary, one has Ned "in the midst of a prairie fire" that stampedes a herd of cattle, "deftly swinging a lariat, roping a steer and throwing it, making the fallen steer a barricade," behind which he and Mary crouch safely as the cattle thunder past.[74] To establish Ned's credentials as a gunfighter, the opening scene has him "'pinking' out the ten spots of clubs on a card at 20 paces in the record time of three seconds, shooting with both right and left hands."[75] Exhibitors were bullish: "Tom Mix has arrived [and] is far ahead of Hart or Fairbanks."[76] And audiences seemed to be enthralled by Mix, with "his nice smile," as the movies' "master cowboy" hero.[77]

The last Fox western starring Mix to consider here, *Fighting for Gold* (April 1919), adapted from William Mcleod Raine's 1915 novel, *The Highgrader*, offers an especially apt conclusion.[78] For one, the trade press used it to mark his extraordinary popularity with audiences.[79] Much more important, however, was Mix's embodiment of Wister's Anglo-Saxon hero. Jack Kilmeny is an Englishman who has traveled to the West seeking his fortune and soon is working a gold mine.[80] While his partner, Curly Brandon, is drunk one day, Jack has to fend off men hired by a British company that owns a neighboring gold mine and wants to seize his claim. Lord Farquar, the aristocratic head of the British company, and his daughter Moya arrive, along with Bobyan Verinder, to inspect the property. Jack meets and falls for Moya and later snatches her from a runaway wagon onto his racing horse. Prodded by a dance hall girl during a rodeo, Curly robs a man and casts blame on Jack by dressing in his coat and riding his horse. When Curly flees to Mexico, Jack follows, escaping a sheriff bent on arresting him. While he is away, Bobyan takes over his claim and hires ruffians as guards. When Jack returns and gives back the stolen money, he finds his claim occupied and the hired guns throwing dice to see who gets Moya whom they have captured. In a shootout, Jack kills the ruffians and rescues Moya once again, but not before Curly, who also has returned, saves him and is mortally wounded. In the end, Curly confesses to the sheriff, and Jack and Moya marry, merging their adjacent properties.

Once more, Mix shows off not only his stunt work but also his marksmanship and especially his skill with horses, which fast were becoming a prerequisite for other cowboy stars.[81] In rescuing Moya, for instance, "he flings his lasso over the roof, ties one end to the saddle of his horse, grabs the other end and makes the animal pull him to the top of the house. Then he drops down the chimney and kills the ruffians."[82] "Here is an actor," one newspaper wrote in aptly comic awe, "who treats his life about as carefully as the average man does a plugged nickel."[83] What's new is the action that provokes the runaway wagon: Inexplicably, Jack has a pet grizzly that gets loose and tumbles downhill to land in the Farquars' picnic gathering, causing hilarious mayhem. If

148 OUR COUNTRY/WHOSE COUNTRY?

this story has Jack and Curly cross the border into Mexico, the country and its inhabitants, given the ongoing revolution, hardly create any problems and merely serve as a backdrop for a convenient plot turn. Instead, with the focus on white men mining for gold, the film sets up a sharp difference between an honest, hard-working Englishman and a devious one working for a British company. That difference, of course, masks the exploitation of a supposedly empty land by settlers in their westward march across the continent. More to the point, the British company's intent on a kind of conquest of the land would, in miniature, reverse the path of American history.

Douglas Fairbanks, "Performing Doug"

Douglas Fairbanks (1883–1939) had an increasingly successful stage career for more than a dozen years before entering the movie industry. That career began with amateur theater in Denver, two years touring with the Frederick Warde company, and then taking leading roles on the Broadway stage, among them in *A Gentleman from Mississippi* (1908–1909). Moving to Hollywood in 1915, he contracted with Triangle to take on leading roles under the supervision of D. W. Griffith. Several early films astonished audiences and newspaper reviewers with his athletic abilities, "adorably diverting stunts," and "dazzling" comedic fervor.[84] Very soon he was working with Anita Loos and John Emerson in a series of feature-length romantic comedies. By late 1916, he had left Triangle and signed with Paramount-Artcraft. In the midst of those increasingly popular comedies, Fairbanks acted in five westerns, a genre he eventually would return to in *The Mark of Zorro* (1920). Remarkably different from those the same company soon produced with Hart, Fairbanks's features offer a surprisingly apt conclusion to this study of westerns within the framework of settler colonialism.

The first of Fairbanks's five-reel westerns, *The Lamb* (October 1915), set a strikingly unique tone for his following films. Based loosely on *The New Henrietta* (1913), a popular stage play in which Fairbanks had starred, *The Lamb* has an unusually ramshackle spoof of a plot that resembled earlier Keystone comedies and shared parallels with Mix's slightly later *The Heart of Texas Ryan*.[85] As the foppish son of the idle rich in New York, Gerald is about to wed when "a young giant from Arizona," Bill Cactus, rescues a friend of his fiancée Mary (Seena Owen) at the beach, revealing the Lamb's "yellow streak." Once she and her friends decamp for Bill's ranch in Arizona, Gerald follows, gets off a train to buy some Indian trinkets, and is left behind.[86] "Two crooks from the east" offer a shortcut to catch the train but rob him, and he's left wandering in the desert. Luckily, an aviator, another guest at the ranch, finds him, but they are captured by Yaqui Indians and taken across the border into Mexico. After Bill and Mary lead an automobile search party across the border, the Yaquis fight off Mexican soldiers and then seize Mary. Bill now turns coward and flees with the others back to report her capture to American troops. Together Gerald and Mary escape, only to face the angry Indians. Finding a machine gun that the Yaquis took from the Mexicans, but think is just junk, Gerald, now a "giddy little lamb," uses it to mow down many of the Indians who try to attack them. When he runs out of ammo, the remaining Yaquis begin crawling nervously toward the desperate Americans. In the nick of time, of course, the US troopers arrive, scatter the Indians, and Gerald and Mary are left in one another's arms. Back home, Gerald can now compare himself favorably to a portrait of his "Old War Horse" of a father.

The time period of *The Lamb* is a mishmash of the present day and an imaginary past that, like the earlier *Yaqui Cur*, also messes gleefully with history.[87] The airplane, automobile, and machine gun contend with Yaqui Indians who had long resisted Mexican soldiers but rarely attacked whites, unless they supported the hated Diaz regime.[88] Instead, the film dismissively turns them into cowering stereotypes, too stupid to recognize a machine gun.[89] Puffing this first Fairbanks vehicle, Triangle's publicity ballyhoos the climactic battle as comparable "to some of the great Civil War moments in 'The Birth of a Nation,'" and harps on Griffith's supposed supervision of its production.[90] As Gerald, Fairbanks plays a helpless, hopeless naif who keeps on smiling, untroubled by any threats thrown his way, much like an indestructible "cartoon" character. By the time he escapes the Yaquis, his "healthy and magnetic personality" emerges, and he suddenly becomes an athletic hero, leaping from the ground onto a cabin roof (in reverse motion) and tossing Indians left and right.[91] In the end, *The Lamb* is the first of these western features to debunk the myth of the West in an outrageous tongue-in-cheek parody.

Released the following year, *The Good Bad-Man* (April 1916) benefited from a more serious scenario written by Fairbanks himself and from deft direction by Allan Dwan.[92] The story is set in Wyoming where "there still remains undisturbed a remnant of life as it was in the days of the pioneers."[93] The film opens with a couple of old-timers reading a newspaper story about the eccentric outlaw, "Passin' Through," and "swappin' stories" about his exploits.[94] Troubled by not knowing anything of his father, he is said to

150   OUR COUNTRY/WHOSE COUNTRY?

engage in daring hold-ups and then give any loot—money or groceries—
to orphaned children like him. Most recently, his "peculiar hobby" led him
to rob the Pacific Express, solely to secure a coveted ticket punch.[95] Riding
through the desert near Maverick City, he meets Pap May, his daughter
Sarah (Bessie Love), and The Wolf, leader of a gang that rules the lawless
region.[96] Asking to bunk in Pap's cabin, he protects Sarah from The Wolf's
advances and then sits to talk with her, sharing the letter from his mother
to Bob Evans, who will tell him the truth about his father. Trying to repress
his attraction to Sarah, Passin' Through rides off to shoot up the rough
town's saloon, is lassoed by the sheriff, and confronts a marshal looking for
him—who happens to be Evans. Shown the letter, Evans, as his mother's
best friend, tells him about how she met and married his father who was
shot by a spurned rival, Bud Frazer. Evans is surprised to recognize Frazer
as The Wolf when the latter confronts him in town and now threatens to kill
the son. Before Passin' Through can try to take Sarah and Pap away from
their cabin, The Wolf and his gang try to shoot him; failing that, after Passin'
Through has to flee, he and his gang seize Sarah, ride into town, and hide
her in a hotel room. Passin' Through returns to find Pap dead, discovers his
mother's photo and a letter to Frazer in The Wolf's cabin, races into town,
and saves Sarah from one of his gang. He and Evans face off against The Wolf
in the saloon; Evans sends him off to safety and then exchanges shots with
Frazer. After a posse captures the gang who were pursuing Passin' Through
and Sarah, Evans discovers that the locket with the mother's photo has
stopped one of Frazer's bullets. In the end, the lovers ride off into the desert,
aiming to cross the border.

Located in an empty desert of scattered cabins around a mine near a lawless town, this story has a relatively clear narrative arc, with several melodramatic coincidences: Passin' Through meeting Pap and Sarah by chance, the
marshal turning out to be Evans, whose memory of the past lets him recognize The Wolf as Frazer.[97] Filling that arc are rival white men in love with the
same woman—one pair in the past, the other in the present—and a lawman
and "eccentric outlaw" pitted against The Wolf and his gang. Passin' Through,
like some of Hart's characters, is haunted by a mother but troubled even more
by her silence about his father. A Robin Hood figure, he robs in order to help
orphaned boys or to collect a few trinkets for himself and already hopes to
go straight before he falls in love with Sarah and learns from Evans how his
father was killed. Perhaps unexpectedly, Evans takes over the revenge plot,
partly because he has been searching not for the wanted outlaw but for his

Figure 5.7 Triangle, *The Good Bad-Man*, 1916 (San Francisco Film Festival/ Cinémathèque française)

father's killer. With newspapers now noting his popularity with audiences, Fairbanks plays both Passin' Through and himself, a very self-confident, insouciant American male actor, skilled with a horse and gun—but eschewing Mix-like stunts—and always ready with a big grin.[98] Strikingly, Dwan has him often occupy a lower position in the frame than Evans and even Sarah, which makes him look boyishly young.[99] (See Figure 5.7.) In his first long scene with Sarah, the two playfully interact like youngsters as he shows her his trinkets, lets her read his mother's letter, and sets his Stetson aslant on her head. While most of the time, Sarah is a demure, put-upon figure, she does once cover Passin' Through's escape by boldly standing and firing a revolver with deadly aim at several of the lurking gang. In the context of settler colonialism, it is telling that The Wolf's gang includes one Indian (who is shot for attacking Sarah) and a Mexican or half-breed, further signs of the representational shift in which such "aliens" are threatening only because they are subordinate members of a white-led gang outside the law. If Passin' Through means to take the willing Sarah across the border, supposedly into Mexico, it is far from clear what awaits them there.

152 OUR COUNTRY/WHOSE COUNTRY?

Although released more than a year later, *The Man from Painted Post* (October 1917) makes a good pair with *The Good Bad-Man*. Adapted by Fairbanks from a recent magazine story while shooting occurred near Laramie, Wyoming, the film was edited in a special train car as the cast and crew traveled to New York.[100] Those conditions sometimes gave the story, like that of *The Lamb*, a decidedly slapdash look.[101] It begins with a crucial short scene in which a bad man called "30.30" Smith assaults and then shoots the sister of detective "Fancy Jim" Sherwood (Fairbanks). Later, Bronson, the leader of a group of Wyoming cattlemen, hires Sherwood to get rid of rustlers in the area, and a flashback explains why: in a saloon scene, he shoots two men at once, "crossing his revolvers in front of him and not looking at either."[102] Adopting the disguise of an Easterner, Sherwood buys Bronson's ranch and pretends to be unfamiliar with western ways. After using a map to locate "Bull" Madden's ranch and a hidden hillside cabin, he realizes Madden heads the "Hole-in-the-Wall" gang of rustlers and sends him a courteous note to desist. Madden wants to marry Jane Forbes, a teacher from the East, but his freckle-faced son warns Sherwood, who comes between them and soon shyly falls in love. Sherwood later scales the steep hillside, drops through the cabin's roof, and discovers its importance: the gang drives cattle into the lower floor and change Bronson's brand V to W. More crucially, he also finds a 30.30 bullet that reveals Madden was his sister's killer. After Madden and his gang seize Jane and hide her in the cabin, at night Sherwood breaks in, leading to a dramatic gun fight. One by one, the gang is dispatched, with Jane once firing a rifle to save Sherwood.[103] While the cattlemen capture Madden and turn him over to the law, Sherwood and Jane ride off together into the sunset.

Much of this story is set on Bronson's ranch, in the hillside cabin, around the isolated schoolhouse, and especially on the plains where horsemen ride furiously, and admittedly far too repeatedly.[104] In the cabin, however, very selective lighting first serves to obscure the branding and then heightens key moments of the gun battle. As Sherwood, Fairbanks makes sure that he initially seems inept by quickly falling backward off a bucking horse the ranch cowboys set him on and, in his first encounter with Madden, "accidentally" shooting holes in his hat.[105] But he soon demonstrates his athletic ability by leaping onto horses and riding hell-bent through empty landscapes. The flashback of Sherwood's amazing gun skills ends with him leaping onto a high rafter to disarm other outlaws who burst into the saloon—evidence of how he will handle himself in the climactic gun battle.[106] As in *The Good*

Bad-Man, the Fairbanks smile marks his character, rather self-deprecatingly early on, but his virile confidence can't be suppressed. That is, except in his early scenes with Jane, where he tries, with bashful stoicism, to avoid revealing his interest in her despite her obvious attraction to him. Again, as in *The Good Bad-Man*, the heroine is a lone white woman threatened by the villain and his gang, dragged off into hiding, and eventually needing to be rescued by the male hero. Here, even more non-white figures appear in minor subordinate roles. Madden's gang includes at least one Mexican and one Indian, and Bronson's ranch seems to have a half-breed Chinese servant. Most striking is the squaw Madden lives with and abuses without any fear of reprisal. By contrast, both Jane and Sherwood dote on his wayward, half-breed boy, who resembles the orphaned recipients of Passin' Through's loot.

The last two Fairbanks westerns to take up could hardly be more different. Unlike the previous films, *The Half Breed* (July 1916) is an unusually "straight drama," in which "the intense personality of Fairbanks does not bulge out of the story."[107] Adapted by Anita Loos from Bret Harte's *In the Carquinez Woods*, the film takes place in "the picturesque days of early California."[108] Fairbanks plays Lo Dorman, the son of an Indian woman betrayed by a white man, who leaves her baby boy with her only friend, an old naturalist, and then kills herself. When the old man dies years later, several "ruthless white men" make Lo, now grown, an outcast because "an Indian can't hold land in this country." In the nearby ironically named town of Excelsior, a number of important characters appear in the Palka Saloon: a hypocritical blowhard, Pastor Wyn; a drunk "specimen of the 'Superior' white man"; and rival suitors, the express manager Jack Brace and Sheriff Dunn. From the hollow interior of an old redwood in which he lives, Lo comes to town, and Wyn invites him to sit beside his daughter Nellie in church as an example of his sermon on "tolerance." After the coquettish, fashion-conscious Nellie invites him to walk with her, Brace, Dunn, and even Wyn denounce Lo to his face: "she's a white woman, you're an Indian." Two other characters now appear: Dick Carson, who sells "snake medicine" to both Indians and whites, and his assistant Teresa (Alma Rubens), a Mexican who is angered by Carson going off with a local blonde.[109] The next morning, she confronts Carson, stabs him in the back, and flees into the woods. When Dunn pursues and finds her, he asks for sexual favors, and she stabs him in the chest. Now she meets Lo, who tells her she will be safe in his redwood hollow. While Carson and Dunn are recovering, Lo asks Nellie for a dress, which he gives to Teresa to wear. After Lo and Teresa sit and talk companionably about his interest in

Figure 5.8 Triangle, *The Half-Breed*, 1916 (San Francisco Film Festival/ Cinémathèque française)

plants, he and Nellie, who has searched for him, also sit to talk—and Teresa imagines the two are lovers. Searching for Nellie, Brace finds the dress Teresa now has discarded and tells Dunn of what he mistakes as a love nest. Barely able to walk, Dunn goes after Lo and finds Teresa, who reveals that he is Lo's father—and Dunn collapses. Drunken Indians set fire to the forest; Lo rescues Teresa who is unable to escape the flames. In the end, Lo says that he can't ask her to share his life as an outcast, but Teresa, as an alien outside the law, insists that she wishes to go with him.

Especially notable in *The Half-Breed* are director Dwan's deep space compositions. (See Figure 5.8.) At least three stand out: a high-angle extreme long shot past Lo's mother to the river curving through a forest far below and then the matching high angle/extreme long shot as Lo slowly walks in the opposite direction as an outcast: the full shot/extreme long shot of the church interior, looking from the pastor's back and congregation to the doorway and distant street where Lo appears; the long shot/extreme long shot of a huge half-fallen tree trunk (in silhouette) seeming to arch over the distant figures of Lo and Teresa at the end. (See Figure 5.9.) After his introduction standing

Figure 5.9 Triangle, *The Half-Breed*, 1916 (San Francisco Film Festival/ Cinémathèque française)

nearly naked by that river, Lo throughout wears a buckskin outfit and coonskin hat, as if modeled after the dime novel cover of *Seth Jones* (1860). As Lo, Fairbanks's performance is quiet and restrained; he indulges in very few stunts; and he only smiles with Nellie and Teresa or to show his initial indifference to the white men's contempt.[110] Much like Hart's *The Narrow Trail*, the film sharply divides the "clean things" of the forest from the ruthless whites of the town who scorn Lo, pursue Teresa, and berate Nellie.

Perhaps most striking are the differences between the film and Harte's novella. Dunn is identified as Lo's father when first introduced in an intertitle, which prepares for his and Teresa's delayed discovery; and Teresa herself shows little fear, as in Harte's story, but rather is quite fiery and aggressive. Surprisingly, the film adds several subordinate non-white characters: an African American man dealing cards in the saloon, a group of Chinese at another card game, and three drunken, dancing Indians apparently working for Carson. The Indians turn out to be crucial characters (already "cursed" by white whiskey traders), performing in stereotypical ways for the whites, which angers Lo. Even if the Indians want revenge for Lo sending them away

156   OUR COUNTRY/WHOSE COUNTRY?

from town, that they set the forest afire is inexplicable—and contradicts the historical way Native Americans used fire to manage their lands.[111] Given the characterization of the whites and Indians, Lo becomes a singular "in-between" figure who combines the educated knowledge of his foster father and the "natural" temperament of his mother's heritage. Yet, he remains an outcast from both worlds. Although in the novella Lo, Teresa, and Dunn all die in a fire of unknown origin, the film's ending is strikingly ambiguous. It's unclear whether Lo ever learns that Dunn was his father and whether Lo will ever accept Teresa, despite their similar position as outsiders, after she slowly follows him, but at a distance, into what he realizes is an "endless exile."[112]

The antithesis of *The Half-Breed*, *Wild and Wooly* (June 1917) makes a fitting conclusion to this study of Fairbanks's early westerns. Full of outrageous comedy, the film that Loos adapted from a Horace B. Carpenter story spins a highly self-aware tale about the lure of the West.[113] It begins with a series of images contrasting the pioneering past and the modern present day before moving to New York City. There the idle son of a railroad king, Jeff Hillington, is sitting before a teepee, eating a plateful of beans, and reading a dime novel in what soon is revealed to be his mansion room. After imitating the action in a Remington painting of cowboys taming a horse, he plays tricks on a butler until his father says they are late getting to the office. While Jeff escapes on Sunday to watch a western movie, the film switches to Bitter Creek, Arizona, to introduce the hotel proprietor Tom Larabee, his daughter Nell (Eileen Percy), the hotel clerk Pedro, and his real boss Steve Shelby (Sam De Grasse), a grafting Indian agent. Hoping to build a railroad spur, the townspeople want Jeff, who is being sent to the West, to report favorably to his father. Nell convinces them to remake the town into a replica of how it looked in the 1880s; they plan a fake hold-up of a stagecoach, along with a fake Indian uprising, and Shelby, warned of an Indian Service audit, prepares for one last theft before he and Pedro escape to Mexico. When Jeff steams into town, dressed in fancy western garb fit for "a masque ball," he is excited to find what he expected of the West.[114] After he chases off a phony Red Eye Dan, manhandling Nell, the townspeople put dummy bullets in his guns to avert real trouble. When Wild Bill (Shelby in disguise) enters the saloon/dance hall, Jeff nonchalantly shoots him and lights a cigar, while Bill pretends to be wounded in the hand. Pedro leads Shelby's generic Indians into town, then seizes Nell, which is "not part of the program," and the Indians begin firing real bullets at Jeff. Once armed with his own real bullets, he rides off in pursuit of Pedro, while the "cursed" Indians hold the townspeople at bay and drink themselves silly. Jeff wounds Pedro and rescues Nell, then lassos Shelby. More Indians, lured by a thirst for drink, now surround Nell, and Jeff has to rescue her again. Returning to the saloon, he has Nell distract the drunken Indians, leaps down from an opening in the floor above, pushes the bar over on them, and returns the money that Shelby had stolen. In the end, the "conquering hero" says he has learned his lesson and will go back to his father's office "where I belong." But there's more.

Wild and Wooly is "an immensely clever burlesque" of the heroic cowboy fearlessly bringing law and order to the uncivilized West.[115] As if one-upping Tom Mix, Fairbanks pulls off stunt after stunt, "without receiving as much as a scratch," like a "wild-riding, quick-shooting, fierce-fighting, Jonnie-on-the-spot cowboy," all with his trademark grin.[116] As the location for his heroism, Bitter Creek becomes a Potemkin-like village that serves as a fantasy backdrop for staged fights, hold-ups, and "savage" attacks on an allegedly threatened community of settlers. All the fun goes wrong, however, at the instigation of the non-white characters. The Mexican Pedro abducts Nell for himself, and the Indian uprising, organized by Shelby, turns into a deadly battle. Although Jeff kills several Indians shooting at the saloon and easily subdues many of the others, they end up being either comic stereotypes addicted to drink or "savages" dancing around an encircled white woman. If Harry's drunkenness in *Hell Bent* led audiences to laugh with him, these many drunk Indians likely provoked derisive snorts. This burlesque of a story comes to an aptly tongue-in-cheek conclusion. After Jeff departs on the back platform of a train, leaving a saddened Nell, one of Loos's clever intertitles pops up. "But wait a minute, this will never do. We can't end a Western romance without a wedding. Yet—after marriage, where will they live? For Nell likes the East. And Jeff like the West. So where are the twain to meet?" In two spliced together shots, the film poses a remarkable answer. In the first LS, the wedded couple strolls through the New York mansion and kisses; in the second, reverse-angle long shot/extreme long shot, they pass out a doorway in western clothes, mount horses, and ride off into a desert landscape. In an editing sleight-of-hand that George Méliès might have admired, East and West are inextricably linked so Jeff and Nell can live happily in a single fantasy space. What a perfect parody of "American Progress," which unites East and West and so neatly resolves the many conflicts inherent to the settler colonialism determining *our country.*

Afterword: Looking Backward to Look Ahead

"Precepts of the Honorable Harvest:
to take only what is given, to use it well, to be grateful for the gift, and
to reciprocate the gift."

Robin Wall Kimmerer, *Braiding Sweetgrass* (2013)

The concept of *settler colonialism*, I have argued, proves invaluable in reframing early westerns as reenactments of this country's repressed and too often unacknowledged past. "In many ways," Janet Flanner wrote, perhaps only partly conscious of her meaning, "the 'Western' is a picturization of the country's suppressed desires."[1] For the modern American world of the early 20th century, that picturization operated in projection much like a nostalgia machine. The concept also reveals a striking shift in those reenactments during the first decades of the last century. In short, the films stage a remarkable vision of white settlers' westward expansion across the continent that reveals a historical transformation in American culture by recapitulating what "American Progress" came to mean in three successive phases. The crucial shift or break occurred between the second and third phases and more or less coincided with the outbreak of the Great War.

Initially, a loose grouping of films tracked settlers moving westward across the Appalachians, the Great Plains, and the Rockies to California. Their often-illegal seizure of "empty land" provoked the continual resistance of Indigenous peoples and later Mexicans; "pioneers" suffered extreme hardships in the inevitable conflicts that arose, but heroic male figures usually scattered those alleged "aliens" or even wiped them out. Some films even began to indulge in the long-held notion of nostalgic empathy for the Indian as the "Vanishing American." In the early 1910s, increasingly popular westerns then spun ever more complicated and contradictory tales. In Indian pictures, Indigenous peoples ranged from devious savages to victims of violent attacks by whites (often now involving the US Army) and agents of sometimes successful resistance, with some acting as "in-between" figures unable

160   AFTERWORD: LOOKING BACKWARD TO LOOK AHEAD

to survive in the clash of opposing cultures and even fewer as "mixed-descent peoples" partnered for the purposes of security and/or advantage. Mexicans and Mexican Americans—and, in rare instances, Chinese—tended to take positions across a similar spectrum. In cowboy and cowgirl films, "ordinary" characters could become heroes and heroines fighting outlaws, and bandits like Broncho Billy could undergo a transformation into "good badmen," but only in relation to other whites.

Finally, the mid- to late 1910s saw the most significant shift or rupture, as Indian pictures and cowgirl films nearly disappeared and male figures, embodied by movie stars, dominated several popular series, from shorts to features. In different ways, William S. Hart and Harry Carey reinvented the "good badman" as a stoic, if sometimes troubled, figure of virile mascu-linity. By contrast, in cowboy stories of often comic romance, Tom Mix not only indulged in dangerous stunts as an expert horseman but also donned costumes that made him a fashionable icon for an increasingly dominant consumer society. In just a few westerns, Douglas Fairbanks turned the myth of American Progress on its head in ramshackle parodies, ever sporting his nonchalant grin of effortless self-confidence. However diverse were these stories, nearly all assumed the context of a settled white community, only occasionally still harassed by Indians or Mexicans; instead, most of the latter now served as secondary characters or extras. Masked as Manifest Destiny, the expropriation of the West's lands and resources seemed settled once and for all.

But now, looking ahead, what potential pathways come into view? One might stake out an exploration of how the concept of settler colonialism could reframe genres other than the western. What about comedies, espe-cially in the 1910s, given the comic mode of some Mix and Fairbanks films? Could Biograph's *The Tourists* (August 1912) really be unique in its satire of white tourists who step off a Santa Fe train at Albuquerque to treat Navajos and their wares as salable commodities?[2] (See Figure A_1.1.) When Mabel Normand is left behind, wanders through the pueblos, and assumes a chief is merely part of a living history exhibit, she is chased away by a mob of "Indian suffragettes on the war-path."[3] Are there comedies either before *The Tourists* or in the years prior to Fatty Arbuckle's "slapstick farce," *Out West* (February 1918), that would merit analysis?[4] And how might *Out West* measure up to Fairbanks's earlier *Wild and Wooly*? After all, the later film has Fatty thrown off a freight train in the desert, quench his thirst by draining a waterhole, sud-denly be struck from behind by Indian arrows, and chased into the frontier

Figure A_1.1 Biograph, *The Tourists*, 1912 (Museum of Modern Art, New York)

town of Mad Dog. There, he halts a hold-up in the saloon, takes over as bartender, and, with the help of Buster Keaton and Al St. John, wildly shoots up the place. Extra bits of scene-stealing have Fatty outperforming Hart by rolling "a cigarette with miraculous ease and rapidity," a white horse with its hooves on the saloon bar rail downing a schooner of beer and then walking out "with an indescribable gait," and Fatty in the end rescuing a Salvation Army lass by tickling the villain into unconsciousness.[5] Moreover, what about an amusing parodic feature like *Two-Gun Betty* (1918), starring Bessie Barriscale, who bets she can pass as a cross-dressed cowboy on the ranch of her girlfriend's brother?[6] Easily spotting her disguise, the ranch hands plot to have fun with her, but she turns the tables on them, roping a steer, riding a broncho, winning at cards, deftly rolling a cigarette, capturing a real "Bad Man," and captured herself by her "good man" boss.[7]

A second pathway could lead to further questioning westerns as well as travel films beyond the 1910s and through the 1920s. How would the concept of settler colonialism reframe an analysis of big spectacle features such as *The Covered Wagon* (1923) and *The Iron Horse* (1924)? The first returns to the familiar story of pioneers threatened by Indians as they cross the plains

162 AFTERWORD: LOOKING BACKWARD TO LOOK AHEAD

and mountains and the quarrel between two white men for the love of a white woman. The second restages the construction of the transcontinental railroad through the interrelations of two Illinois men named Brandon and Marsh. Brandon, a surveyor, discovers a pass through the Black Hills but is killed by a Cheyenne war party. Years later, after President Lincoln authorizes the Union Pacific and Central Pacific to build the railroad's western and eastern sections, respectively, Marsh is the principal contractor overseeing crews of Chinese, Italians, and Irish repeatedly ambushed by Indians who have been divested of their ancestral lands. Brandon's son Davy, a pony express rider, rediscovers his father's pass, which enables Marsh to use it as a shortcut, countering the greedy maneuvers of a big landowner and his own chief engineer. In parallel with the completion of the railroad, Davy wins the hand of Marsh's daughter. Especially striking is the film's inclusion of ethnic groups—non-white "aliens" at the time—as railway workers who have to fend off the angered Indians, in sharp contrast to the famous photograph commemorating the railroad's construction, which excluded the Chinese. What about less well-known features such as *The Vanishing American* (1925) or *The Devil Horse* (1926)?[8] And those starring western figures from Mix and Carey to Hoot Gibson, Buck Jones, Ken Maynard, Fred Thomson, and others, including the legendary Black rodeo and trick rider Bill Pickett? What about all the serials from *Go-Get-Em Hutch* (1922), *In the Days of Buffalo Bill* (1922-1923), and *Galloping Hooves* (1924–1925) to *Ruth of the Rockies* (1921–1922) and *The Timber Queen* (1922)? In addition, did travel pictures continue to transform the western wilderness into spectacular uninhabited landscapes— and new ways of getting there—for the consuming pleasure of actual and virtual tourists? Finally, following the paths promoted by earlier exposition *actualités*, did others begin to track the emerging reach of settler colonialism to lands overseas, from the Caribbean to the Philippines and Asia?

A third pathway could shift attention to questions of exhibition and reception. How extensively were early westerns screened in movie theaters and other venues, in which cities and towns, accompanied by what other films, on what days of the week, and for how long? How did their circulation differ within and between the biggest cities, mid-sized cities, and small towns, perhaps in the context of run-zone patterns? What would be the result of comparing, for instance, the circulation of one-reel Broncho Billy films and multiple-reel Indian pictures such as *Indian Massacre* or the features of William S. Hart and those of Tom Mix? Although far from easy to determine, what was the response of audiences to early westerns? How might that

AFTERWORD: LOOKING BACKWARD TO LOOK AHEAD   163

have differed between the late 1900s, the early 1910s, and the late 1910s as well between the kinds of westerns released, series with well-known players and stars, and even specific titles? This book has relied mostly on trade press reviews and exhibitor comments, which could often be contradictory and perhaps less than representative of audiences. But what would come from researching newspaper articles and reviews more than has been done in Chapters 4 and 5? In the *Chicago Tribune*, Mae Tinée was scathing in writing about Hart's *The Devil's Double*: the story seemed concocted by "a bunch of youngsters" playing in a barn.[9] By contrast, in the *Des Moines Tribune*, Dorothy Day enthused, along with young boys, over the personal appearance in several theaters of Harry Carey, "one of the greatest screen idols."[10] In a different mode, despite the grim final shot in *The Half-Breed*, many newspapers told moviegoers the film ended happily for Douglas Fairbanks as Lo Dorman. Could such columns really represent actual audiences—and what kinds of audiences? That's hard to tell. At least one more source worth examining would be surveys of schoolchildren who attended the movies. In the early 1910s, in San Francisco, those in grades three through eight, for instance, preferred Wild West films far above any other kind, but whether the kinds of westerns or else the children were differentiated in any way was unclear.[11]

A fourth pathway might explore the relations between early westerns and similar stories in other cultural forms. Those could include novels, magazine and newspaper stories, theatrical productions, poems, pulp fiction, popular songs, cartoons, and even scrapbooks. One vantage point on this path would involve looking at scenario sources, following the lead of Josephine Rector, who claimed that many of her own scripts came from pulp magazines. A second would set up an analysis of any striking differences between a source story and a later film, as in the adaptation of a Bret Harte story for Douglas Fairbanks's *The Half-Breed* (1916). Another would take in stories published around the same time yet never sourced, such as B. M. Bower's "Like a Knight of Old," included in *Popular Magazine* on August 15, 1910, in which a naïve cowboy mistakes a film crew staging a gunfight for the real thing and gallops gallantly to the rescue.[12] This pathway also would raise another salient question: Were novels and magazine stories about Indians, cowboys, and cowgirls as popular as similar stories were in the movies—or were they much less frequent, and, if so, why? A fourth would focus on juvenile series fiction, from *The Rover Boys Out West* (1900), *The Motor Boys Across the Plains* (1907), and *The Moving Picture Boys in the West* (1913) to *The Motor Maids Across the*

164 AFTERWORD: LOOKING BACKWARD TO LOOK AHEAD

Continent (1911), and the *Ruth Fielding* series (beginning in 1913), whose central character entered the film industry as a scriptwriter and eventually became a director and producer.[13] Could this pathway even lead to parallel phenomena such as popular songs, from "Cheyenne" (1906) to others like "Starlight Sioux," "Indian Summer," and "Orinoco"?[14] Or even to comic strips such as "Haphazard Helen" (1915), one of which, in several adventures out West, has the heroine punch out a Mexican bandit?[15] In terms of live performance, what about "Lakota activist and author Luther Standing Bear" who starred as Charging Hawk in H. A. Brunswick's Great Wild West Indian Vaudeville, which, in 1909, included "a complete lecture on the Western pictures" that changed each night?[16]

Finally, what if we twist the conceptual lens of settler colonialism, and its myths of white supremacy, to reframe early American films within what Cedric Robinson has called "racial capitalism"?[17] Simply put, Robinson argues that "slavery and the slave trade constituted the basis of US capitalist development" and continues to do so today.[18] And the acquisition of land or territory, Roxanne Dunbar-Ortiz adds, was central to the US capitalist system.[19] Specifically, following Walter Johnson, she identifies the South as "the site for the rise of the fully articulated US capitalist state."[20] In the early 19th century, creating such conditions meant forcibly expelling Indigenous peoples—Cherokee, Creek, Chickasaw, and Choctaw—from their homelands so that slaveholders could transform the southeastern region of the Mississippi Valley, which had been in economic decline, into what became the Cotton Kingdom by increasing the population of enslaved Africans from elsewhere.[21] In other words, racial capitalism depended on a crucial linkage between Black slaves and Indigenous peoples in the cultivation and confirmation of white supremacy.[22]

How might this linkage lead to new ways of viewing early westerns? That could involve more than studying the representation of Blacks and Indians together and instead exploring their historical bonding as a determining structural absence.[23] How might early westerns look differently if we considered that both Indigenous peoples and Blacks had to move against their will to lands west of the Mississippi? The expulsion of Indigenous peoples redefined tribal territories and their interrelations, creating new alliances and conflicts, especially as white settlers continued to invade the West. The parallel movement of escaping or former slaves led to a large number of Black cowboys and to a smaller Black population in Mexico because of the latter's opposition to slavery.[24] How might early Civil War films in particular look differently, once the absence of most Indigenous peoples and the continued historical presence of some tribes, especially those who themselves owned slaves, were taken into account? How might this twist of the lens lead us to review other genres, from domestic melodramas and films of labor vs. capital to a variety of comedies, serials with female stars, advertising films, and even cartoons?

Given the multiple pathways sketched here, and those that others could scope out, perhaps the quote attributed to Yogi Berra is especially apt: "When you come to a fork in the road, take it."

Notes

Introduction

1. Richard Abel, "Our Country/Whose Country?" in *The Red Rooster Scare: Making Cinema American, 1900–1910* (Berkeley: University of California Press, 1999), 151–174.
2. "An American School of Moving Picture Drama," *Moving Picture World* (November 20, 1909): 712.
3. Richard Abel, "The 'Usable Past' of Westerns," in *Americanizing the Movies and "Movie Mad" Audiences, 1910–1914* (Berkeley: University of California Press, 2006), 61–82, 105–123.
4. Rick Altman, *Film/Genre* (London: British Film Institute, 1999), 36–38.
5. Roxanne Dunbar-Ortiz, *An Indigenous Peoples' History of the United States* (Boston: Beacon Press, 2016).
6. Lorenzo Veracini, *Settler Colonialism: A Theoretical Overview* (London: Palgrave Macmillan, 2010), 3. See also Lorenzo Veracini, "Introduction: Settler Colonialism as a Distinct Mode of Domination," in *Routledge Handbook of the History of Settler Colonialism*, eds. Edward Cavanagh and Lorenzo Veracini (New York: Routledge, 2016), 1–8.
7. Dunbar-Ortiz also makes a crucial distinction between emigrants as settlers and immigrants in which the latter migrate into a country with an existing political order, while the former invade a land where they destroy a society of longstanding inhabitants and build a new one reinforced by later waves of settlement. See *Not "A Nation of Immigrants": Settler Colonialism, White Supremacy, and a History of Erasure and Exclusion* (Boston: Beacon Press, 2021), 49–50.
8. Patrick Wolfe, *Settler Colonialism and the Transformation of Anthropology: The Politics and Poetics of an Ethnographic Event* (London: Cassell, 1999), 163; and Wolfe, "Settler Colonialism and the Elimination of the Native," *Journal of Genocide Research* 8.4 (2006): 387–409.
9. Mark Rifkin, *Manifesting America: The Imperial Construction of U.S. National Space* (New York: Oxford University Press, 2009), 6.
10. John L. O'Sullivan, "Statue to Jackson," *United States Magazine and Democratic Review* (July–August 1845), 5. See also Maura L. Jortner, "Playing 'America' on the Nineteenth-Century Stage" (Ph.D. dissertation, University of Pittsburgh, 2005). These references come from Steve Inskeep, "Introduction," in *Imperfect Union: How Jessie and John Frémont Mapped the West, Invented Celebrity, and Helped Cause the Civil War* (New York: Penguin, 2020), xxii.

168   NOTES

11. Frederick Jackson Turner, "The Significance of the Frontier in American History," in the American Historical Association's *Annual Report for the Year 1893* (Washington, D.C.: Government Printing Office, 1894), 199–227.

12. Walter Prescott Webb, *The Great Plains* (Boston: Ginn, 1931). The concept of a "blank space" comes from Jane Tompkins, *West of Everything: The Inner Life of Westerns* (New York: Oxford University Press, 1992), 75. Tompkins was shocked to find that Indians were simply absent from the later sound westerns she remembered liking so much in the past. For the impact of 19th-century painting on this "blank space" of the western wilderness, see also Virginia Wright Wexman, "The Family on the Land: Race and Nationhood in Silent Westerns," in *The Birth of Whiteness: Race and the Emergence of U.S. Cinema,* ed. Daniel Bernardi (New Brunswick: Rutgers University Press, 1996), 141.

13. Sarah Deutsch, "Landscape of Enclaves: Race Relations in the West, 1850–1900," in *Under an Open Sky: Rethinking America's Western Past*, eds. William Cronon, George Miles, and Jay Gitlin (New York: W.W. Norton, 1992), 113. See also Dina Gilio-Whitacker, *As Long as Grass Grows: The Indigenous Fight for Environmental Justice, from Colonization to Standing Rock* (Boston: Beacon Press, 2019), 58.

14. "American Progress" boasts a large central figure floating in the air and gazing left, apparently to the future: a luminous white woman partly veiled in white with the "Star of Empire" fronting her long auburn hair, holding in one arm a schoolbook and a spool of telegraph wire strung on poles from the far-right background where the sun is rising over a distant city on a bay. Following her are farmers plowing a field with oxen, a stagecoach, and three parallel trains. Slightly ahead of her are a small group of miners, a settler's wagon, one lone cowboy, and in the distance a wagon train in front of snow-capped mountains, dark clouds, and the hint of a sea at the edge of the left frame. Tiny Indian figures dance near several teepees in the distance, while deer, buffalo, an elk, and a bear flee before her, led by half a dozen "primitive" Indigenous peoples—three warriors, a mother and papoose, and a bare-breasted woman. A chromolithograph of the painting is located in the Prints and Photographs Division of the US Library of Congress.

15. William Cronon, "A Place for Stories: Nature, History, and Narrative," *Journal of American History* 78 (March 1992): 1357. The sidebar sections of this book also draw on Carolyn Merchant, *The Columbia Guide to American Environmental History* (New York: Columbia University Press, 2002).

16. Wolfe, "Settler Colonialism and the Elimination of the Native," n.p.

17. Patricia Nelson Limerick, "Making the Most of Words: Verbal Activity and Western America," in *Under an Open Sky*, 174.

18. Limerick, "Making the Most of Words," 176. She quotes Richard Henry Dana Jr.'s alarm at San Diego's "'Babel' of English, Spanish, French, Indian," and other languages in the early 19th century—in *Two Years Before the Mast* (New York: New American Library, 1964), 176.

19. John Mack Faragher, "Americans, Mexicans Métis: A Community Approach to the Comparative Study of North American Frontiers," in *Under an Open Sky*, 91.

NOTES 169

20. Jay Gitlin, "On the Boundaries of Empire: Connecting the West to Its Imperial Past," in *Under an Open Sky*, 75.
21. Faragher, "Americans, Mexicans Métis," 96, 100–101.
22. Gitlin, "On the Boundaries of Empire," 87.
23. Here, without any direct references, many of the historians I cite implicitly invoke the perspective of "critical race theory" initially developed as an interpretive lens in legal history. This book obviously aligns with the general parameters of the concept.
24. Owen Wister claimed that Americans were a new, culminating "breed of Anglo-Saxon" in "The Evolution of the Cow-Puncher," *Harper's Monthly* 91 (September 1895): 602–617. The concept of *white* or *Anglo* encompassed a range of migrants of largely European descent and often ignored a hierarchy of differences among them.
25. "On the discovery of this immense continent, the great nations of Europe were eager to appropriate to themselves so much of it as they could respectively acquire. Its vast extent offered an ample field to the ambition and enterprise of all, and the character and religion of the inhabitants afforded the apology for considering them [the Indians] as a people over whom the superior genius of Europe might claim an ascendency."—quoted in Gilio-Whitacker, *As Long as Grass Grows*, 56. For an excellent analysis of the little known Doctrine of Discovery, "the legal framework that informs the US colonial system," see Dunbar-Ortiz, *Not "A Nation of Immigrants*," 32–34. A slightly later Supreme Court case, *Cherokee Nation v. Georgia* (1831), asserted "a sovereign settler claim against *both* federal interference and indigenous resilience"—Patricia Wild, "Terms of Assimilation: Legislating Subjectivity in the Emerging Nation," in *Cultures of the United States* Imperialism, eds. *Amy* Kaplan and Donald E. Pease (Durham, NC: Duke University Press, 1993), 75.
26. See, for instance, Limerick, "Making the Most of Words," 180–182. For a stunningly benign image of assimilation that masks its cruelty, see William Fuller's grid-like design for *Crow Creek Agency, Dakota Territory* (1884), held by the Amon Carter Museum, Fort Worth, Texas. This large painting serves as the front cover of William H. Truettner, ed., *The West as America: Reinterpreting Images of the Frontier, 1820–1920* (Washington, DC: Smithsonian Institution, 1991), an amazing catalog for the major exhibition of that same title organized by the National Museum of American Art, March 15–July 7, 1991.
27. For a good sense of the great diversity of Indigenous peoples in North America, see Pekka Hämäläinen's sweeping history, *Indigenous Continent: The Epic Contest for North America* (New York: Liveright, 2022). His book also includes a useful series of maps that sketch the movements and shifting locations of Native American tribes. See also Fatimah Tobing Rony's concept of the racialized bodies of Indigenous peoples becoming "metonyms for an entire category of people," in *The Third Eye: Race, Cinema, and Ethnographic Spectacle* (Durham, NC: Duke University Press, 1996), 71.
28. For concise definitions of *Mexican*, from a white American perspective, that masked its diversity, see Laura E. Gómez, *Manifest Destinies: The Making of the Mexican American Race* (New York: New York University Press, 2007), 1–6, 82–83; Katherine Benton-Cohen, "Making Americans and Mexicans in the Arizona Borderlands," in *Mexico and Mexicans in the Making of the United States*, ed. John Tutino

170 NOTES

(Austin: University of Texas Press, 2012), 172–173; and Devra Weber, "Keeping Community, Challenging Boundaries: Indigenous Migrants, International Workers, and Mexican Revolutionaries, 1900–1920," in *Mexico and Mexicans in the Making of the United States*, 209. See also Mark Reisler, *By the Sweat of Their Brow: Mexican Immigrant Labor in the United States, 1900–1940* (Westport, CN: Greenwood Press, 1976), 14; Neil Foley, *Mexicans in the Making of America* (Cambridge: Harvard University Press, 2014), 25–26; and Kelly Lytle Hernández, *Bad Mexicans: Race, Empire, and Revolution in the Borderlands* (New York: W.W. Norton, 2022), 79. A typical racist description at the time went like this: "The Mexican laborer is unambitious, listless, physically weak, irregular, and indolent [but] docile, patient, usually orderly in camp, fairly intelligent under competent supervision, obedient, and cheap"—Victor S. Clark, "Mexican Labor in the United States," *Bulletin of the Bureau of Labor* 78 (Washington, DC: Government Printing Office, 1908), 496. By contrast, Mexican *vaqueros* were the first cowboys working on ranch lands that covered much of the Southwest between Texas and California into the mid-19th century—Jonathan Haeber "Vaqueros: The First Cowboys of the Open Range," *National Geographic News* (August 15, 2003).

29. Chinese immigrants initially joined the search for gold but then were recruited to construct the continental railroad; by 1870 there were 63,000 in California. See Dunbar-Ortiz, *Not "A Nation of Immigrants,"* 186, 188–189. The Page Act of 1875 barred the immigration of Chinese women as "undesirable," notably out of fear they would engage in prostitution. Similarly, Mexican migrants did "most of the railroad construction work in southern California, Arizona, New Mexico, and Texas." See Reisler, *By the Sweat of Their Brow*, 3–4.

30. See, for instance, Bruce A. Glasrud, "Introduction: 'Don't Leave Out the Cowboys!'" in *Black Cowboys in the American West: On the Range, on the Stage, Behind the Badge*, eds. Bruce A. Glasrud and Michael N. Searles, (Norman: University of Oklahoma Press, 2016), 10. Similar laws and policies aimed at Mexicans were dubbed "Juan Crow." See Hernández, *Bad Mexicans*, 9–10, 80–83.

31. As long has been known, with the exception of Indians on the Great Plains, many Indigenous peoples actually relied on agricultural practices.

32. Ronald Takaki, *Iron Cages: Race and Culture in 19th-Century America*, rev. ed. (New York: Oxford University Press, 2000), 13. The Dawes Severalty Act of 1887 forced "tribal land to be broken down into individual allotments whose proprietors would eventually sell to White people"—Wolfe, "Settler Colonialism and the elimination of the native," n.p. Good sources for the concept of *commons* are David Bollier, *Silent Theft: The Private Plunder of Our Common Wealth* (New York: Routledge, 2002); and Bollier, *Think Like a Commoner: A Short Introduction to the Life of the Commons* (Gabriola Island, BC: New Society Publishers, 2014). For very different studies of Indigenous peoples who either shared or fought over their territories, see Richard White, *The Middle Ground: Indians, Empires, and Republics in the Great Lakes Region, 1650–1815* (New York: Cambridge University Press, 1991); and Pekka Hämäläinen, *Comanche Empire* (New Haven: Yale University Press, 2008).

NOTES 171

33. Alan Trachtenberg, *The Incorporation of America: Culture and Society in the Gilded Age* (New York: Hill and Wang, 1982): 17–18.

34. This large mural depicts a struggling but excited group of wagon train settlers poised on a mountain pass looking toward the "promised land" of a fertile plain and sliver of ocean in the left background, suffused by a sky of golden light that also illuminates white-capped mountains in the right background. A revealing analysis of the mural— "What Do You See?"; What Does the Painting Tell You?"; "What the Painting Does Not Tell You"—appears in *The West as America: A Guide for Teachers* (Washington, DC: Smithsonian Art Museum), 6–8.

35. This poster is reprinted in Paul Reddin, *Wild West Shows* (Urbana: University of Illinois Press, 1999): between pp. 85 and 86.

36. My analyses and arguments extend earlier research by many others, but especially the following historians: Robert Anderson, "The Role of the Western Film Genre in Industry Competition, 1907–1911," *Journal of the University Film Association* 31.2 (1979): 19–26; Gregg Mitman, *Reel Nature: America's Romance with Wildlife on Film* (Seattle: University of Washington Press, 1999); Scott Simmon, *The Invention of the Western: A Cultural History of the Genre's First Half-Century* (Cambridge: Cambridge University Press, 2003); Andrew Brodie Smith, *Shooting Cowboys and Indians: Silent Western Films, American Culture, and the Birth of Hollywood* (Boulder: University of Colorado Press, 2003); Nana Verhoeff, *The West in Early Cinema: After the Beginning* (Amsterdam: University of Amsterdam Press, 2006); Jennifer Lynn Peterson, *Education in the School of Dreams: Travelogues and Early Nonfiction Film* (Durham, NC: Duke University Press, 2013); Michelle H. Raheja, *Reservation Reelism: Redfacing, Visual Sovereignty, and Representations of Native Americans in Film* (Lincoln: University of Nebraska Press, 2010); and Joanna Hearne, *Native Recognition: Indigenous Cinema and the Western* (Albany: SUNY Press, 2012).

37. Gilio-Whitacker, *As Long as Grass Grows*, 39.

38. The classic study of the concept is found in this work: Brian W. Dippie, *The Vanishing American: White Attitudes & U.S. Indian Policy* (Lawrence: University of Kansas Press, 1982).

39. Verhoeff, *The West in Early Cinema*, 16.

40. For a concise summary of the concept of the "Noble Savage," see Julie Schimmel, "Inventing the 'Indian,'" in *The West as America*, 151–154. The consummate Noble Savage portrait is Charles Bird King's *Young Omahaw, War Eagle, Little Missouri, and Pawnees* (1822). For a timely study of the range of "mixed-descent peoples" and their relations, see Anne F. Hyde, *Born of the Lakes and Plains: Mixed-Descent Peoples and the Making of the American West* (New York: W.W. Norton, 2022).

41. These were not the *magonistas* that President Porfirio Diaz called *malos Mexicanos* or "bad Mexicans," who helped provoke the Mexican Revolution in 1910. However, the bad Mexicans resisting whites in early westerns could be seen as displacements for the *magonistas* who did threaten American interests, specifically the investors who had taken over lands that Diaz had seized from many rural and Indigenous communities, which, in turn, led to the large low-wage labor migration into the United States. For a summary of the forces that led to the revolution, see Hernández, *Bad Mexicans*, 4–9.

172 NOTES

42. For an excellent study of the creation of the first national parks, see Mark David Spence, *Dispossessing the Wilderness: Indian Removal and the Making of the National Parks* (New York: Oxford University Press, 1999). My own study also cannot ignore this: nitrate film stock used during this period was composed of cellulose, crushed animal bones, and silver salts, so that, from the beginning, as Paolo Cherchi Usai concisely puts it, "cinema was fundamentally at odds with environmental concerns." Paolo Cherchi Usai, *Silent Cinema: A Guide to Study, Research and Curatorship*, 3rd edition (London: British Film Institute/Bloomsbury, 2019), 21–22.

43. When I first began to study the concept of "white supremacist entertainments" applied to early westerns, I consulted this work: Robert W. Rydell, *All the World's a Fair: Visions of Empire at American International Expositions, 1876–1916* (Chicago: University of Chicago Press, 1984), 6. For an excellent analysis of Buffalo Bill's Wild West as a white supremacist entertainment operating in parallel with world's fairs, see Jonathan Martin, "'The Grandest and Most Cosmopolitan Object Teacher,' Buffalo Bill's Wild West and the Politics of American Identity, 1883–1899," *Radical History Review* 66 (Fall 1996): 92–123.

44. Timothy Snyder, *On Tyranny: Twenty Lessons from the Twentieth Century* (New York: Tim Duggan Books, 2007), 125.

Chapter 1

1. See, for instance, Steve Inskeep, *Imperfect Union: How Jessie and John Frémont Mapped the West, Invented Celebrity, and Helped Cause the Civil War* (New York: Penguin, 2020).

2. The Apaches in particular, along with the unnamed Comanches, threatened white pioneers on the Santa Fe Trail that ran through Mexican and Indian territory during the early and mid-1800s. See Walter Johnson, *The Broken Heart of America: St. Louis and the Violent History of the United States* (New York: Basic Books, 2021), 69.

3. Citing royalty and/or an ancient worthy figure in such titles was a typical attempt to elevate an American historical hero.

4. Albert Johannsen, *The House of Beadle and Adams and Its Dime and Nickel Novels: The Story of a Vanished Literature,* vol. 1 (Norman: University of Oklahoma Press, 1950), 5.

5. "Kit Carson," *Biograph Bulletins, 1896–1908*, compiled with notes by Kemp R. Niver and edited by Bebe Bergsten (Los Angeles: Locare Research Group, 1971), 24–25.

6. No print survives, so the following summary is based on tableaux descriptions in *Biograph Bulletins*. AM&B did not use intertitles at the time, which meant an off-screen lecturer could use the descriptions to explain the story to those unfamiliar with it. See also Nanna Verhoeff, *The West in Early Cinema: After the Beginning* (Amsterdam: University of Amsterdam Press, 2006), 142.

7. Throughout this chapter I use the terms *Indian* and *Indians* because they circulated in all the trade press descriptions and exhibitors' comments at the time.

8. "The entire Hispano ruling class collaborated with the Anglo invasion" in what was still a part of Mexico—Roxanne Dunbar-Ortiz, *Not "A Nation of Immigrants": Settler*

NOTES 173

Colonialism, White Supremacy, and a History of Erasure and Exclusion (Boston: Beacon Press, 2021), 113.

9. No print survives, so the following summary again is based on tableaux descriptions in *Biograph Bulletins*, 25–26. See also Verhoeff, *The West in Early Cinema*, 142–143.

10. Large historical paintings such as George Caleb Bingham's *Daniel Boone Escorting Settlers through the Cumberland* (1849) and William Tylee Ranney's *Boone's First View of Kentucky Gap* (1851–1852) commemorated this legendary trail.

11. John Mack Faragher, *Daniel Boone: The Life and the Legend of an American Pioneer* (New York: Holt, 1992), 92–93—cited in Woody Holton, *Liberty Is Sweet: The Hidden History of the American Revolution* (New York: Simon & Schuster, 2021), 362. For a recent analysis of Native American alignments in the Seven Years War between the French and British, see Pekka Hämäläinen, *Indigenous Continent: The Epic Contest for North America* (New York: Liveright, 2022), 268–286.

12. The capture and rescue of Jemima and her friends are recounted in great detail in Matthew Pearl, *The Taking of Jemima Boone: Colonial Settlers, Tribal Nations, and the Kidnap that Shaped America* (New York: HarperCollins, 2021), 20–75. See also, Carl or Charles Ferdinand Wimar's *The Abduction of Daniel Boone's Daughter by the Indians*, 1853.

13. Peter Cozzens, *The Earth Is Weeping: The Epic Story of Indian Wars for the American West* (New York: Vintage, 2016), 17–19. See also the Iroquois "mourning wars" that expelled many rival tribes into the Great Lakes region in the mid- to late 17th century—Hämäläinen, *Indigenous Continent*, 101–107. For an excellent study of enslavement practices by Indigenous peoples, Mexicans, and white settlers, see Andréa Reséndez, *The Other Slavery: The Uncovered Story of Indian Enslavement in America* (New York: Houghton Mifflin Harcourt, 2016).

14. Boone's capture, life among the Shawnee, and escape, aided by his tribal "mother," as well as the Shawnee siege of Boonesboro are recounted in Pearl, *The Taking of Jemima Boone*, 111–165, 190–209.

15. In the latter novel, Boone has to rescue a plantation owner's daughter whom his brother wants to marry, after the owner has gambled away his estate in pro-slavery North Carolina. Johannsen, *The House of Beadle and Adams*, 96–97.

16. Jon T. Coleman, *Nature Shock: Getting Lost in America* (New Haven: Yale University Press, 2020), 139. See also Richard Slotkin, *Regeneration through Violence: The Mythology of the American Frontier, 1600–1860* (Middletown, CT: Wesleyan University Press, 1973), 42.

17. Charles Musser has a good analysis of this film's production in *Before the Nickelodeon: Edwin S. Porter and the Edison Manufacturing Company* (Berkeley: University of California Press, 1991), 336–340. See also "World of Players," *New York Clipper* (December 29, 1906): 1178.

18. Because no print seems to survive, this plot summary is based on the synopsis published in "Film Review," *Moving Picture World* (April 6, 1907): 74–75. Musser mentions trade press complaints that *Daniel Boone* and other films "required an accompanying lecture to be understood," in *Before the Nickelodeon*, 366–367.

174 NOTES

19. The plot synopsis is unclear about what happens to the daughters' mother. Captivity narratives of white women were popular in the early 19th century. See, for instance, *A Narrative of the Captivity of Mrs. Mary Jemison* (1824), who lived all her life with the Seneca, and Eliza Fraser's *Narrative of the Capture, Sufferings, and Miraculous Escape of Mrs. Eliza Fraser* (1837).

20. Often mistakenly called the "first western," Edison's *The Great Train Robbery* (1903) did introduce figures similar to the cowboy. Musser still offers the best analysis of *The Great Train Robbery* in *Before the Nickelodeon*, 253–256, and in *The Emergence of Cinema: The American Screen to 1907* (New York: Scribner's, 1991), 352–355, 360.

21. Gast's "American Progress" has a tiny, lone cowboy on a bucking broncho in the distance.

22. Owen Wister, "The Evolution of the Cowpuncher," *Harper's Monthly* 91 (September 1895): 602–617. See also Richard Abel, *The Red Rooster Scare: Making Cinema American* (Berkeley: University of California Press, 1999), 159–160.

23. Edison ad, *New York Clipper* (July 21, 1906): 596. See also Musser, *Before the Nickelodeon*, 363. Perhaps the Edison company was hoping to make up for the absence of the entertaining action long popular in Buffalo Bill's Wild West, which was on a lengthy tour of Europe. See, for instance, Paul Reddin, *Wild West Shows* (Urbana: University of Illinois Press, 1999), 148–150.

24. This plot summary comes from a review in *Variety* (January 19, 1907): 9, reprinted in Musser, *Before the Nickelodeon*, 360–362.

25. It is worth noting that Williams and Van Alstyne's cowboy love songs (i.e., "Cheyenne") and Indian love songs (i.e., "Navaho" and "Seminole") were popular at the time— Shapiro, Remick & Company ads, *New York Clipper* (February 13, 1904): 1228, and (July 16, 1904): 478; and Jerome H. Remick and Company ad, *New York Clipper* (February 17, 1906): 1340.

26. Selig Polyscope ads, *New York Clipper* (April 29, 1905): 264, and *Billboard* (June 3, 1905): 36.

27. Glenn Adamson, *Craft: An American History* (New York: Bloomsbury, 2021), 147.

28. In a stunt that played on the authenticity of location shooting, according to a Selig puff piece placed in Hearst newspapers, an unsuspecting tourist supposedly found the "killing" of the child so real that he began shooting at the robbers—see Andrew Brodie Smith, *Shooting Cowboys and Indians: Silent Western Films, American Culture, and the Birth of Hollywood* (Boulder: University of Colorado Press, 2003).

29. Although confined to shooting in the Catskills, AM&B drew on the Selig film's popularity in *From Leadville to Aspen: Hold-Up in the Rockies* (1906), a curious combination of phantom ride, comedy between a blackface porter and a small "ugly" woman in a train car, and a robbery by two gunmen who are captured after a long chase involving the train, a hand car, and their horse and buggy. Unlike other train crime films, this one often was exhibited in the amusement ride rail cars of Hale's Tours— Scott Simmon, "From Leadville to Aspen," *More Treasures from American Film Archives, 1894–1931* (San Francisco: National Film Preservation Foundation, 2004), 56. A print of this film is included on the second DVD accompanying this brochure.

NOTES   175

30. "Working to Boom Colorado," *Colorado Springs Gazette* (January 9, 1905): 5—quoted in Smith, *Shooting Cowboys and Indians*, 22.

31. "New Films," *Views and Films Index* (April 20, 1907): 6; and "Moving Pictures," *New York Clipper* (April 20, 1907): 251.

32. Possible precedents for this cowgirl heroine include David Belasco's play, *Girl of the Golden West* (1905) and female performers skilled with horses and guns in Wild West shows—see Smith, *Shooting Cowboys and Indians*, 28.

33. Selig ad, *Variety* (March 9, 1907): 15; H. H. Buckwalter, "The Show World Is Given Hearty Greeting at Denver," *Show World* (July 6, 1907): 9. See also Selig's *A Montana Schoolmarm* (1908), in which a young Easterner hired to teach a rowdy bunch of kids turns out to be an "accomplished horsewoman" and has no trouble handling a "Colts 44"—"Films of the Week," *Film Index* (December 19, 1908): 9.

34. This plot summary comes from "Film Review," *Moving Picture World* (June 29, 1907): 268.

35. Selig ads, *Moving Picture World* (June 22, 1907): 251, and (June 29, 1907): front cover.

36. This sense of bad Mexican men suppressed the fact that most Mexican migrants returned home to their families after working in the southwestern United States; between 1900 and 1910, an estimated 100,000 migrants crossed the border in search of work—Hernández, *Bad Mexicans*, 79–80.

37. Joanna Hearne stresses this point about families: "The 'West' of the Western is a theatrical space in which family formation and the shaping of youth take place within a politicized mise-en-scène"—*Native Recognition: Indigenous Cinema and the Western* (Albany: SUNY Press, 2012), 7.

38. Richard Slotkin was one of the first to argue that violence crucially defined the frontier—*Gunfighter Nation: The Myth of the Frontier in Twentieth-Century America* (New York: Atheneum, 1992).

39. "Film Review," *Moving Picture World* (March 7, 1908): 195. Robert Anderson highlights Selig's claim in "The Role of the Western Film Genre in Industry Competition, 1907–1911," *Journal of the University Film Association* 31.2 (1979): 23.

40. See Samuel Bowles's explicit assumptions of white supremacy about the government's only responsibility: feed and educate the Indian "to such elevation as he will be awakened to, and then let him die—as die he is doing and die he must"—*The Parks and Mountains of Colorado: A Summer's Vacation in the Switzerland of America, 1868*, ed. James H. Pickering (Norman, OK: University of Oklahoma Press, 1991): 145–147. Rarely, except in pseudo-ethnographic films that presumed to produce "authentic reenactments," are "Native people [perceived] as survivors—as peoples with viable, living cultures"—Gilio-Whitacker, *As Long as Grass Grows*, 59.

41. For an excellent history of the more than 30 years of wars against specific tribes, mainly on the Great Plains, see Cozzens, *The Earth Is Weeping*, 2016.

42. See the Edison ad's "Synopsis of Scenes" in *Moving Picture World* (July 4, 1908): back cover.

43. Indian attacks on pioneer wagon trains on the Great Plains also were the subject of captivity narratives of white women such as *Rachel Plummer's Narrative of Twenty One Months' Servitude as a Prisoner Among the Commanchee Indians* (1838) and

176 NOTES

Sarah Ann Horn with E. House, *A Narrative of the Captivity of Mrs. Horn, and Her Two Children, With Mrs. Harris, by the Camanche Indians* (1839). See also paintings such as John Mix Stanley's *Osage Scalp Dance* (1845) and George Caleb Bingham's *Captured by Indians* (1848).

44. Mazeppa was a Tartar chieftain who suffered this fate in the climactic scene of the equestrian melodrama, *Mazeppa* (1831); the figure also was depicted in paintings.

45. "Reviews of Late Films," *New York Dramatic Mirror* (July 11, 1908): 7. This and other films were what Scott Simmon dubbed "Eastern Westerns," produced by companies with "wild" locations outside New York City—Simmon, "Eastern Westerns," *The Invention of the Western Film: A Cultural History of the Genre's First Half-Century* (Berkeley: University of California Press, 2003), 12–18. See also Verhoeff, *The West in Early Cinema*, 77–95.

46. "Film Review," *Moving Picture World* (August 8, 1908): 110.

47. "Stories of the Films," *Moving Picture World* (April 10, 1909): 457.

48. In Bison's *Iona, the White Squaw* (1909), a white girl raised by Indians, becomes the object of a search and reward, is retrieved by a cowboy, and is "safely secured among her [white] friends."—"Independent Reviews," *New York Dramatic Mirror* (October 30, 1909): 16. Fred Balshofer seems to have directed this and other early Bison films in the wooded hills and fields near Fort Lee, New Jersey. See Fred Balshofer and Arthur Miller, *One Reel a Week* (Berkeley: University of California Press, 1967), 27, 32.

49. Of course, white actors played nearly all of these films' important Indian roles and retained their white identity beneath the "redskin" masquerade.

50. Michelle Raheja argues that the "redface performances by white actors" served "to efface Native Americans to the point that they never seemed to have existed at all," another sign of their assumed "vanishing." See Michelle H. Raheja, *Reservation Reelism: Redfacing, Visual Sovereignty, and Representations of Native Americans in Film* (Lincoln: University of Nebraska Press, 2010), 70–72. Red makeup normally registered as black on positive prints of orthochromatic film stock (standard throughout the silent period), so white actors may have used what was called "Indian red" to lightly darken their skin—"How the Movie Queen Makes Up," *Cleveland Sunday Leader* (January 24, 1915): Feature section, 1.

51. Joseph Norman Heard, "The Assimilation of Captives on the American Frontier in the Eighteenth and Nineteenth Centuries," (doctoral thesis, Louisiana State University, 1977). See also Benjamin Franklin's letter to Peter Collinson (May 9, 1753)—quoted in David Graeber and David Wengrow, *The Dawn of Everything: A New History of Humanity* (New York: Farrar, Straus and Giroux, 2021), 19–20.

52. "Film Stories," *Moving Picture World* (January 9, 1909): 45–46. Historically, the Santa Fe Railroad that followed the Santa Fe Trail led to "the rapid industrialization of mining and cattle ranching beginning in the late nineteenth century, destroy[ing] much of the irrigated subsistence farming that had dominated the land"—Dunbar-Ortiz, *Not "A Nation of Immigrants,"* 104. *In Old Arizona* was shot partly in Colorado, with Sioux, who performed in *On the Warpath* about the same time, acting as Apaches. A production photo of the cowboys' campsite apparently uses a backdrop of treeless hills to cover whatever was of less interest in the location background— Seaver Center for Western History Research, Los Angeles, P-26, L.1361–15.

53. Often in these westerns, "the category 'Mexican' comes to serve," Mark Rifkin writes, "as a racialized figure of ingrained alienness and tendencies toward migrancy" rather than settledness. —*Manifesting America: The Imperial Construction of U.S. National Space* (New York: Oxford University Press, 2009), 6. At the time, the racial hierarchy of the Southwest set Mexican Americans above Indians such as the Apaches— Laura E. Gómez, *Manifest Destinies: The Making of the Mexican American Race* (New York: New York University Press, 2007), 82.

54. "Film Stories," *Moving Picture World* (February 20, 1909): 214–215.

55. I use the term *"half breed"* or *"half-breed"* throughout this chapter and those following because it was common throughout the early 20th century. A much more accurate and felicitous term is "mixed-descent," as Anne F. Hyde (who is also the editor) explains in "A Note on Terms," *Born of the Lakes and Plains: Mixed-Descent Peoples and the Making of the American West* (New York: W.W. Norton, 2022), xii.

56. "Coming Headliners," *Moving Picture World* (February 13, 1909): 173. For a good summary of the Lakota Sioux "empire" (a "confederacy" that included the Dakota Sioux) that controlled the upper Great Plains in the mid-1800s, see Hämäläinen, *Indigenous Continent*, 430–452. With few exceptions, noted here and elsewhere in the text, the trade press subsumed a number of tribes under the generic term, Sioux.

57. Bison's *The Ranchman's Wife* (1909) has another "half breed" abduct a ranch owner's bride, who proves a plucky adversary; after his capture, the rancher's cowboys, in "a striking novelty," tar and feather him—"Independent Films," *Moving Picture World* (November 13, 1909): 699; "Comments on the Week's Films," *Moving Picture World* (November 27, 1909): 700.

58. Joy S. Kasson, *Buffalo Bill's Wild West: Celebrity, Memory, and Popular History* (New York: Hill and Wang, 2000): 244–248. The 1904 Louisiana Purchase Exposition in St. Louis also daily restaged "The Battle of the Little Big Horn." See Walter Johnson, *The Broken Heart of America: St. Louis and the Violent History of the United States* (New York: Basic Books, 2020), 208.

59. "Stories of the Films," *Moving Picture World* (November 27, 1909): 773.

60. "Films of Custer Massacre," *Nickelodeon* (November 1909): 154. See also "Custer's Last Stand," *Moving Picture World* (November 27, 1909): 755.

61. Often it was unclear whether the Indians came from reservations, beginning to be instituted in 1868, or from other parts of the vast "Indian Territory"—Hyde, *Born of the Lakes and Plains*, 280–282.

62. As the head of a peripatetic western unit, G. M. Anderson was making several films for Essanay in the foothills outside Denver, Colorado.

63. "Stories of the Films," *Moving Picture World* (March 13, 1909): 312. See also *The James Boys of Missouri* (1908), which simply staged nine "sensational" episodes depicting major events in the lives of Jesse and Frank James—"Latest Films of All Makers," *Views and Films Index* (April 4, 1908): 11; "Film Reviews," *Variety* (April 25, 1908): 13.

64. One trade press reviewer found the story so "incoherent" that a New York City audience "did not seem to know what it was about"—"Moving Picture Reviews," *Variety* (April 10, 1909): 13.

65. "Licensed Reviews," *New York Dramatic Mirror* (September 19, 1908): 9. A 35mm print survives at the National Film Archive in London.

178 NOTES

66. "Latest Films of All Makers," *Views and Films Index* (September 12, 1908): 11. The surviving scenario for the film lists 27 scenes (some shot more than once), and the last has the "Indian girl" alone with the chief rustler's body, here named Bill—"The Cattle Rustlers," William H. Selig Collection, Folder 186, Margaret Herrick Library. The National Film Archive print has no intertitles. His name suggests that Cherokee may have come from Oklahoma, where the Cherokees had been relocated forcibly in the 1830s.

67. Although his analysis of the reception of Hollywood greaser films in Mexico focuses on the 1920s, see Angel Miquel, "A Difficult Assimilation: American Silent Movies and Mexican Literary Culture," *Film History* 29.1 (2017): 84–109 [especially 91–92].

68. "Film Review," *Moving Picture World* (July 18, 1908): 49; and "Stories of the Films," *Moving Picture World* (May 15, 1909): 646. A 35mm paper print of *Fight for Freedom* survives at the US Library of Congress.

69. "Stories of the Films," *Moving Picture World* (September 19, 1908): 221. See also Tom Gunning, "The Red Girl," in *The Griffith Project*, vol. 1, ed. Paolo Cherchi ., (London: British Film Institute, 1997), 93–95. A 35mm paper print survives at the US Library of Congress. With reason, film historians have tended to focus, in these and other titles, on Griffith's development of film narrative and cinematic features (mise-en-scène, camerawork, editing); still the best such analysis is Tom Gunning's *D.W. Griffith and the Origins of American Narrative Film: The Early Years at Biograph* (Urbana: University of Illinois Press, 1991).

70. The partnering of this white woman and native woman against a doubly deceitful Mexican woman seems relatively unusual for the time. The two main characters are played by Florence Lawrence and Linda Arvidson, with one of them in redface.

71. "Film Review," *Moving Picture World* (August 15, 1908): 126. The engineers are part of a crew building a railroad between the United States and Mexico. See also Cooper Graham, "The Greaser's Gauntlet," in *The Griffith Project*, vol. 1, 75–76. A 35mm paper print survives at the US Library of Congress.

72. "Stories of the Films," *Moving Picture World* (May 1, 1909): 563.

73. "Comments on Film Subjects," *Moving Picture World* (May 15, 1909): 636.

74. Gregory S. Jay was probably the first to offer an extensive analysis of Griffith's Indian melodramas in "'White Man's Book No Good': D.W. Griffith and the American Indian, *Cinema Journal* 39.4 (2000): 3–26.

75. "Stories of the Films," *Moving Picture World* (October 31, 1908): 344. Scott Simmon, "The Call of the Wild," in *The Griffith Project*, vol. 1 (London: British Film Institute, 1997): 135–136. A 35mm paper print survives at the US Library of Congress.

76. Adamson, *Craft: An American History*, 92, 110. See also Hyde, *Born of the Lakes and Plains*, 306–308. Charles Inslee played Redfeather in redface. For a timely biography, see David Maraniss, *Path Lit by Lightning: The Life of Jim Thorpe* (New York: Simon & Schuster, 2022), especially 95–100.

77. Daniel Bernardi (ed.), "The Voice of Whiteness: D.W. Griffith's Biograph Films (1908–1913)," in *The Birth of Whiteness: Race and the Emergence of U.S. Cinema* (New Brunswick: Rutgers University Press, 1996), 119; and Simmon, "The Call of the Wild," 136.

78. Jay, "'White Man's Book No Good,'": 11. This dejected figure soon would be epitomized in James E. Fraser's iconic sculpture *The End of the Trail* (1915).

NOTES   179

79. See also the history lesson that opens Biograph's *The Indian Runner's Romance* (1909). "Stories of the Films," *Moving Picture World* (August 28, 1909): 287. A 35mm paper print survives at the US Library of Congress; a 35mm nitrate negative survives at the AFI/Mary Pickford Collection.

80. "Stories of the Films," *Moving Picture World* (August 7, 1909): 203. Patrick Loughney, "The Mended Lute," in *The Griffith Project*, vol. 3 (1999): 3–4. While a 35mm paper print survives at the US Library of Congress; a 35mm nitrate negative survives at the Museum of Modern Art, New York.

81. Although this snapshot "history lesson" is relatively accurate, the story's Indians seem more like an agricultural tribe like the Otoes than the Sioux "confederacy" that was displacing them—Hämäläinen, *Indigenous Continent*, 403–404.

82. All four Indian characters are played by white actors in redface: Owen Moore, Florence Lawrence, James Kirkwood, and Frank Powell. Unlike the similar practice of blackface, redface on whites could work to ennoble Indian characters in these early Griffith Indian pictures—Raheja, *Reservation Reelism*, 70–72.

83. See, for instance, the concept of "Native storytelling" in Michael Witgen, *An Infinity of Nations*, 10; and the analysis of Curtis's photographs and films in Fatimah Tobing Rony, *The Third Eye: Race, Cinema, and Ethnographic Spectacle* (Durham, NC: Duke University Press, 1996), 90–98. Rony also mentions a less famous contemporary of Curtis, Joseph K. Dixon, and his "photographs of the noble Plains Indian warrior," 92, 242.

84. "Stories of the Films," *Moving Picture World* (September 11, 1909): 349. This description reproduces that in the *Biograph Bulletin* #273 (September 9, 1909), reprinted in Ben Brewster, "Comata the Sioux," in *The Griffith Project*, vol. 3, 39. An incomplete 35mm acetate fine grain master survives at the Museum of Modern Art; a 35mm paper print survives at the US Library of Congress.

85. James Kirkwood and Marion Leonard, respectively, played Comata and Clear Eyes in redface.

86. "Comments on the Week's Films," *Moving Picture World* (October 2, 1909): 450–451. The mountains of the Black Hills were a sacred site for the Sioux.

87. Brewster, "Comata the Sioux," 40.

88. Brewster, "Comata the Sioux," 41.

89. The 1887 Dawes Act made the Bureau of Indian Affairs issue regulations that sought to forbid and punish marriages between whites and Native Americans, which further fueled white settler fears of miscegenation—Hyde, *Born of the Lakes and Plains*, 311–312.

90. "Stories of the Films," *Moving Picture World* (December 11, 1909): 847. This description reproduces that in the *Biograph Bulletin* (December 9, 1909), reprinted in Tom Gunning, "The Redman's View," in *The Griffith Project*, vol. 3, 123–124. A 35mm nitrate negative survives at the Museum of Modern Art; a 35mm paper print survives at the US Library of Congress.

91. Owen Moore and Lottie Pickford played the two main Indian characters, in redface.

92. This attribution of family relations reverses that of the earlier Edison and AM&B films.

180 NOTES

93. "Licensed Reviews," *New York Dramatic Mirror* (December 18, 1909): 16; "Film Reviews," *Film Index* (December 25, 1909): 6; and "Comments on the Films," *Moving Picture World* (December 25, 1909): 920.

94. The union of white men and Indian women (rather than the reverse) through marriage could be an acceptable means of harmonizing relations between the "races" in the 19th century, if often expedient in one way or another, as Hyde explains: see, for instance, Alfred Jacob Miller's painting *The Trapper's Bride* (1850).

95. Agata Frymus, "Pocahontas and Settler Colonialism in Early Film, 1907–1908, *Journal of Cinema and Media Studies* 60.3 (Spring 2021): 83–103. Unfortunately, only fragments of this film survive—Musser, *Before the Nickelodeon*, 424–425.

96. An early claim of the romance between Pocahontas and Smith occurs in John Davis, *Travels in the United States*, 1803.

97. William Watson Waldron, *Pocahontas, American Princess: and Other Poems*, 1841. For a superb analysis of this influential Pocahontas myth, see Rayna Green, "The Pocahontas Perplex: The Image of Indian Women in American Culture," *Massachusetts Review* 16.4 (Autumn 1975): 698–714. See also Frymus, "Pocahontas and Settler Colonialism," 92.

98. *Variety* (October 3, 1908): 11.

99. "Stories of the Films," *Moving Picture World* (March 7, 1908): 195. Although panned by an exhibitor, Selig's *On the Border* (1909) tells a complicated story that ends with a white man convincing a Mexican woman, whom he earlier loved, to leave her wealthy Mexican husband and join him crossing the border—"Stories of the Films," *Moving Picture World* (November 27, 1909): 773; "Comments on the Films," *Moving Picture World* (December 4, 1909): 799.

100. "An American School of Moving Picture Drama," *Moving Picture World* (November 20, 1909): 712. Dunbar-Ortiz makes this intriguing point: because of the 1787 Northwest Ordinance, "the 'wild west' originated in the Northwest Territory, east of the Mississippi, not in the West"—Dunbar-Ortiz, *Not "A Nation of Immigrants,"* 31.

101. Raheja, *Reservation Reelism*, 65.

102. Raheja, *Reservation Reelism*, 43.

103. Hearne, *Native Recognition*, 31.

104. Hearne, *Native Recognition*, 31.

105. Raheja, *Reservation Reelism*, 65, 67.

106. Hearne, *Native Recognition*, 81.

107. Paul Chaat Smith, *Everything You Know about Indians Is Wrong* (Minneapolis: University of Minnesota Press, 2009), 178.

108. See also Bison's *The Paymaster* (1909) and Selig's *On the Border* (1909).

109. Hearne, *Native Recognition*, 51.

West 1

1. Charles Musser, *The Emergence of Cinema: The American Screen to 1907* (New York: Scribner's, 1990), 232.

NOTES 181

2. Edison ad, *New York Clipper* (1903). This is a late instance of the phantom rides that were frequent in the late 1890s.

3. Charles Musser, *The Emergence of Cinema*, 234. The train may have been on the South Pacific railroad, which transported the cameramen to California—Charles Musser, *Before the Nickelodeon: Edwin S. Porter and the Edison Manufacturing Company* (Berkeley: University of California Press, 1991), 110.

4. Here, Captain Richard Pratt's infamous 1892 assertion is apt: "All the Indian there is in the race should be dead. Kill the Indian in him and save the man."—quoted in Patrick Wolfe, "Settler Colonialism and the Elimination of the Native," *Journal of Genocide Research* 8.4 (2006: n.p. *Indian Day School*, originally in a paper print, is viewable in a digital version in the "America at Work, America at Leisure" series on the US Library of Congress website. See also Edison's very different *Circle Dance* (1898), with unidentified Plains Indians performing in the Black Maria.

5. Robert W. Rydell, *All the World's a Fair: Visions of Empire at American International Expositions, 1876–1916* (Chicago: University of Chicago Press, 1984), 127, 129–130.

6. Claude Bragdon, "Some Pan-American Impressions," *American Architecture and Building News* 72 (1901): 43–44, quoted in Rydell, 135. *Panorama View of the Electric Tower from a Balloon* and *Circular Panorama of the Electric Tower* shows well-dressed couples and others walking among a series of buildings. Both of these 1901 films, along with the other titles, are viewable in digital versions on the US Library of Congress website.

7. Musser, *Before the Nickelodeon*, 317–318.

8. Rydell, *All the World's a Fair*, 131.

9. *Japanese Village* actually "stars" a team of three boy acrobats in front of a "Japanese" structure. For an excellent analysis of the Filipino Village, see Rydell, *All the World's a Fair*, 139–144.

10. Only Part 1 of *Sham Battle at the Pan-American Exposition* survives in a digital version on the US Library of Congress website. After a rather close shot of Indians on horseback riding past the camera, a long shot depicts the battle from behind lines of soldiers firing into the background.

11. Walter Johnson, *The Broken Heart of America: St. Louis and the Violent History of the United States* (New York: Basic Books, 2020), 201–215.

12. *Opening Ceremonies, St. Louis Exposition, Parade of Floats, St. Louis Expedition*, and *Asia in America, St. Louis Exposition* are viewable in digital versions on the US Library of Congress website. Kleine Optical also sold nine St. Louis Fair films—Kleine Optical ad, *New York Clipper* (July 2, 1904): 444.

13. For excellent analyses, see Rydell, *All the World's a Fair*, 168–178; and Johnson, *The Broken Heart of America*, 206–208. Naming the Philippine enclosure as a "reservation" explicitly forged a link to Native Americans.

14. Raymond Fielding, "Hale's Tours: Ultrarealism in the Pre-1910 Motion Picture," in *Film Before Griffith*, ed. John L. Fell (Berkeley: University of California Press, 1984), 116–130; and Lauren Rabinovitz, "'Bells and Whistles': The Sound of Meaning in Train Travel Rides," in *The Sounds of Early Cinema*, eds. Richard Abel and Rick Altman (Bloomington: Indiana University Press, 2001), 167–180.

182 NOTES

15. Selig Polyscope ad, *New York Clipper* (November 22, 1902): 875; and "Colorado's Best Advertisement," *Views and Films Index* (January 26, 1907): n.p. Selig advertised at least two of these films, *Panoramic View of Royal Gorge* and *Ute Pass*, along with *Georgetown Loop*, in the *New York Clipper* (1902). Andrew Brodie Smith, *Shooting Cowboys and Indians: Silent Western Films, American Culture, and the Birth of Hollywood* (Boulder: University of Colorado Press, 2003), 12–19. Perhaps recalling Edison's 1894 kinetoscope films featuring Lakota performers from Buffalo Bill's Wild West—*Sioux Ghost Dance, Buffalo Dance,* and *Indian War Council*—Buckwalter also shot *Indian Fire Dance, Shoshone Indians in Scalp Dance,* and *Ute Indian Snake Dance* (all 1902).

16. Fielding, "Hale's Tours," 127.

17. Fielding, "Hale's Tours," 127. Fielding reprints the catalog description for *Ute Pass*.

18. Fielding, "Hale's Tours," 128. This quote comes from the 1906 Selig catalog.

19. Yellowstone National Park was established in 1872, Yosemite National Park in 1880. Before their removal, Indigenous peoples inhabited the territories of most national parks and viewed them as sacred places as well as hunting and gathering grounds. In 1870, the US government sponsored the Washburn Expedition to survey the Yellowstone territory—Mark David Spence, *Dispossessing the Wilderness: Indian Removal and the Making of the National Parks* (New York: Oxford University Press, 41–43. See also John T. Coleman, *Nature Shock: Getting Lost in America* (New Haven: Yale University Press, 2020), 207–209.

20. The most influential books included George Perkins Marsh, *Man and Nature, or the Physical Geography as Modified by Human Action,* ed. David Lowenthal (Cambridge: Harvard University Press, 1965 [1864], and Samuel Bowles, *Across the Continent: A Summer's Journey to the Rocky Mountains the Mormons, and the Pacific States, with Speaker Colfax* (Springfield, MA: Samuel Bowles, 1865). For references to the paintings of Thomas Moran and John James Audubon, see Spence, *Dispossessing the Wilderness,* 17–18, 34. For a brief reference to influential photographs, see William Welling, *Photography in America: the Formative Years, 1839–1900* (New York: Crowell, 1977), 221.

21. Spence, *Dispossessing the Wilderness,* 55–60, 102–108.

22. More women than men, heavily dressed in black, step off the coach closest to the camera.

23. *Biograph Bulletins,* 67. Musser, *The Emergence of Cinema,* 306. Panoramas of *The Gap of the Rocky Mountains* and *The Steamboat Rocks* were still available for sale three summers later—AM&B ad, *New York Clipper* July 30, 1904): 532.

24. *New York Clipper* ads, 1902.

25. *Biograph Bulletins,* 145–147. Edward Sheriff Curtis also "made a film in 1904 of a Navajo Yeibichai ceremony"—Fatimah Tobing Rony, *The Third Eye: Race, Cinema, and Ethnographic Spectacle* (Durham, NC: Duke University Press, 1996), 70.

26. Rony, *The Third Eye,* 146–147. Whether any of these films were shown outside the exposition is unclear.

27. Selig Polyscope ad, *New York Clipper* (February 23, 1907): 15.

NOTES 183

28. Edison ads, *New York Clipper* (March 9, 1907): 94; and "Film Review," *Moving Picture World* (March 23, 1907): 47.
29. Spence, *Dispossessing the Wilderness*, 4, 7.
30. Selig Films ads, *Moving Picture World* (August 10, 1907): front cover, and (August 24, 1907): front cover.

Chapter 2

1. Robert Anderson, "The Role of the Western Film Genre in Industry Competition, 1907–1911," *Journal of the University Film Association* 31.2 (Spring 1979): 25, n. 65.
2. Essanay ad, *Moving Picture World* (October 21, 1911): 226, and "Manufacturers' Bulletins," *Film Index* (March 19, 1910): 13.
3. "Manufacturers' Bulletins," *Film Index* (June 11, 1910): 18.
4. Hired in 1910 by Pathé as its chief filmmaker in Fort Lee, Young Deer set up and managed the company's West Coast Studio from 1911 to 1913, making dozens of short Indian pictures in the environs. Born James Young Johnson, he was the son of white, African American, and Native American parents. Posing as fully "Indian," specifically Winnebago, Young Deer could hide his African American heritage in the movie industry. For good research on Young Deer, see Angela Aleiss, "Who Was the Real James Young Deer?," *Bright Lights Film Journal* (May 2013): 1–10.
5. "Film Charts," *Motion Picture News* (April 29, 1910): 21, and (May 20, 1910): 20.
6. Fatimah Tobing Rony, *Race, Cinema, and Ethnographic Spectacle* (Durham, NC: Duke University Press, 1996), 10. Her inspiration for the label came from Susan Sontag's influential essay, "Fascinating Fascism."
7. "Comments on the Films," *Moving Picture World* (July 16, 1910): 142.
8. "Comments on the Films," *Moving Picture World* (August 20, 1910): 406.
9. "Variety's Own Picture Reviews," *Variety* (February 25, 1910): 15.
10. "Indians in 'Uprising': Moving Pictures, Not White Man," *Washington Post* (February 16, 1911): 1. What allegedly sparked this protest was a screening of Selig's *Curse of the Red Man*.
11. "Poor Lo on the Warpath," *Moving Picture World* (March 4, 1911): 10–11.
12. "The Indian and the Cowboy," *Moving Picture World* (December 17, 1910): 1399.
13. See also W. Stephen Bush, "Overproduction of 'Western Pictures,'" *Moving Picture World* (October 21, 1911): 189.
14. "Pictures That Children Like," *Film Index* (January 21, 1911): 3.
15. "The Passing of the Western Subject," *Nickelodeon* (February 18, 1911): 181–182.
16. "Facts and Comments," *Moving Picture World* (December 2, 1911): 700.
17. "Manufacturers' Bulletins," *Film Index* (March 12, 1910): 15; and especially Selig Supplement #226, William H. Selig Collection, Folder 554, Margaret Herrick Library. See also Selig's *Early Settlers* (1910), which is even more specific in tracking a white family from a home on the Ohio River to farmland on the Mississippi River in Minnesota, where Indians warn them to move on, abduct them, and a troop of soldiers guided by a lone trapper rescues them. See "The Early Settlers: Selig's Strong Story of Pioneer Days, Period of 1847," *Film Index* (October 22, 1910): 12.

184   NOTES

18. To make audiences feel that they too were under attack, Andrew Brodie Smith writes that director Otis Turner "placed the camera directly outside the wagon train, looking in on the migrants [as] they load and fire their guns" at the faceless, circling "savages"—Smith, *Shooting Cowboys and Indians: Silent Western Films, American Culture, and the Birth of Hollywood* (Boulder: University of Colorado Press, 2003), 62. Smith's analysis was based on viewing a US Library of Congress print of *Across the Plains* under the title "Unidentified Selig."

19. See also Biograph's *Fighting Blood* (1911), in which a disobedient son visits his sweetheart after being thrown out of his father's house, spies a distant Indian attack on a settler's cabin, and finds patrolling soldiers who save his own family from the continuing Indian attack. Shot in and around Lookout Mountain, Griffith made these Southern California landscapes central to the film's story. Unlike *Across the Plains*, however, the fraught relations of a father and son crucially define this settler family, while the son's mother and sweetheart play minor roles. "Fighting Blood—Biograph," *Moving Picture World* (July 8, 1911): 1575. J. B. Kaufman, "Fighting Blood," in *The Griffith Project*, vol. 5, ed. Paolo Cherchi Usai (London: British Film Institute, 2001), 79–81. A 35mm nitrate negative survives at the George Eastman Museum; 28mm and 16mm diacetate positives survive at the US Library of Congress.

20. Joanna Hearne, *Native Recognition: Indigenous Cinema and the Western* (Albany: SUNY Press, 2012), 48.

21. "Reviews of Notable Films," *Moving Picture World* (July 29, 1911): 193. See also Kaufman, "The Last Drop of Water," in *The Griffith Project*, vol. 5, 82–84. A 35mm nitrate positive print survives at the US Library of Congress.

22. "Reviews of Notable Films," 193. In a bit of pretentious hype, the company's publicity cited Sir Philip Sydney's legendary gift of a last drop of water to a dying common soldier.

23. "Reviews of Notable Films," 193. See also Essanay's *Under Western Skies* (1910), in which a "badman" (G. M. Anderson), reformed by his wife, becomes a prospector who has to rescue her from a former fiancé, who, after persuading her to flee, loses their way in a desolate desert. See "Comments on the Films," *Moving Picture World* (August 20, 1910): 406.

24. For an analysis of *Romance of the Western Hills*, see Gregory S. Jay, "'White Man's Book No Good': D.W. Griffith and the American Indian," *Cinema Journal* 39.4 (2000):12–14; for *Ramona*, see Chon Noriega, "Birth of the Southwest: Social Protest, Tourism, and D.W. Griffith's *Ramona*," in *The Birth of Whiteness: Race and the Emergence of U.S. Cinema*, ed. Daniel Bernardi (New Brunswick: Rutgers University Press, 1996), 218; for *Isola's Promise*, see Hearne, *Native Recognition*, 66–69.

25. "Manufacturers' Bulletins," *Film Index* (September 24, 1910): 19; "Synopses of Current Films," *Nickelodeon* (October 1, 1910): 133. A restored 35mm print found in the New Zealand Film Archive is included in *Treasures 5: The West, 1898–1938* (San Francisco: National Film Preservation Foundation, 2011), DVD. This is one of the few surviving films directed by Francis Boggs.

26. For more information on the film's production, see Scott Simmon, "The Sergeant," in *Treasures 5*, 4–7.

NOTES   185

27. See also Pathé's *The Flag of Company H* (1910), in which a cavalry regiment, alerted by his bulldog mascot, rescues a badly wounded sergeant from drunken Indians who have overrun an outpost—"Manufacturers' Bulletins," *Film Index* (June 11, 1910): 16.

28. Mark David Spence, *Dispossessing the Wilderness: Indian Removal and the Making of the National Parks* (New York: Oxford University Press, 1999), 101–108. See also Dina Gilio-Whitacker, *As Long as Grass Grows: The Indigenous Fight for Environmental Justice, from Colonization to Standing Rock* (Boston: Beacon Press, 2019), 98.

29. The army became the park's police force once Yosemite National Park was established in 1890—Simmon, "The Sergeant," 5. As early as 1847, the state was under martial law, which required "California Indians either to be employed by non-Indians or to be defined as 'thieves and marauders' "—Walter Johnson, *The Broken Heart of America: St. Louis and the Violent History of the United States* (New York: Basic Books, 2020), 137. See also Damon B. Akins and William J. Bauer Jr., *We Are the Land: A History of Native California* (Oakland: University of California Press, 2022) and Ed Vulliamy, "Reclaiming Native Identity in California," *New York Review of Books* (June 22, 2023): 45-48.

30. "Recent Films Reviewed," *Nickelodeon* (October 1, 1910): 199See also the publicity photo of Yosemite Falls in *Moving Picture World* (September 10, 1910): 577.

31. "Comments on the Films," *Moving Picture World* (October 8, 1910): 813.

32. Michelle Raheja, *Reservation Realism: Redfacing, Visual Sovereignty, and Representations of Native Americans in Film* (Lincoln: University of Nebraska Press, 2010), 65.

33. "Synopses of Current Films," *Nickelodeon* (February 25, 1911): 228. See Eileen Bowser, "The Heart of a Savage," in *The Griffith Project*, vol. 5, 9. A 35mm-nitrate negative survives at the Museum of Modern Art. See also *The Squaw's Love* (1911), "an Indian poem of love in pictures"— David Mayer, "The Squaw's Love," in *The Griffith Project*, vol. 5, 117–119.

34. "Recent Films Reviewed," *Nickelodeon* (March 11, 1911): 280; and "Comments on the Films," *Moving Picture World* (March 18, 1911): 602. See also Bison's *Little Dove's Romance* (1911), in which a white trapper rescues Little Dove (played by Mona Darkfeather) from his half-breed cook, but a young brave from her tribe pursues and kills the half-breed and then persuades her that she is better off with him than with the departing trapper with whom she has fallen in love. See "Little Dove's Romance," *Moving Picture World* (September 2, 1911): 602. See an analysis of the film in Raheja, *Reservation Realism*, 66.

35. "Synopses of Current Films," *Nickelodeon* (November 15, 1910): 291. A 35mm acetate fine-grain master of this film survives at the Museum of Modern Art.

36. "Variety's Picture Reviews," *Variety* (December 3, 1910): 14.

37. Sumiko Higashi, "The Song of the Wildwood Flute," in *The Griffith Project*, vol. 4 (2000), 219.

38. See also Biograph's *The Broken Doll* (1910), in which the daughter of a white prospector family gives a little Indian girl a doll that a vengeful warrior smashes; the girl, badly wounded, warns the family of an attack and then collapses by the grave where she had buried her doll. "Synopses of Current Films," *Nickelodeon* (October

186   NOTES

15, 1910): 230. See also David Mayer, "The Broken Doll," in *The Griffith Project*, vol. 4, 191–194. A 35mm-nitrate positive print survives at the National Film Archive (London); a 35mm paper print survives at the US Library of Congress.

39. "Manufacturers' Bulletins," *Film Index* (January 1, 1910): 17.

40. "Variety's Own Picture Reviews," *Variety* (January 8, 1910): 12, the reviewer blasted this film: "full of inconsistencies," not well acted, with an army outpost that is such "a flimsy looking affair . . . it's a wonder the Indians didn't carry it off to build campfires with."

41. At least one reviewer tartly dismissed this kind of story as "the same old thing," in which a "grateful Indian" keeps on saving one or more whites—and often dying—"Recent Films Reviewed," *Nickelodeon* (March 11, 1911): 280.

42. See also Kalem's *The Conspiracy of Pontiac* (1910), focused, from a white perspective, on the Odawa chief's siege of Fort Detroit in the Six Nations' 1763 rebellion against the British in the Seven Years War, already familiar to children in "Webster's Third Reader"—"The Conspiracy of Pontiac," *Film Index* (August 27, 1910): 5.

43. "Synopses of Current Films," *Nickelodeon* (August 1, 1910): 74; "The Red Girl and the Child," *Film Index* (August 13, 1910): 3. See also the analysis of Biograph's *Isola's Promise* (1912), in which Isola (Mary Pickford again in redface) saves a captured white woman by donning the latter's clothes, only to be shot by her own tribe's warriors as she leads them to confront a threatened group of prospectors. See Hearne, *Native Recognition*, 66–69.

44. For a good study of Red Wing, see Linda Waggoner, *Starring Red Wing: The Incredible Career of Lilian M. St. Cyr, the First Native American Film Star* (Lincoln: University of Nebraska Press, 2019).

45. "Licensed Film Stories," *Moving Picture World* (September 23, 1911): 905. A 35mm print of this film survives at the National Film Archive, London. Alice Joyce played the half-breed. See also Kalem's *Her Indian Mother* (1911), in which a half-breed daughter, after being educated in Montréal, returns, in a reverse trajectory, to her Indian village. A 35mm print of this film, from the US Library of Congress, was shown at the 2015 Giornate del cinema muto, Pordenone, Italy.

46. Charlie Keil, "The Blackfoot Halfbreed," *Le Giornate del cinema muto 34* (Pordenone, 2015), 135.

47. "Stories of the Films," *Moving Picture World* (February 11, 1911): 320; "Comments on the Films," *Moving Picture World* (February 18, 1911): 370. This was one of the last films directed by Francis Boggs. A 35mm print survives at the National Film Archive, London.

48. Could the conflation of Mariposa (California) and Apache (Southwestern border) serve to demonize all or many Indians?

49. "Reviews of the Films," *Nickelodeon* (February 11, 1911): 169.

50. Mark Lawrence Schrad, *Smashing the Liquor Machine: A Global History of Prohibition* (New York: Oxford University Press, 2021), 260–263. See also the complaints of Chief Little Turtle of the Miami Confederacy, who actively supported the 1802 law, found in Charles H. L. Johnston, *Famous Indian Chiefs: Their Battles, Treaties, Sieges, and Struggles with the Whites for Possession of America* (Boston: L.C. Page & Company, 1909), 307—cited in Schrad, *Smashing the Liquor Machine*, 260.

NOTES 187

51. Schrad, *Smashing the Liquor Machine*, 284, 304.

52. Schrad, *Smashing the Liquor Machine*, 265, 269. He even goes so far as to describe this system as "American ethnic cleansing," 281.

53. For an analysis of the little-known *Maya, Just an Indian* (1913), see Hearne, *Native Recognition*, 69–72.

54. G. Harrison Orians, *The Cult of the Vanishing American: A Century View, 1834–1934* (Toledo: H.J. Chittenden, 1934)—cited in Brian W. Dippie, *The Vanishing American: White Attitudes & U.S. Indian Policy* (Lawrence: University of Kansas Press, 1982), 21.

55. "Reviews of Notable Films," *Moving Picture World* (July 29, 1911): 191.

56. Joseph Norman Heard, "The Assimilation of Captives on the American Frontier in the Eighteenth and Nineteenth Centuries," (doctoral thesis, Louisiana State University, 1977).

57. "Independent Film Stories," *Moving Picture World* (July 20, 1912): 276. A 35mm print of this film survives at the National Film Archive, London. It was directed by Allan Dwan.

58. Both the photograph and film blur distinctions among Indians however, making Navajos and Hopi stand in for various Plains Indians, who really were vanishing. See Dippie, *The Vanishing American*, 285–286. Dippie reproduces this photograph among several dozen illustration inserts.

59. Charlie Keil, "The Vanishing Race," *Le Giornate del cinema muto* 34 (Pordenone, 2015), 138.

60. In American Film's *The Poisoned Flume* (1911), directed by Allan Dwan, a rancher named Martinez is intent on gaining control of a neighbor's property by illegal means—see my analysis of the film in *Americanizing the Movies and "Movie Mad" Audiences, 1910–1914* (Berkeley: University of California Press, 2006), 111–112.

61. "Licensed Film Stories," *Moving Picture World* (June 22, 1912): 1154. A 35mm print, from the EYE Museum (Amsterdam), was shown at the Giornate del cinema muto in 2016. See also Vitagraph's *A Bit of Blue Ribbon* (April 1913), which has a villainous Mexican try, unsuccessfully, to frame a white cowboy for killing a ranch owner.

62. Unlike Indians and Mexicans, major Chinese characters almost disappeared from early westerns during this period. An exception was Biograph's *That Chink at Golden Gulch* (1910), adapted from a stage play with that stereotypical title. A mining camp laundryman named Charlie Lee captures a robber and has to tie him up with his cut-off "sacred queue," which will prohibit him from ever returning to China. Making a further sacrifice, he leaves the reward money for a white couple who earlier befriended him. Then he vanishes, an "alien figure," into a strange land that remains foreign to him. Invoking racist slurs, reviewers and exhibitors were dismissive.

63. "Manufacturers' Bulletins," *Film Index* (March 12, 1910): 9. A 35mm paper print survives at the US Library of Congress.

64. "Stories of the Films," *Moving Picture World* (May 6, 1911): 1022. Jon T. Coleman, *Nature Shock: Getting Lost in America* (New Haven: Yale University Press, 2020), 174–175.

188 NOTES

65. "Licensed Film Stories," *Moving Picture World* (December 21, 1912): 1222. Rollin S. Sturgeon directed this and other Vitagraph westerns in 1912. Anne Schaeffer plays the mother of the sick child. See also Scott Simmon, "The Better Man (1912)," in *Treasures 5*, 49–52. A 35mm print, repatriated from the New Zealand Film Archive, is included in the *Treasures 5: The West, 1898–1938* DVD.

66. "Manufacturers' Synopses," *Motion Picture News* (May 13, 1911): 17. A 35mm print of this film, from the EYE Museum in Amsterdam, was shown at the 2015 Giornate del cinema muto.

67. "Notable Films," *Moving Picture World* (May 13, 1911): 1067; "Motion Picture Reviews," *Bioscope* (May 20, 1911): 13. Whether or not Allan Dwan directed *The Ranchman's Vengeance* remains unclear.

68. "Licensed Film Stories," *Moving Picture World* (November 11, 1911): 494.

69. A 35mm print of this film survives at the National Film Archive, London.

70. W. Stephen Bush, "The Mexican Joan of Arc," *Moving Picture World* (July 15, 1911): 19. An independent production, *Ammunition Smuggling on the Mexican Border* (1914) is worth noting because it reenacted historical events that occurred in September 1913. The smugglers probably were Yaqui Indians who supported the Mexican Revolution. See Devra Weber, "Keeping Community, Challenging Boundaries: Indigenous Migrants, International Workers, and Mexican Revolutionaries, 1900–1920," in *Mexico and Mexicans in the Making of the United States*, ed. John Tutino (Austin: University of Texas Press, 2012), 217. In the film, however, white lawmen intercept Mexican smugglers, are captured and rescued, and then jail the survivors after a gunfight. See Scott Simmon, "Ammunition Smuggling on the Mexican Border," *Treasures 5*, 52–54.

71. Agata Frymus, "Pocahontas and Settler Colonialism in Early Film, 1907–1910," *Journal of Cinema and Media Studies* 60.3 (Spring 2021): 96–102. Lydia Sigourney's poem, "Pocahontas" (1841), "served as the official source for Thanhouser's adaptation." No print of this film survives.

72. "Thanhouser Company," *Moving Picture World* (October 15, 1910): 892.

73. "Independent Film Stories," *Moving Picture World* (November 26, 1910): 1251. A 35mm print, in poor condition, survives at the US Library of Congress.

74. "Comments on the Films," *Moving Picture World* (December 10, 1910): 1360.

75. "Recent Films Reviewed," *Nickelodeon* (December 15, 1910): 335.

76. "Stories of the Films," *Moving Picture World* (November 19, 1910): 1186. Unlike *Kit Carson* (1904), which ignored the frontiersman's three Indian wives, this film acknowledges that Bridger historically did initially marry a Flathead Indian woman. After her death from a fever, he later married the daughter of a Shoshone chief and, after her death in childbirth, the daughter of another Shoshone chief.

77. "Manufacturers' Bulletins," *Film Index* (February 19, 1910): 12. See also David Kiehn, *Broncho Billy and the Essanay Film Company* (Berkeley: Farwell Books, 2003), 306.

78. For a good analysis of the stereotype, see David D. Smits, "The 'Squaw Drudge': A Prime Index of Savagism," in *Native Women's History in Eastern North America before 1900*, eds. Rebecca Krugel and Lucy Eldersveld Murphy (Lincoln: University of Nebraska Press, 2007), 29–49.

NOTES   189

79. "Pathé's American Productions," *Film Index* (June 18, 1910): 6. A 35mm print from the US Library of Congress is included in the National Film Preservation Foundation's *Treasures from American Film Archives DVD* (2000). See also Scott Simmon, "White Fawn's Devotion (1910)," in *Treasures from American Film Archives* (San Francisco: National Film Preservation Foundation, 2000), 69–71.

80. "Pathé's American Productions," 6.

81. Hearne, *Racial Recognition*, 92–93.

82. Hearne, *Racial Recognition*, 94.

83. "Manufacturers' Bulletins," *Film Index* (March 11, 1911): 18.

84. "Recent Films Reviewed," *Nickelodeon* (March 25, 1911): 336.

85. "Comments on the Films," *Moving Picture World* (March 25, 1911): 656.

86. "Two Pathé Indian Pictures," *Film Index* (June 17, 1911): 13. In startling contrast to his Indian pictures that promoted interracial marriage, Young Deer's career came to an end in early 1913 when he was linked to a white slave ring and later accused of raping a 15-year-old white girl. See Aleiss, "Who Was the Real James Young Deer?," 8.

87. Licensed Film Stories," *Moving Picture World* (June 24, 1911): 1457.

88. Raheja, *Reservation Realism*, 21.

89. "Recent Films Reviewed," *Motography* (July 1911): 41.

90. See also Pathé's *Romance of the Desert* (1911), which reversed the outcome of miscegenation. Indians find a white man collapsed in the desert who has lost his memory, can't recall who gave him a rosary, and weds an Indian woman. Later, as he passes through a town, his white wife recognizes the rosary. In the end, he returns to the white woman, and, in one exhibitor's words, "the [Catholic] religion that he had taught to the squaw prevents a tragedy." "Comments on the Films," *Moving Picture World* (October 28, 1911): 290.

91. "Licensed Film Stories," *Moving Picture World* (April 20, 1912): 262. A deteriorating 35mm print from the Dawson City Collection survives at the US Library of Congress. According to a Library of Congress card, George Gebhardt played the squawman; it is difficult to tell whether Indian or white actors in redface played most of the Indian roles. See also Hearne's description, perhaps based on another print at the George Eastman Museum, in *Racial Recognition*, 94–96.

92. In suggesting some music for this film, Clarence E. Simm indicates that the "man is seen dead" before the brother returns the daughter to his sister. See "Music for the Pictures," *Moving Picture World* (June 8, 1912): 92.

93. An exhibitor was disappointed in the film's lack of "extensive natural scenes" and of "artistic" photography. See "Comments on the Films," *Moving Picture World* (May 11, 1912): 527.

94. Here, *For the Papoose* stages a justified act of punishment similar to that in *The Ranchman's Vengeance*.

95. James Mooney, "Population," in *Handbook of American Indians North of Mexico*, B.A.E. Bulletin 30, volume 2, ed. Frederick Webb Hodge (Washington, DC: Bureau of American Ethnology, 1910). Mooney's work is discussed in Dippie, *The Vanishing American*, 236–241.

96. Francis E. Leupp, *The Indian and His Problem* (New York: Scribner's, 1910), 343–344.

190 NOTES

97. Dippie, *The Vanishing Indian*, 260.

98. "Essanay Features," *Film Index* (June 4, 1910): 29.

99. "Manufacturers' Bulletins," *Film Index* (June 4, 1910): 23.

100. See also Essanay's *The Little Prospector* (1910). According to company publicity, the film's appeal, especially to "eastern Americans," was the scenic beauty of its location shooting in the Rocky Mountains. See "The Little Prospector," *Film Index* (November 12, 1910): 11.

101. "Manufacturers' Bulletins," *Film Index* (May 7, 1910):10.

102. Linda Arvidson Griffith, *When the Movies Were Young* (New York: E.P. Dutton, 1925), 167–168. This work was cited in Eileen Bowser, "The Gold-Seekers," *The Griffith Project*, vol. 4, 72. See also *In the Days of '49*, adapted from another Bret Harte story—Biograph Bulletin (May 8, 1911)—reprinted in Lea Jacobs, "In the Days of '49," in *The Griffith Project*, vol. 5, 44–46.

103. "Licensed Stories," *Moving Picture World* (April 12, 1912): 158.

104. Charlie Keil, "The Female of the Species," in *The Griffith Project*, vol. 6 (2002), 27–29.

105. Examples include Essanay's *The Girl on the Triple X* (1910), Biograph's *The Twisted Trail* (1910), American Film's *The Ranch Girl* (1911), Vitagraph's *The Greater Love* (1912), and Kalem's *The Driver of the Deadwood Stage* (1912).

106. Edwin M. La Roche, "A New Profession for Women," *Motion Picture Magazine* (May 1914): 85. One of her first credited scenarios was for *Across the Plains* (1911). See Kiehn, *Broncho Billy and the Essanay Company*, 315. Adept at riding and "swinging a lariat," Rector also could play lead roles in the company's westerns. See "Answers to Inquiries," *Motion Picture Story Magazine* (October 1913): 152, and (November 1913): 156. For more information on her life and career, see Viktoria Paranyuk, "Josephine Rector," Women Film Pioneers website (2013).

107. Bill Strobel, "Niles Days as Film Capital Recalled by Oakland Woman," *Oakland Tribune* (May 21, 1958): S8—quoted in Kiehn, *Broncho Billy and the Essanay Company*, 97. How many of these and other early cowboy films actually were drawn from or inspired by popular magazines, perhaps with relevant differences, could be the subject of future research.

108. As Smith first argues, Broncho Billy also could serve as a surrogate father in slightly later films, as in *Broncho Billy's Heart* (1912). See Smith, *Shooting Cowboys and Indians*, 146–147.

109. "Synopses of Current Films," *Nickelodeon* (July 15, 1910): 49; "Manufacturers' Bulletins," *Film Index* (July 30, 1910): 20. For production information, see Kiehn, *Broncho Billy and the Essanay Company*, 309.

110. "Manufacturers' Bulletins," *Film Index* (November 5, 1910): 23.

111. See also Essanay's *The Loafer* (1912)—"Manufacturers' Advance Notes," *Moving Picture World* (January 13, 1912): 129. A 35mm print of this film survives at the National Film Archive, London. Both Barry Salt and Kristin Thompson first noted the film's extended shot/reverse shot sequence, perhaps the earliest extent use of this device.

112. "Manufacturers' Advance Notes," *Moving Picture World* (August 12, 1911): 381. A 35mm print of this film survives at the US Library of Congress.

NOTES **191**

113. "Licensed Film Stories," *Moving Picture World* (July 6, 1912): 176. A 35mm print, from the EYE Museum (Amsterdam), was shown at the Giornate del cinema muto in 2016.

114. "Comments on the Films," *Moving Picture World* (August 3, 1912): 445.

115. "Essanay Western Offerings," *Film Index* (October 8, 1910): 6.

116. "Manufacturers' Bulletins," *Film Index* (August 27, 1910): 20.

117. "Comments on the Films," *Moving Picture World* (September 10, 1910): 574.

118. "Manufacturers' Bulletins," *Film Index* (February 12, 1910): 12.

119. *Broncho Billy's Narrow Escape* (1912) also makes its heroine an expert horsewoman who saves the falsely accused Billy from a lynching. Yet the film is unusual when, at the end, they sing together to a guitar and banjo and Billy slides a ring onto her finger—which an exhibitor found too conventional and unnecessary. "Licensed Film Stories," *Moving Picture World* (June 29, 1912): 1250; "Comments on the Films," *Moving Picture World* (July 20, 1912): 243. A 35mm print, from the EYE Museum (Amsterdam), was shown at the Giornate del cinema muto in 2016.

120. "Manufacturers' Synopses of Films," *Moving Picture World* (July 1, 1911): 22. For other active heroines, see the left-behind woman, who single-handedly captures a stage robber, in Kalem's *The Girl Deputy* (1912), and the two sisters, who burn down the shack where a thief and wife-beater is holed up, in Solax's *Two Little Rangers* (1912). See the extended analysis of *Two Little Rangers* in Verhoeff, *The West in Early Cinema*, 395–397.

121. "From El Cajon Valley," *Moving Picture World* (July 22, 1911): 128.

122. At least two other films also stage this stunning bit of climactic shooting. One is American Film's *The Ranchman's Nerve* (1911), directed by Dwan—Jas. S. McQuade, "Reviews of Notable Films," *Moving Picture World* (July 29, 1911): 190–191. The more fanciful is Selig's *Sallie's Sure Shot* (1913), in which the heroine keeps two thieves at bay with a rifle and then spins, fires, and cuts the fuse on dynamite set to blow up her father's cabin. See "Selig Releases for Week of June 30," *Motography* (June 28, 1913): 482. A 35mm print of this film survives at the National Film Archive, London.

123. Clifford Weldon, "A Western of Unusual Strength," *Motography* (September 1911): 120–121.

124. See my analysis of this film in *Americanizing the Movies and "Movie-Mad" Audiences*, 70.

125. "Manufacturers' Synopses of Films," *Moving Picture World* (December 16, 1911): 836. A 35mm print, from the US Library of Congress, was shown at the Giornate del cinema muto in 2015.

126. Laura Horak, "A Range Romance," *Le Giornate del cinema muto 34* (Pordenone, 2015), 141–142.

127. "Licensed Film Stories," *Moving Picture World* (April 13, 1912): 156. A 35mm print, from the EYE Museum (Amsterdam), was shown at the Giornate del cinema muto in 2016. Anne Schaeffer played the no-nonsense woman here as she did the mother in *The Better Man*.

192 NOTES

128. Vitagraph ad, *Moving Picture World* (April 20, 1912): 199; "Comments on the Films," *Moving Picture World* (May 4, 1912): 425.

129. H.F.H., "How States Are Made," *Moving Picture World* (February 17, 1912): 565. See also "Reviews of Licensed Films," *New York Dramatic Mirror* (March 13, 1912): 29. A 35mm print from the EYE Museum (Amsterdam) was show at the Giornate del cinema muto in 2016.

130. For the best study of the US government's infamous expulsion of the Cherokee, Creek, Chicksaw, Choctaw, and Seminole from their tribal lands in the South, see Claudio Saunt, *Unworthy Republic: The Dispossession of Native Americans and the Road to Indian Territory* (New York: W.W. Norton, 2020).. See also Mark Rifkin, *Manifesting America: The Imperial Construction of U.S. National Space* (New York: Oxford University Press, 2009), 37–74.

131. For concise information on the 1893 land rush, see also Roxanne Dunbar-Ortiz, *An Indigenous Peoples' History of the United States* (Boston: Beacon Press, 2016) 112–114.

132. "Comments on the Films," *Moving Picture World* (March 23, 1912): 1062–1063.

133. See an initial argument of this point in my *Americanizing the Movies and "Movie-Mad" Audiences*, 118–119.

West 2

1. Marguerite S. Shaffer, *See America First: Tourism and National Identity, 1880–1940* (Washington, DC: Smithsonian Institution, 2001), 4.

2. For a rich survey of the pre-colonial landscape inhabited by Indigenous peoples, see Roxanne Dunbar-Ortiz, *An Indigenous Peoples' History of the United States* (Boston: Beacon Press, 2016), 15–31.

3. Many of the Miwok returned to live in the valley, usually on the margins of white settlements and working to support the tourist trade—Mark David Spence, *Dispossessing the Wilderness: Indian Removal and the Making of the National Parks* (New York: Oxford University Press, 1999), 104–108. See also David Treuer, "Return the National Parks to the Tribes," *The Atlantic* (May 2021): 32.

4. Jennifer Lynn Peterson, *Education in the School of Dreams: Travelogues and Early Nonfiction Film* (Durham, NC: Duke University Press, 2013), 236.

5. Shaffer, *See America First*, 16, 36–37.

6. The following sentences are based on Shaffer's informative analysis in *See America First*, 26–32.

7. "Stories of the Films," *Moving Picture World* (April 3, 1909): 414; and Kalem ad, *Moving Picture World* (April 3, 1909): 415. Months later, Lubin released its own very short *Glimpses of Yellowstone Park*, whose view of the major falls an exhibitor found "not so successful"—Lubin ad, *Moving Picture World* (September 11, 1909): 352; and "Comments on the Films," *Moving Picture World* (October 2, 1909): 452.

NOTES 193

8. August 16, 1909 letter from Francis Boggs to W. N. Selig—Clarke Collection, Margaret Herrick Library, Academy of Motion Picture Arts and Sciences. A year earlier, a potential film producer noted that "40 moving picture artists" already were working in the Park—"A Dark Horse," *Views and Films Index* (August 15, 1908): 6. Tourism in the national parks now overwhelms its mandate to conserve these wild lands; in 2019, there were a total of 327 million visitors—Christopher Ketcham, "The Business of Scenery: Why America's national parks need new management," *Harper's* (April 2021): 46.

9. "Stories of the Films," *Moving Picture World* (August 21, 1909): 261.

10. Wilson Mayer, "Moving Picture Work of the Railroads," *Nickelodeon* (February 1909): 42.

11. Selig ads, *Variety* (February 27, 1909): 31, and *Moving Picture World* (February 27, 1909): 226.

12. Theodore T. Kling, "Motography at the Seattle Fair, *Nickelodeon* (March 1909): 76.

13. Fatimah Tobing Rony, *The Third Eye: Race, Cinema, and Ethnographic Spectacle* (Durham, NC: Duke University Press, 1996), 83.

14. Theodore T. Kling, "Motography in the Government Service," *Nickelodeon* (September 1909): 73–74. Thompson may have shot AM&B's Yellowstone films in 1904.

15. August 16, 1909 letter from Francis Boggs to W. N. Selig—Clarke Collection, Margaret Herrick Library. He also revealed how he traveled by rail on the O.R.&N. so as to "get around the Inter-state law." For the importance of salmon fishing to Indigenous peoples of the region, shown as "primitive" in the film, see Dina Gilio-Whitacker, *As Long as Grass Grows: The Indigenous Fight for Environmental Justice, from Colonialization to Standing Rock* (Boston: Beacon Press, 2019), 62, 73.

16. Selig ad, *Moving Picture World* (December 25, 1909): 919.

17. "Selig Notes," *Film Index* (July 16, 1910): 10. Apparently this film led Mix to ask Selig to work on westerns—September 26, 1910 letter from Tom Mix to William Selig, William H. Selig Collection, Folder 453: Correspondence from Actors, Margaret Herrick Library. The African American trick rider George Hooker performed in several of these westerns, *A Romance of the Rio Grande* and *Why the Sheriff Is a Bachelor* (both 1911), but played Mexican Americans—Roger D. Hardway, "Oklahoma's African American Rodeo Performers," in *Black Cowboys in the American West*, eds. Bruce A. Glasrud and Michael N. Searles (Norman: University of Oklahoma Press, 2016), 117.

18. "Life on a Ranch," *Moving Picture World* (July 9, 1910): 78.

19. Kevin Brownlow, *The War, the West, and the Wilderness*, (New York: Knopf), 243.

20. Scott Simmon, "Life on the Circle Ranch in California," *Treasures 5: The West, 1898–1939* (San Francisco: National Film Preservation Foundation, 2011), 38–40. This may have been the first film produced by the Circle Ranch Film Company and directed by John B. O'Brien—"John B. O'Brien, Director," *Moving Picture World* (December 14, 1912): 1091. Whether the film was exhibited or where remains unclear. A 35mm print, from the UCLA Film & Television Archive, is included in *Treasures 5: The West, 1898–1939* DVD (2011).

194 NOTES

21. Simmon, "Life on the Circle Ranch," 40.
22. Peterson, *Education in the School of Dreams*, 245.
23. Jas. S. McQuade, "Picturesque Colorado (Rex)," *Moving Picture World* (September 23, 1911): 891. A surviving three-minute excerpt, from the National Archive, is included in the National Film Preservation Foundation's *Treasures 5: The West, 1898–1938* DVD (2011). In her insightful analysis, Peterson reveals that the Colorado and Southern Railway published a guidebook with the same title (1899–1913) and the Greater Colorado Industrial Parade (July 18, 1911) initially lured the filmmakers—Peterson, *Education in the School of Dreams*, 260, 264.
24. Scott Simmon, "The West in Promotional Travelogues," *Treasures 5: The West, 1898-1938* (San Francisco: National Film Preservation Foundation, 2011), 94. A surviving one-minute excerpt, from the Library of Congress, is included in the *Treasures 5* DVD.
25. "Kinemacolor Company Branches Out," *Moving Picture World* (May 25, 1912): 716; "Kinemacolor in Travel Field," *Moving Picture World* (October 27, 1912): 354. The US Department of Agriculture, sometimes in conjunction with the Department of Interior, also produced and distributed films, a few of which took national parks as their subject—Raymond Evans, "The U.S.D.A. Motion Picture Service, 1908–1943," *Business Screen* 1 (1943): 19–21.
26. "Cross Country Tour Pictures," *Motography* (May 1912): 232.
27. Watterson R. Rothacker, "Yellowstone Park on the Screen," *Motography* (April 1912): 169–170; Watterson R. Rothacker, "Seeing America First in Pictures," *Motography* (December 7, 1912): 429–430. The publicist Lloyd W. McDowell "cemented the alliance between the Great Northern Railway and moving pictures"—"Brevities of the Business," *Motography* (June 13, 1914): 437. Other railroads quickly adopted the slogan as well—Peterson, *Education in the School of Dreams*, 243.
28. "Pathe Freres," *Moving Picture News* (November 9, 1912): 30; G. F. Blaisdell, "At the Sign of the Flaming Arrow," *Moving Picture World* (November 9, 1912): 540; "The Waterfalls of Idaho [See America First Series]," *Motography* (March 1, 1913): 166; "Current Educational Releases," *Motography* (October 4, 1913): 251. McDowell wrote stories for popular magazines as well as newspapers that accompanied these and other Pathé films—"Brevities of the Business," 437.
29. Peterson, *Education in the School of Dreams*, 239, 251. Members of the Crow Indians were called "primitive Americans" because they "were so delighted with the bit of glass" in a monocle—"Kinemacolor in Travel Field," 354. This was evidence of "a common trope of early ethnographic cinema," that indigenous people were ignorant of "civilized" technologies, including "film technology"—Rony, *The Third Eye*, 12.
30. George Blaidell, *"At the Sign of the Flaming Arcs,"* *Moving Picture World* (September 20, 1913): 128. For an excellent study of what led up to, in 1910, the creation of Glacier National Park, formerly inhabited by Blackfoot Indians, see Spence, *Dispossessing the Wilderness*, 71–82.

Chapter 3

1. Richard Abel, *Americanizing the Movies and "Movie-Mad" Audiences, 1910–1914* (Berkeley: University of California Press 2006), 22–26.

2. "Bison Company Gets 101 Ranch Wild West," *Motion Picture News* (December 2, 1911): 24; "Bison Company Gets 101 Ranch," *Moving Picture World* (December 9, 1911): 810; "What Bison Wants," *Moving Picture World* (January 13, 1912): 119. Some Sioux are featured in "Western Operations of the New York Motion Picture Company," *Moving Picture World* (August 24, 1912): 777.

3. Thomas Ince headed the Inceville studio (hence the name). For a good study of Ince and the Bison 101 films, see Andrew Brodie Smith, *Shooting Cowboys and Indians: Silent Western Films, American Culture, and the Birth of Hollywood* (Boulder: University of Colorado Press, 2003), 105–132.

4. "Reviews of Special Feature Subjects," *New York Dramatic Mirror* (April 24, 1912): 27.

5. A 16mm viewing print of *Blazing the Trail* is available at the US Library of Congress.

6. "Pick of the Programmes," *Bioscope* (April 25, 1912): 291. A similar ending tableau in *The Deserter* (March 1912) has silhouetted cavalry in the distance above a foreground burial site where they earlier had honored an exonerated army deserter. A 35mm viewing print of the surviving second reel is available at the US Library of Congress.

7. Whether or not they were asked or forced to adopt the practice of redfacing remains unclear.

8. Ernest A. Dench, *Making the Movies* (New York: Macmillan, 1919 [1915]), 94.

9. "Bison-101 Feature Pictures," *Moving Picture World* (January 27, 1912): 298.

10. Bison 101 ads, *Motion Picture News* (May 11, 1912): 28, and *Moving Picture World* (May 18, 1912): 588. See also Nana Verhoeff, *The West in Early Cinema: After the Beginning* (Amsterdam: Amsterdam University Press, 2006): 65–66.

11. "The Lieutenant's Last Fight—Wonderful Military Film," *Motion Picture News* (May 25, 1912): 24–25; "Stories of Licensed Films," *Moving Picture World* (June 1, 1912): 868–869. A slightly incomplete 35mm print, from the EYE Museum, was shown at the 2016 Giornate del cinema muto.

12. Does Ford also adopt and then erase even a slight trace of redface?

13. The intertitle (in Dutch in the surviving print) is quoted in "Stories of the Films," *Moving Picture World* (June 1, 1912): 868.

14. Louis Reeves Harrison, "The Indian Massacre," *Moving Picture World* (March 9, 1912): 854–856. A 35mm print, from the US Library of Congress, is included in *Saved from the Flames*.

15. Louis Reeves Harrison, "The Invaders," *Moving Picture World* (November 9, 1912): 542. Harrison also praised Anna Little who played Ravenwing in redface.

16. Scott Simmon offers an extended analysis of the film in "Pocahontas Meets Custer: The Invaders," *The Invention of the Western Film*, 55–78. The latter storyline, Simmon argues, evokes the defeat of Custer's Seventh Cavalry as well as "Fetterman's massacre," which took place 10 years earlier (President Grant's portrait appears on the wall behind the colonel).

196 NOTES

17. Joanna Hearne makes much of these paired voyeurs in *Native Recognition: Indigenous Cinema and the Western* (Albany: SUNY Press, 2012), 50–51.

18. This perspective, Simmon argues, was similar to that of post-Civil War officers such as General George Cook, who described the army's position as "an impossible [one] between put-upon Indians [with whom he empathized] and western business interests who wanted them swept out of the way"—Simmon, *Invention of the Western*, 80.

19. At least one trade press review seemed unmoved by the film's ambiguity, chiefly calling attention to several historical inaccuracies—"Reviews of Film Supply Co. Films," *New York Dramatic Mirror* (November 27, 1912): 31.

20. For the film's release, see the NYMP ad, *Motion Picture News* (October 19, 1912): 4–5. The Sales Company breakup led New York Motion Picture (NYMP) to contract with Mutual Film, but the struggle with Universal, which wrested away control of the Bison brand, kept the company from releasing any "special features" until that fall. NYMP then reorganized its production under new brand names, Kay-Bee and Broncho. See "Universal Bison Litigation," *New York Dramatic Mirror* (August 7, 1912): 27; "Bison Pictures to Be Real Features," *New York Morning Telegraph* (August 11, 1912): 4.2: 4; and the Broncho ad, *Motion Picture News* (August 17, 1912): 27.

21. New York Motion Picture Company ad, *Motion Picture News* (September 21, 1912): back cover. See also Verhoeff, *The West in Early Cinema*, 136–137.

22. "Custer's Last Fight," *Photoplay Magazine* (September 1912): 25–32.

23. Louis Reeves Harrison, "Custer's Last Fight," *Moving Picture World* (June 22. 1912): 1116–1118; "Important Films of the Week," *New York Morning Telegraph* 4.2 (September 29, 1912): 10; and "Reviews of Supply Co. Films," *New York Dramatic Mirror* (October 2, 1912): 32.

24. "Famous Indian War in Pictures," *Motography* (July 6, 1912): 23–24; Jas. S. McQuade, "The Fall of Black Hawk," *Moving Picture World* (July 6, 1912): 31–34. For detailed information on the historical figure of Black Hawk, see Rifkin, *Manifesting America*, 75–108; and Johnson, *The Broken Heart of America*, 57–65.

25. Perry Armstrong, *The Sauks and the Black Hawk War, with Biographical Sketches, Etc.* (Springfield, IL: H.W. Rokker, 1887), 148—cited in Mark Lawrence Schrad, *Smashing the Liquor Machine: A Global History of Prohibition* (New York: Oxford University Press, 2021), 295–298.

26. "Historic Ground for Pictures," *Moving Picture World* (June 15, 1912): 1018.

27. "Famous Indian War in Pictures," 23.

28. A similar privileging of white characters marked American Film's two-reel *Geronimo's Last Raid* (September 1912), outsourced to W. D. Emerson and shot on the Starved Rock Reservation west and south of Chicago. "'Geronimo's Last Raid' A Big Historic," *Motography* (August 3, 1912): 110; and Jas. S. McQuade, "Geronimo's Last Raid," *Moving Picture World* (September 14, 1912): 1054–1055. A 35mm print, rather deteriorated and from an unknown source, is included on Powerhousefilms' DVD of Walter Hill's *Geronimo, An American Legend* (2021).

29. "Independent Film Stories," *Moving Picture World* (October 19, 1912): 282.

30. "Independent Film Stories," *Motion Picture News* (November 23, 1912): 30.

31. Repressed here is the historical record of white whiskey traders who have already "cursed" the Apaches into an addiction to liquor.

NOTES 197

32. See also "Western Jottings," *Universal Weekly* (November 23, 1912): 28; and "Manufacturers' Advance Notes," *Moving Picture World* (November 23, 1912): 782.

33. "Manufacturers' Synopses of Films," *Motion Picture News* (October 26, 1912): 26; and "Independent Film Stories," *Moving Picture World* (November 2, 1912): 492.

34. *The Man They Scorned* does not survive, which makes any firm conclusion about its handling of Jewishness and Jewish assimilation tentative. At the time, Jewish and Irish immigrants, unlike Italians, were becoming more accepted as "white" Americans.

35. "Manufacturers' Synopses of Films," *Motion Picture News* (October 5, 1912): 33; and "Independent Film Stories," *Moving Picture World* (October 12, 1912): 182.

36. "Plots of the Plays," *Photo Playwright* (December 1912): 55.

37. "Licensed Film Stories," *Moving Picture World* (May 10, 1913): 624. Claribel Egbert, "A Yaqui Cur," *Motion Picture Story Magazine* (June 1913): 29–36. Biograph's *The Massacre* and *The Battle of Elderbush Gulch* are excluded here for two reasons. Although produced in 1912, both were inexplicably delayed release until Griffith and many of his actors had left the company in 1914. By then, their stories also looked anachronistic. *The Massacre* has the 8th cavalry attack an Indian village without justification, provoking a later Indian attack that fills so much of the film's second reel that it erases what initially seemed a strong critique of the US Army's actions in the Plains wars. Surprisingly, *The Massacre* was distributed much earlier in France— "Nouveautés Cinématographiques," *Ciné-Journal* (November 2, 1912): 80. As if anticipating *The Birth of a Nation*, *The Battle of Elderbush Gulch* makes the Indians into thoroughly stereotypical savages, ludicrously demonized further as "uncivilized" eaters of dogs. The settlers instead are sentimentalized in the figures of two orphan girls, a young couple, their missing baby, and especially two overly cute puppies.

38. Unnamed in the film, the youth is called "Strong Heart" in *Motion Picture Story Magazine* and "Kira" in the 1916 reissue by the Aywon Company—Tom Gunning, "The Yaqui Cur," in Paolo Cherchi Usai, ed., *The Griffith Project*, vol. 7 (London: British Film Institute, 2003), 80. Egbert's fictionalization, unlike the film, has the youth's own tribal chief condemn him as a "cowardly cur," lessening the belittling impact of the white prospectors.

39. Gunning, "The Yaqui Cur," 80–81.

40. Gunning, "The Yaqui Cur," 83.

41. For an excellent summary of this Yaqui history, expanded in Chapter 6, see Evelyn Hu-DeHart, *Yaqui Resistance and Survival* (Madison: University of Wisconsin Press, 2016), 7–10. See also Kelly Lytle Hernández, *Bad Mexicans: Race, Empire, and Revolution in the Borderlands* (New York: W.W. Norton, 2022),145–146.

42. "Stories of the New Photoplays," *Reel Life* (December 19, 1914): 10; "Brief Stories of the Week's Film Releases," *Motography* (December 26, 1914): 912. A 35mm print, from the Museum of Modern Art, is included in the *Treasures 5: The West, 1898–1938* DVD.

43. Critics praised the 80-year-old Joe Goodboy who played Gray Otter. Following an industry convention, the Japanese American actor Sessue Hayakawa played Tiah, and Hayakawa's wife, Tsuru Aoki, played the Indian woman whom Tiah accosted. Whether either appeared in redface is unclear.

198 NOTES

44. See also Scott Simmon's analysis of the film in "The Last of the Line," *Treasures 5: The West, 1898–1938*, 20–24.

45. Stephen W. Bush, "No Lowering of Standards," *Moving Picture World* (January 24, 1914): 389.

46. A 35mm print of *The Life of Buffalo Bill*, re-edited by Blackhawk Films, survives at the US Library of Congress. For an extended analysis and the legal difficulties that hampered the film's release, see Sandra K. Sagala, *Buffalo Bill on the Silver Screen* (Norman: University of Oklahoma Press, 2013), 42–51.

47. This pairing collapsed the difference between the Cheyenne located in the northern Great Plains and the Santa Fe Trail whose trajectory lay closer to the southern border in the Southwest.

48. Sagala, *Buffalo Bill on the Silver Screen*, 46–47.

49. "First 'Broncho Billy' Multiple Reel," *Motography* (October 18, 1913): 269–270.

50. "A Great Film's Second Edition," *Motography* (January 18, 1913): 49–51. The "first edition" of the film was released in late October 1909—"Stories of the Films," *Moving Picture World* (October 23, 1909): 583. A 35mm print of the later film survives at the EYE Museum, Amsterdam.

51. The painting is reproduced on a full page in *Motography* (January 18, 1913): 4.

52. "Selig Releasing Western Thriller," *Motography* (May 31, 1913): 395–396. Mix already had appeared in other Selig single-reel westerns such as *Saved by the Pony Express* (1911), in which he plays a pony express rider who has to leap from one galloping horse to another as he carries a confession that will exonerate a man about to be convicted of murder. A 35mm print, from the US Library of Congress, was shown at the 2015 Giornate del cinema muto.

53. "Dakota" serves as another appropriation of Native American tribal names.

54. "The Escape of Jim Dolan," *Motography* (November 15, 1913): 353–354.

55. "The Toll of Fear," *Moving Picture World* (April 5, 1913): 28. For a rare study of Fielding's career, see Linda Kowall Woal, "Romaine Fielding: The West's Touring Auteur," *Film History* 8.4 (1995): 401–425.

56. "Comments on the Films," *Moving Picture World* (April 26, 1913): 379. See also *The Rattlesnake—A Psychical Species* (November 1913), another of Fielding's psychological studies, which the trade press described as "extremely repulsive"—"Important Films of the Week," *New York Morning Telegraph* (November 2, 1913): 5:2.

57. "California M.P. Company's First Release," *Moving Picture World* (July 4, 1914): 68. The film premiered in San Francisco in October 1914—"A De Luxe Booklet," *Motography* (October 31, 1914): 600. See also "'Salomy Jane' to Be Seen at Grand," *Trenton Times-Advertiser* (November 1, 1914): 3.7; and "At the Movies," *San Diego Tribune* (November 20, 1914): 8. For the film's production, see Scott Simmon, "Salomy Jane," *Treasures 5*, 7–11.

58. "Feature Film Stories," *Moving Picture World* (November 7, 1914): 836. Beatriz Michelina, a young opera singer and stage actress, played the spirited Salomy Jane. A 35mm print, from the US Library of Congress, is included in the *Treasures 5: The West, 1898–1938* DVD.

59. Trade press writers consistently called attention to the California scenery in their unusually positive reviews: "Feature Film Reviews," *Variety* (October 31,

1914): 27; Louis Reeves Harrison, "Salomy Jane," *Moving Picture World* (November 7, 1914): 768; Charles R. Condon, "'Salomy Jane' a Masterpiece," *Motography* (November 14, 1914): 649–650. See also "'Salomy Jane,' a Story of Early Days in California, Being Shown at Liberty Theater," *San Jose News* (November 11, 1914): 2.

60. See also Selig's *The Spoilers*, set in Alaska during the 1898 gold rush. Specially advertised in Chicago, the film ran for nearly three months at the downtown Studebaker Theater—Studebaker ad, *Chicago Tribune* (April 17, 1914): 5; and "News Notes of Plays and Players," *Chicago Sunday Tribune* (June 21, 1914): 8.2.

61. Louis Reeves Harrison, "The Squaw Man," *Moving Picture World* (February 28, 1914): 1068–1069. See also "The Jefferson," *Fort Wayne Journal-Gazette* (April 19, 1914): 22. Just weeks earlier, Essanay's *The Indian Wars*, which restaged several battles between 1876 and 1891, was shown privately to US government officials. This six-reel feature received very limited commercial distribution—Sandra K. Sagala, *Buffalo Bill on the Silver Screen* (Norman: University of Oklahoma Press, 2013), 130. For a succinct discussion of that film's production, distribution, and exhibition, see Joy S. Kasson, *Buffalo Bill's Wild West: Celebrity, Memory, and Popular History* (New York: Hill & Wang, 2000), 257–263.

62. In the play, Wynnegate renames himself Jim Carson, buys the Red Butte Ranch in Montana, and is rescued several times by the "Ute Indian Maiden Nat-U-Rich" before they have a son and marry. While Dustin Farnum received accolades for his performance, Red Wing was singled out in newspapers, as "a full blood Indian," for her "exquisite fidelity and great depth of feeling"—"Dustin Farnum Will Be Seen at the Rex," *Salt Lake City Telegram* (March 7, 1914): 15; and "Surprise and Delight Is 'The Squaw Man,'" *Anaconda Standard* (March 20, 1914): 11.

63. A different photo from Figure 3.8 showing Cash about to shoot Jim accompanies the short article "Dustin Farnum in the Famous Play of Indian Life, The Squaw Man, Will Be Shown at the Theater De Luxe, Elaborately Staged," *San Jose News* (April 3, 1914): 2.

64. In the play, Jim and Diana already have been secretly in love, and he escapes to America partly to protect her from any guilt.

65. Again in the play, Jim returns to England with his son and marries Diana.

66. Hearne, *Native Recognition*, 54.

67. Hearne, *Native Recognition*, 56.

68. Hearne, *Native Recognition*, 55.

69. Hearne, *Native Recognition*, 56.

70. Robert C. McElravy, "The Virginian," *Moving Picture World* (September 19, 1914): 1648; "Feature Film Stories," *Moving Picture World* (September 26, 1914): 1828. In England, the film may have been released in four-reels—"The Virginian," *Picture Stories Magazine* (January 1915): 281–294. An incomplete print of the film is available from Alpha Movie Classics, from an unknown source.

71. "Rex," *Duluth News Tribune* (September 27, 1914): 6. Most of this article, likely a press release, is reprinted in "Dustin Farnum Is Big Feature Monday," *Hot Springs* [Arkansas] *Sentinel-Record* (October 11, 1914): 6.

72. The capture occurs at a campfire that Alvin Wyckoff shot at night, an early dramatic use of low-key lighting that became known as "Lasky lighting"—Sumiko Higashi,

200 NOTES

Cecil B. DeMille and American Culture: The Silent Era (Berkeley: University of California Press, 1994), 14–15.

73. Perhaps because Wister, along with Kirke La Shelle, wrote the scenario, the film follows the novel and play relatively closely.

74. Peter Milne, "The Virginian," *Motion Picture News* (September 19, 1914): 46.

75. Milne, "The Virginian," 46; "Film Reviews," *Variety* (September 11, 1914): 22; and "Dustin Farnum in the 'Virginian' at the Broadway Theater Today," *Salt Lake City Telegram* (September 17, 1914): 3. Accentuating one scene, with the Virginian "silhouetted against the western sky," was the nostalgic melody, "Carry Me Back to Old Virginia"—W. Stephen Bush, "The Art of Exhibition," *Moving Picture World* (November 21, 1914): 1063.

76. "Lincoln Carter's First," *Variety* (February 14, 1913): 14.

77. "News and Reviews of Feature Films," *New York Dramatic Mirror* (March 12, 1913): 29; and "Comments on the Films," *Moving Picture World* (March 22, 1913): 1221. A 35mm print of the film survives at the National Film Archive, London.

78. For an extended analysis of these Civil War films, see Abel, *Americanizing the Movies*, 141–167.

79. Historical studies of the dominance of "The Lost Cause" are extensive, but see especially David W. Blight, *Race and Reunion: The Civil War in American Memory* (Cambridge: Harvard University Press, 2001), 255–299.

80. An incomplete 35mm print of this film, retitled *The Fiftieth Anniversary of the Battle of Gettysburg*, survives at the US Library of Congress. One trade press review admitted that it would "be hard pressed for any audience to forgive the Northerner for his low-down trick"—"Reviews of Universal Films," *New York Dramatic Mirror* (August 6, 1913): 31.

81. "Patriotic Confederate Veterans," Independent 52 (July 5, 1900): 1629—quoted in Nina Silber, *The Romance of Reunion: Northerners and the South, 1865–1900* (Chapel Hill: University of North Carolina Press, 1993), 180.

82. "Music for Indian Pictures," *Motion Picture News* (August 3, 1918): 779. This later article took note of the earlier popularity of Indian pictures and their recent absence but compiled a list of 21 tunes that an exhibitor would want an orchestra to play, in case one showed up.

West 3

1. Sponsored by the Smithsonian Institution and financed by Andrew Carnegie, former President Roosevelt's expedition aimed to collect flora and fauna for the National Museum in Washington, DC—Gregg Mitman, *Reel Nature: America's Romance with Wildlife on Film* (Seattle: University of Washington Press, 1999), 5.

2. A "special descriptive lecture" for the film described each of these 36 scenes— "Roosevelt in Africa," *Film Index* (April 2, 1910): 6–7. For more information on Kearton, see "Cherry Kearton and His Work," *Moving Picture World* (September 10, 1910): 567–568.

NOTES   201

3. "Hunting African Big Game in the Jungles of Chicago," *Moving Picture World* (July 31, 1909): 156–157. The success of this film led Selig to produce a number of "sensational" jungle pictures, often starring Kathlyn Williams, in the early 1910s.

4. A "big game hunter, naturalist, millionaire, and sportsman-extraordinaire," Rainey spent over $250,000 to finance his expedition that depended on a New York animal photographer and adventurer, J. C. Hemment, a hundred specially trained American hunting dogs, and unnumbered and little mentioned "natives." George Fortiss, "Paul Rainey, Sportsman," *Outing Magazine* 58 (1911) 746—quoted in Mitman, *Reel Nature*, 16. "Paul J. Rainey Jungle Pictures," *Moving Picture News* (April 13, 1912): 10.

5. "The Paul Rainey African Pictures," *Moving Picture World* (April 20, 1912): 214–215. This synopsis was based on the eight reels shown to the trade press and exhibitors before they were edited into the released five reels.

6. "The Paul Rainey African Pictures," 215. The *New York Times* review, for instance, was reprinted in *The "Implet"* (May 11, 1912): 4.

7. "Paul J. Rainey Jungle Pictures," 10.

8. "Washington, D.C.," *Moving Picture News* (October 12, 1912): 15.

9. "Rainey Pictures' Remarkable Run," *New York Dramatic Mirror* (August 21, 1912): 27; William Harris ad, *New York Dramatic Mirror* (September 25, 1912): back cover; Rev. W.H. Jackson, "Moving Picture Educator," *Moving Picture World* (July 11, 1914): 245.

10. See also *Lady Mackenzie's Big Game Pictures* (1915), which at first simply recorded a well-known sportswoman's trip to British East Africa and then was edited into a seven-reel feature shown at the New York Lyceum, but where else remains unclear. "State Rights Buyers After McKenzie Animal Picture," *Motion Picture News* (May 29, 1915): 58; "Boys [Boy Scouts] See MacKenzie Films," *Motography* (June 5, 1915): 935; Charles R. Condon, "MacKenzie Big Game Films," *Motography* (June 19, 1915): 1016–1017; George D. Proctor, "Lady MacKenzie's Big Game Pictures," *Motion Picture News* (June 19, 1915): 66.

11. W. Stephen Bush, "Wild Life in Films," *Moving Picture World* (March 6, 1915): 1462–1463. Helping to capture a treed mountain lion was an "Indian guide," who remained unidentified. The California Fish and Game Commission was likely the government agency supporting Salisbury.

12. Kitty Kelly, "Flickerings from Film Land," *Chicago Tribune* (March 12, 1915): 12. In that interview, she mentions that Salisbury is "a University of California man," but was he a faculty member or a prior student?

13. The first trade press ad promoted the film's "six thrilling reels"; the version shown in Chicago had seven reels; a later trade press ad again listed "six thrilling reels." All Star Features ad, *Moving Picture World* (January 30, 1915): 739; Kitty Kelly, "Flickerings from Film Land," *Chicago Tribune* (March 2, 1915): 10; All Star Features ad, *Motion Picture News* (October 16, 1915): insert between pages 65 and 66.

14. Studebaker ad, *Chicago Sunday Tribune* (February 28, 1915): 8.2. Salisbury himself reported that the film already had played for two weeks at the Tivoli in San Francisco, to 120,000 people—Bush, "Wild Life in Films," 1463.

15. All Star Features ad, *Moving Picture World*, 739; "American Film of Exceptional Interest," *Motography* (March 13, 1915): 396.

202 NOTES

16. All Star Features ad, *Motion Pictures News*, insert.

17. The National Film Preservation Foundation "repatriated" and restored this surviving excerpt, along with a dozen other films, in 2012. My description and analysis of the "Hunting Geese" sequence draws on a commentary written by Amanda Getty in my Seminar in Cinema Historiography, Winter 2013.

18. Legal protection finally did appear several years later—"New Game Bird Law Bars Pot Shooting," *New York Times* (August 18, 1918): 14.

19. One of the four pages in the second All Star Features ad is adamant about this "romance."

Chapter 4

1. "William S. Hart," *Le Giornate del Cinema Muto Catalogue* (October 2019): 37–80. The following pages draw on and revise the Koszarskis' catalogue entries as well as my own.

2. Despite having appeared in *The Squaw Man* and starring in *The Virginian* on stage, Hart had no experience acting in movies and probably was not considered when those two features went into production. For more extensive information on Hart, see Andrew Brodie Smith, *Shooting Cowboys and Indians: Silent Western Films, American Culture, and the Birth of Hollywood* (Boulder: University of Colorado Press, 2003), 157–185.

3. Paramount ad, *Moving Picture World* (November 28, 1914): 1136. Reginald Barker directed the film—Diane Kaiser Koszarski, *The Complete Films of William S. Hart: A Pictorial Record* (New York: Dover, 1980), 3.

4. W. Stephen Bush, "The Bargain," *Moving Picture World* (December 5, 1914): 1390.

5. "At the Nesbitt," *Wilkes Barre Times-Leader* (December 28, 1914): 6.

6. Koszarski, *The Complete Films of William S. Hart*, 5.

7. Paramount Pictures ad, *Moving Picture World* (November 28, 1914): 1136. This photo also was reproduced in "'The Bargain,' Story with Scenes in Arizona, Is Big Feature of New Program at the De Luxe," *San Jose News* (December 23, 1914): 4.

8. Hart appears as a gold miner slowly crossing a desert on his way to a lawless town.

9. Indians assumed major roles as threats to white men in only three Hart films made within a few months of one another in 1916—and only one, *The Captive God* (July 1916) survives. Tellingly, all of their stories were located outside the United States, two in Canada and one in Mexico, which erased any explicit reference to this country as a nation built on the conquests of settler colonialism. Only in *The Dawn Maker* (September 1916) would Hart take on the rare role of a sacrificial "half breed."

10. "The Passing of Two-Gun Hicks," *Reel Life* (December 19, 1914): 16; Louis Reeves Harrison, "The Passing of Two-Gun Hicks," *Moving Picture World* (December 19, 1914): 1695. Harrison disparages the film, the first to be directed by Hart, as an attraction for small boys. No print seems to survive.

NOTES   203

11. "Interesting Film Reviews," *Motion Picture News* (December 26, 1914): 51. Compared with that of Dustin Farnum in *The Virginian*, for instance, Hart's acting here is strikingly restrained.

12. "Brief Stories of the Week's Film Reviews," *Motography* (December 26, 1914): 912; "Interesting Film Reviews," *Motion Picture News* (December 26, 1914): 51. A 35mm print of *In the Sage Brush Country*, a reconstruction drawn from versions at the EYE Museum and at the George Eastman Museum, was shown at the 2019 Giornate del cinema muto, Pordenone.

13. The Lost Hope Mine is one of several ironic or tongue-in-cheek names sometimes given to towns and companies in these Hart films.

14. Janet Flanner, "Comments on the Screen," *Indianapolis Sunday Star* (July 14, 1918): 5.33.

15. In contrast to these stereotypes, one of the 101-Ranch Sioux in Ince's company also plays the Indian maid quietly washing dishes in a background room of the mine owner's office.

16. The film follows a film industry convention of having a non-Mexican play a Mexican character, here a Japanese American actor, Thomas Kurihara.

17. Gossip item, *Cleveland Sunday Plain Dealer* (April 2, 1916): Metropolitan/ Photoplays, 7.

18. A 35mm print of this film, from the Danish Film Institute (Copenhagen), was shown at the 2019 Giornate del cinema muto.

19. Clarence J. Caine, "Mutual's 'On the Night Stage,'" *Motography* (April 24, 1915): 656–657. Briefly, "Silent Texas" Smith, a stage robber, shoots a gambler threatening to seduce a dance hall woman he loves so that she and the parson she has married can be reunited. In the final tableau, Smith is left alone, sadly wondering "what is left for me."

20. A press release, on the occasion of *On the Night Stage*'s release, touted Hart's growing fame—"William S. Hart Has Become Really Famous," *Albuquerque Journal* (April 23, 1915): 8. See also a short article on *The Man From Nowhere*, "What the Press Agents Say," *Colorado Springs Gazette* (May 6, 1915): 11.

21. "Stories of the New Photoplays," *Reel Life* (April 3, 1915): 12. A 35mm print of this film, from the Museum of Modern Art, New York, was shown at the 2019 Giornate del cinema muto.

22. Two different plot synopses suggest that changes were made to the ending between the film's advance publicity and its release. In *Reel Life*, "Luke, a revolver in either hand, is sitting, propped against a sand hill, his arm riddled with bullets . . . across his knees is the body of the dead sheriff." In *Motography*, by contrast, "in a thrilling scene," Luke and the sheriff "repulse an Indian attack," which sets up an unexpectedly "happy ending."

23. "Stories of the New Photoplays," *Reel Life* (April 24, 1915): 12; "Mutual Program," *Motography* (May 15, 1915): 762.

24. Intriguingly, the trade press named Johnson Pasquale, making him less "American" than Buck, Emma, Frazer, and the other townspeople.

25. The surviving archive print is missing several scenes at the end, so the resolution has to be gathered from Mutual's publicity.

204 NOTES

26. "Mutual Program," *Motion Picture News* (May 8, 1915): 77.

27. "Stories of the New Photoplays," *Motography* (May 8, 1915): 12. A 35mm print of *"Bad Buck" of Santa Ynez*, from the US Library of Congress, was shown at the 2019 Giornate del cinema muto. Santa Ynez was a canyon near Inceville, so the title serves as an in-joke for the film's production.

28. Peter Milne, "Bad Buck of Santa Inez," *Motion Picture News* (May 22, 1915): 69.

29. An anomaly in these films, *Pinto Ben* has Hart regaling a bunch of cowboys with the poem of his favorite horse, whose story is told in a series of flashbacks. In *A Knight of the Trails*, Hart is a road agent engaged to a waitress who discovers his hidden cache of stolen money and breaks with him. A rival comes courting, persuades her to marry him and entrust her savings with him, and then runs off to meet an eastbound train. In pursuit, Hart takes a shortcut, stops the thief near the railroad station, knocks him down, recovers the money, but has to shoot him when the thief draws his gun. Once her savings are returned, the couple renews their engagement.

30. "Banner Features in the Mutual Program," *Reel Life* (September 4, 1915): 5. A 35mm print, from the Museum of Modern Art, New York, was shown at the 2019 Giornate del cinema muto.

31. "There is nothing in history like the Western cinema dance-hall scenes," so goes Flanner's ironic words, "how unfortunate history was written before motion pictures were invented. They could have helped color it so."—Flanner, "Comments on the Screen," 14.

32. Louise Glaum, darkened with makeup, plays Anita with flamboyant excess, ensuring that the "alienness" of her character contrasts sharply with the white hero and heroine.

33. "The Darkening Trail," *Reel Life* (May 22, 1915): 16; George D. Proctor, "The Darkening Trail," *Motion Picture News* (May 29, 1915): 70.

34. *The Disciple* is available for purchase on DVD, drawn from a 35mm print in either the US Library of Congress or the George Eastman Museum.

35. For this and later films, Ince had an even larger "western dance hall, saloon, and gambling place erected in Santa Ynez Canyon"—J. C. Jensen, "In and Out of Los Angeles Studios," *Motion Picture News* (July 24, 1915): 47.

36. Louis Reeves Harrison, "The Disciple," *Moving Picture World* (October 30, 1915): 810.

37. "The Man with the Face That Talks," comes from "Facts and Fancies about the Films," *New Orleans Times-Picayune* (April 19, 1916): 16.

38. Louis Reeves Harrison, "Hell's Hinges," *Moving Picture World* (February 5, 1915): 1146–1147; "Film Reviews," *Variety* (February 11, 1915): 21. The trade press signaled *Hell's Hinges*' importance by highlighting Victor L. Schertzinger's film score—"Pacific Coast Notes," *Motography* (March 18, 1915): 656. A 35mm tinted print, from the Museum of Modern Art, New York, is included in the *Treasures from the American Film Archives* DVD.

39. "'Hell's Hinges' Real Place," *Motography* (March 4, 1915): 528.

40. "The Stage: Majestic," *Detroit Times* (May 1, 1916): 6.

41. Harvey F. Thew, "Hell's Hinges," *Motion Picture News* (February 19, 1915): 1029.

NOTES   205

42. "Hart Strong in 'Hell's Hinges,'" *Montgomery* [Alabama] *Advertiser* (March 19, 1916): 34.

43. Scott Simmon, "Hell's Hinges (1916)," in *Treasures from the American Film Archives* (San Francisco: National Film Preservation Foundation, 2000), 14.

44. See what likely was a puff piece of publicity in "Thrilling Ride in 'Hell's Hinges' Film," *Duluth News Tribune* (March 24, 1916): 14.

45. A full-page ad even boasts that everyone "Loves Bill (w.s.) Hart"—*Moving Picture World* (October 21, 1916): 329. In an interview, Hart claimed, as a boy, to "having known, of bad men being converted—particularly by good womanhood"—"Wm. S. Hart, the Star, in Great Play Now at the Pastime," *Albuquerque Journal* (December 26, 1916): 6. A 35mm print of *The Return of Draw Egan*, from the US Library of Congress, was shown at the 2019 Giornate del cinema muto.

46. Hart's regular cameraman Joe August created several notable lighting effects: the night scene of cowboys carousing outside the saloon, timely sunset shots setting up the climactic gunfight, artificial "sunlight" slanting across Blake's office table and then on Joe waiting at the saloon bar.

47. One trade press review praised the story's "simplicity" and alluded to these scenes for their "intimate human, heart-effecting situations"—George W. Graves, "The Return of 'Draw Egan,'" *Motography* (September 30, 1916): 785.

48. Richard F. Lussier, "'Draw' Egan," *Birmingham Age-Herald* (November 9, 1916): 3.

49. Peter Milne, "Two Triangle Pictures from Kay-Bee," *Motion Picture News* (December 30, 1916): 4235. See also "Hart as Newspaper Man in Ince Film," *Motography* (January 6, 1917): 35; and George Graves, "Truthful Tulliver," *Motography* (January 6, 1917): 40.

50. "Miscellaneous Subjects," *Moving Picture World* (January 20, 1917): 426. A 35mm print of the film survives at the George Eastman Museum. Some of the following quotes come from intertitles in that print.

51. "Romantic Settings in Kay-Bee Films," *Motography* (February 17, 1917): 369. See also Dorothy Donnell's fictionalization, based on J. G. Hawks's scenario, in "Truthful Tulliver," *Motion Picture Classic* (February 1917): 25–29, 68.

52. "Item Daily Movies," *New Orleans Item* (January 8, 1917): 4.; and "Hart Rides Horse Through Window," *Trenton Times* (January 10, 1917): 7. Vachel Lindsay used several images from the latter stunt to describe sculpture and architecture in motion— quoted as a "Lindsayism" in Epes Winthrop Sargent, "The Photoplaywright," *Moving Picture World* (April 21, 1917): 420.

53. Christopher Bird program notes for *The Gun Fighter* in the 2019 Giornate del cinema muto catalogue.

54. Louis Reeves Harrison, "Triangle Program," *Moving Picture World* (February 10, 1917): 869. For a more positive review, see George W. Graves, "The Gun Fighter," *Motography* (February 17, 1917): 373.

55. "Hart Featured in New Liberty Bill," *Seattle Sunday Times* (February 11, 1917): 3.4.

56. Peter Milne found the "night effects" in this scene superb—"Screen Examinations," *Motion Picture News* (February 17, 1917): 1088.

57. "Theatres," *Ogden Standard* (March 7, 1917): 11. The theater's "capacity audiences" included "large numbers of youthful local 'movie' fans."

206 NOTES

58. George W. Graves, "Wolf Lowry," *Motography* (June 16, 1917): 1289. Much of the film was shot "in Calexico on the Mexican border"—"Hart Continues at St. Regis Today," *Trenton Times* (July 12, 1917): 7. A 35mm print, drawn from a later 28mm Pathescope version licensed to S. A. Lynch and recently preserved at the US Library of Congress, was shown at the 2019 Giornate del cinema muto. Unlike most Hart films, which were scripted by C. Gardner Sullivan, J. G. Hawks, or other scenario writers, *Wolf Lowry* was based on "The Rancher," a story by Charles Turner Dazey, best known for his play, *In Old Kentucky* (1893), and for his scenario for Douglas Fairbanks's *Manhattan Madness* (1916).

59. Louis Reeves Harrison, "Triangle Program," *Moving Picture World* (June 9, 1917): 1625. Harrison is writing shortly after the United States entered the Great War and precisely when Hart was making personal appearances, as at the Metropolitan in Cleveland—"Film Event of Week is W.S. Hart's Appearance," *Cleveland Plain Dealer* (May 20, 1917): 4; and Robert Izart, "Managers Meet to Conform with Patriotic Movie," *Cleveland Plain Dealer* (May 28, 1917): 4.

60. This 35mm fragment is preserved at the US Library of Congress.

61. Diane Koszarski includes a summary of the troubled relations with Triangle in her 2019 Giornate del cinema muto catalogue entry for *The Silent Man*. Hart himself warned exhibitors about these unauthorized reissues in several ads, one in *Moving Picture World* (July 20, 1918): 438, and another in *Motion Picture News* (March 30, 1918): 1802.

62. "William S. Hart Film Next Artcraft Offering," *Motography* (October 20, 1917): 822; "Injunction Bars Hart Picture," *Motography* (October 27, 1917): 872; "Artcraft Restrained from Showing Wm. Hart Picture," *Motion Picture News* (October 27, 1917): 2882. Several newspapers stories, however, suggest some prints of the film were circulating in October.

63. "Reviews of Current Productions," *Moving Picture World* (December 15, 1917): 1641–1642; "Screen Examinations," *Motion Picture News* (December 15, 1917): 4222; Helen Rockwell, "The Silent Man," *Motography* (December 22, 1917): 1306. A less than complete 35mm print, from the US Library of Congress, was shown at the 2019 Giornate del cinema muto.

64. "Forsyth to Offer 'The Silent Man' New Hart Picture," *Atlanta Journal* (November 25, 1917): N10.

65. "The Narrow Trail Tells True Story," *Baltimore American* (November 18, 1917): C24.

66. A 35mm print of *The Narrow Trail*, from the George Eastman Museum, was shown at the 2019 Giornate del cinema muto.

67. "Tense Scenes in Hart Picture," *Montgomery Advertiser* (February 3, 1918): 19.

68. "Hart Has Narrow Escape," *Motography* (September 29, 1917): 647. In her praise of the film and Hart's pinto, Mary Pickford briefly describes this accident in her syndicated column, "Pickford's Comments," *Canton Repository* (March 18, 1918): 10.

69. "'Blue Blazes Rawden' Is Hart's Next," *Moving Picture World* (January 26, 1918): 537; "Hart in 'Blue Blazes Rawden,'" *Moving Picture World* (February 2, 1918): 693. A 35mm print, from the US Library of Congress, was shown at the 2019 Giornate del cinema muto.

NOTES 207

70. This film was shot by Joe August in "the Northern Woods," which apparently did not please the actors. "Weather Attacks Hart Players," *Oregonian* (February 24, 1918): 3.3; Edward Witzel, "Blue Blazes Rawden," *Moving Picture World* (March 2, 1918): 1269; "Ready Made Ad Talks," *Motion Picture News* (March 2, 1918): 1282; and L. J. Bourstein, "Blue Blazes Rawden," *Motography* (March 9, 1918): 473.

71. "Different Hart Play at Strand," *New Orleans Times-Picayune* (February 24, 1918): C8.

72. The *Chicago Tribune* reviewer strangely assumed that Rawden would "take up a better life," "inspired by the trust and love of the white-haired mother"—Mae Tinée, "They've Taken All His Old Time Stuff Away from Wm. S.," *Chicago Tribune* (February 25, 1918): 10.

73. Smith includes a short analysis of this film in *Shooting Cowboys and Indians*, 171.

74. Not all reviewers praised this film. One thought the story overly extended and Hart less restrained in his acting; another wondered whether he was "homesick for that pinto pony of his"—Mae Tinée, "They've Taken All His Old Time Stuff," 10; Peter Milne, "Blue Blazes Rawden," *Motion Picture News* (March 2, 1918): 1315.

75. For an example, see "William S. Hart Needs a Change of Subjects. The Sameness of His pictures is Beginning to Tell," written by S. M. Weller in the *New York Review* (October 12, 1918)—quoted in Koszarski, *The Complete Films of William S. Hart*, 98.

76. "Hart at State in 'The Tiger Man,'" *Trenton Times* (May 6, 1918): 11. This reviewer added that Hart's unique western type "is as near the real thing as art and historical research can suggest."

77. "Hart's New Picture 'The Tiger Man,'" *Motography* (January 23, 1918): 372; and "The Story of the Picture: Synopsis of Current Releases," *Motography* (April 20, 1918): 777. See also "Moving Pictures," *Variety* (April 26, 1918): 42. A 35mm print of this film survives at the Museum of Modern Art, New York.

78. Hart would return to a story of settlers crossing the plains in *Wagon Tracks* (August 1919).

79. *Wid's Daily* (April 25, 1918)—quoted in Koszarski, *The Complete Films of William S. Hart*, 86.

80. "Moving Pictures," *Variety* (May 10, 1918): 42; Louis Reeves Harrison, "Selfish Yates," *Moving Picture World* (May 18, 1918): 1036. See also "The Story of the Picture: Synopsis of Current Releases," *Motography* (May 25, 1918); 1014; "Ready-Made Ad Talks," *Motion Picture News* (June 1, 1918): 3270; and "Hart at State as 'Selfish Yates,'" *Trenton Times* (June 26, 1918): 7. A 35mm print of this film survives at the Museum of Modern Art, New York.

81. Peter Milne, "Selfish Yates," *Motography* (May 18, 1918): 3001.

82. Harrison, "Selfish Yates," 3001. An unsigned newspaper review also praised the film and Hart himself for taking "his art and its mission very seriously—"Films," *Los Angeles Times* (2 July 1918): 2.3.

83. Triangle ad, *Moving Picture World* (April 15, 1916): 368.

84. Andrés Levinson, "William S. Hart: The Print," *Le Giornate del Cinema Muto Catalogue* (2019): 58–59.

85. Ignoring the film's overt hymn to white supremacy, the *Chicago Tribune* reviewer assumed that Hart's character, "very bad indeed," was why "some people may not care

208 NOTES

for this picture"—Kitty Kelly, "Flickerings from Film Land," *Chicago Tribune* (March 21, 1916): 14.

86. Genevieve Harris's review is particularly pertinent in singling out the "wonderful desert scenes" and the atmospheric intertitles. Like Kelly, she also finds the story cruel but argues that it is "so well sustained" that "the drama gives the effect of a stirring poem"—see "The Aryan," *Motography* (April 1, 1916): 766. Much of the film was shot on location in the Mojave Desert.

87. Richard Koszarski, "The Aryan," *Le Giornate del cinema muto Catalogue* (2019): 54. Koszarski also asks whether Sullivan was amplifying the notorious title card that asserted an "Aryan birthright" in Griffith's *The Birth of a Nation* (1915). See also Smith's analysis of the film, based on *The Aryan* scenario, folder "The Aryan," box 1, Dunston Collection, US Library of Congress, in *Shooting Cowboys and Indians*, 166–167.

88. Hart himself sometimes was accused of misogyny both within and outside the industry.

89. A popular source of this ideology at the time was Joseph P. Widney's *Race Life of the Aryan Peoples* (1907)—Koszarski, "The Aryan," 54.

90. Oscar Cooper highlights this epigram in "The Aryan," *Motion Picture News* (April 8, 1916): 2064.

91. Hart's first choice to take the role of Mary Jane was Mae Marsh, whose preference for death rather than dishonor as Flora Cameron, evidenced another connection to *The Birth of a Nation*. Impressed by *The Aryan*, released in France as *Pour sauver sa race*, Louis Delluc promoted the film as high art with an analogy to Greek tragedy that compared Louise Glaum to Clytemnestra and Bessie Love to Electra—"D'Orestre à Rio Jim," *Cinéa 31* (December 9, 1921): 15.

92. Richard Slotkin, *Gunfighter Nation: The Myth of the Frontier in Twentieth-Century America* (New York: Atheneum, 1992). See also Michael Kimmel, *Manhood in America: A Cultural History* (New York: Free Press, 1996)—which surprisingly says almost nothing about the impact of World War I.

West 4

1. Marguerite S. Shaffer, *See America First: Tourism and National Identity, 1880–1940* (Washington, DC: Smithsonian Institution, 2001), 100.

2. Shaffer, *See America First*, 101.

3. Stephen Tyng Mather, "Introduction," in *The National Parks Portfolio* (New York: Scribner's, 1916), n.p.—quoted in Shaffer, *See America First*, 103.

4. Shaffer, *See America First*, 101.

5. Carl Louis Gregory, "Motion Picture Photography," *Moving Picture World* (September 18, 1915): 1994.

6. "'See America First' Film for Interior Department," *Moving Picture World* (October 1915): 297.

NOTES 209

7. "Scenics Becoming Very Popular," *Motion Picture News* (November 14, 1914): 29.

8. "Gaumont Makes Extensive Plans for Fall and Winter," *Motion Picture News* (October 30, 1915): 54.

9. "See America First," *Moving Picture World* (November 6, 1915): 1157. This was #8 in the series.

10. "New Releases on Mutual Program," *Reel Life* (November 27, 1915): 7.

11. "In the Heart of the Blue Ridge," *Reel Life* (January 6, 1917): 9; Rev. W. H. Jackson and Margaret I. MacDonald, "Motion Picture Educator," *Moving Picture World* (January 27, 1917): 523. The Blue Ridge Parkway, constructed a few years earlier, was a model for a national system of good roads—Shaffer, *See America First,* 158.

12. "Scenes Along Oregon Coast," *Reel Life* (March 3, 1917): 6. This was #78 in the series.

13. "All Rothacker Organization Is on the Jump," *Motion Picture News* (August 18, 1917): 1139. A year earlier, a railway agent promoted this park in "Why Glacier National Park is the Goal of Summer Tourists," *Cleveland Plain Dealer* (June 4, 1916): 4.

14. "Our National Parks Pictured," *Moving Picture World* (February 2, 1918): 680; Rev. W. H. Jackson and Margaret MacDonald, "Motion Picture Educator," *Moving Picture World* (March 16, 1918): 1502. General Grant later was renamed Kings Canyon. A 35mm print of *Our National Parks—Yellowstone Park: The Geysers* survives at the EYE Museum, Amsterdam.

15. Jennifer Lynn Peterson, *Education in the School of Dreams: Travelogues and Early Nonfiction Film* (Durham, NC: Duke University Press, 2013), 252–253. A 35mm print of this film, titled *Our National Parks—Glacier*, also survives at the EYE Museum, Amsterdam.

16. Shaffer, *See America First,* 39.

17. Watterson R. Rothacker, "Seeing America First in Pictures," *Motography* (December 7, 1912): 429. See also William J. McGrath, "Chicago News and Comment," *Motion Picture News* (August 18, 1917): 1139. Rothacker released another half dozen films of the Rocky Mountains in 1919—Rothacker ad, *Motion Picture News* (January 4, 1919): 45.

18. W. Stephen Bush, "Seeing America," *Moving Picture World* (February 19, 1916): 1148–1149. Curtis already was famous for his photographs and films (often staged) of North American Indians.

19. Paramount Pictures ad, *Motion Picture News* (January 22, 1916), 326; "New Distribution for Ditmars Films," *Moving Picture World* (January 6, 1917): 80.

20. See, for instance, "Ditmar Animal Pictures Gave Book of Nature to Motion Pictures," *Detroit News-Tribune* (March 4, 1917): n.p.

21. "Educationals," *Reel and Slide* (March 1918): 15. In other travel films, such humor also came "at the expense of the dignity of people of color"—Fatimah Tobing Rony, *The Third Eye: Race, Cinema, and Ethnographic Spectacle* (Durham, NC: Duke University Press, 1996), 84–85.

210 NOTES

22. "Outing-Chester Series to Start June 30," *Motography* (June 22, 1918): 1174. The series ran until 1919—see the *Outing-Chester Pictures* ad, *Moving Picture World* (June 14, 1919): 1586.

23. "Outing Editor Discusses Value of Chester Pictures," *Moving Picture World* (August 31, 1918): 1288.

24. Educational Films ads, *Motion Picture News* (August 30, 1919): 1791, and (December 20, 1919): inside front cover.

25. In 1920, Bruce began shooting scenic outside North America—see, for instance, Lillian May's praise for the new series in "The Soul of Europe," *Motion Picture Magazine* (May 1921): 46–47.

26. Rev. W. H. Jackson and Margaret I. MacDonald, "Motion Picture Educator," *Moving Picture World* (January 27, 1917): 523.

27. A 35mm print of this film, preserved by the Library of Congress, is included in the National Film Preservation Foundation's *Treasures 5, The West, 1898–1938* DVD.

28. This was the first railroad to reach Oregon, just a few years earlier—Scott Simmon, "The West in Promotional Travelogues," in *Treasures 5: The West, 1898–1938* (San Francisco: National Film Preservation Foundation, 2011): 17–20.

29. Simmon, *Treasures 5*, 55–57. A 35mm print of this film, preserved by the Library of Congress, is included in *Treasures 5: The West, 1898–1938* DVD.

30. Simmon, *Treasures 5*, 95. A short excerpt from a 35mm print of this film, preserved by the Library of Congress, is included in *Treasures 5: The West, 1898–1938* DVD.

31. Simmon, *Treasures 5*, 95–96. A short excerpt from a 35mm print of this film, preserved by the Library of Congress, is included in *Treasures 5: The West, 1898–1938* DVD.

32. Simmon, *Treasures 5*, 96. A short excerpt from a 35mm print of this film, preserved by the National Archives, is included in *Treasures 5: The West, 1898–1938* DVD.

33. Simmon, *Treasures 5*, 96–97. A short excerpt from a 35mm print of this film, preserved by the National Archives, is included in *Treasures 5: The West, 1898–1938* DVD.

Chapter 5

1. I have decided to exclude the serials of western subjects, which began to appear in the late 1910s and became prominent by the early 1920s.

2. "Decided Hit at 3rd Ave. Theatre," *New York Telegraph* (September 5, 1906): n.p.—Harry Carey Scrapbook, Robinson Locke Collection, Library of the Performing Arts, Lincoln Center, New York.

3. "'Two Women and That Man' Revealed at the Majestic Theatre," *New York Sun* (October 19, 1909): n.p.—Harry Carey Scrapbook, Robinson Locke Collection, Library of the Performing Arts, Lincoln Center, New York.

4. It was during this period that Carey finally became a recognized star, at least in small towns—"Royal [theater]," *Mansfield* [Ohio] *News-Journal* (June 25, 1917): 9.

5. Ford first directed Carey in the two-reel *Cheyenne's Pal* (August 1917).

NOTES 211

6. "Movie Stars No. 9—Harry Carey," *Cleveland Leader* (April 6, 1919): n.p.—Harry Carey Scrapbook, Robinson Locke Collection, Library of the Performing Arts, Lincoln Center, New York.

7. "Brief Stories of the Week's Film Releases," *Motography* (February 27, 1915): 337. A 35mm print survives at the US Library of Congress. Other than Carey's name, I've found no information on the cast and the crew shooting the film.

8. "Comments on the Films," *Moving Picture World* (March 6, 1915): 1447.

9. This canyon was located near Newall, California, where Carey had a small ranch.

10. J. C. Jessen, "A Knight of the Range," *Motion Picture News* (December 11, 1915): 95.
    The occasion for this article was an advance screening for the Universal Ranch staff of cowboys and others. The exclamation comes from the Ark-Way Theatre ad in the *Log Cabin* [Conway, Arkansas] *Democrat* (June 16, 1916): 2.

11. "Columbia Management Very Much Pleased with Red Feather Features," *Arizona Republican* (March 12, 1916): 2.5. Likely a publicity piece, this article claims the film "cost the producers more money for hospital fees than most pictures cost to make."

12. Neil G. Caward, "A Knight of the Range," *Motography* (February 12, 1916): 375. See also Peter Milne, "A Knight of the Range," *Motion Picture News* (February 5, 1916): 715.

13. "'Straight Shooting' A Whale of a Western Drama," *Moving Picture Weekly* (August 11, 1917): 19; "Harry Carey in 'Straight Shooting,'" *Moving Picture World* (September 1, 1917): 1397; Peter Milne, "Straight Shooting," *Motion Picture News* (September 8, 1917): 1668. In 2020 Kino Lorber released a Blu-ray of the film, NBCUniversal's restoration drawn from a 35mm safety fine grain print from the US Library of Congress and a 35mm silent print from the Museum of Modern Art.

14. These and the following quotes come from the intertitles in the Kino Lorber print.

15. Virginia Wright Wexman singles out this "much admired point of view shot" in "The Family on the Land: Race and Nationhood in Silent Westerns," in *The Birth of Whiteness: Race and the Emergence of U.S. Cinema*, ed. Daniel Bernardi (New Brunswick: Rutgers University Press 1996), 159.

16. See also Robert C. McElravy, "Straight Shooting," *Moving Picture World* (September 8, 1917): 1519.

17. "Official Cut-Outs Made by the Chicago Board of Censors," *Exhibitors Herald* (September 22, 1917): 33.

18. A Chinaman may be glimpsed briefly in the crowd frightened by Harry and Fremont's duel.

19. "At the Elm Today," *Greensboro* [North Carolina] *Record* (November 2, 1917): 6. See also "At the Local Playhouses," *Anaconda Standard* (September 9, 1917): n.p.

20. "Harry Carey in 'The Secret Man,'" *Moving Picture World* (October 6, 1917): 102; "Ready Made Ad-Talks," *Motion Picture News* (October 6, 1917): 2344; "Reviews," *Exhibitors Herald* (October 13, 1917); Genevieve Harris, "The Secret Man," *Motography* (October 13, 1917): 780; Peter Milne, "The Secret Man," *Motion Picture News* (October 13, 1917): 2583. Milne thought the film too drawn out and the characters "generally unskillfully drawn."

21. "The Secret Man," *Pueblo Chieftain* (December 21, 1917): 4.

212 NOTES

22. Billy Leyser, "It's the 'Little Things' That Count: Details Essential, Says Jack Ford," *Moving Picture Weekly* (February 21, 1920): 30.

23. "Harry Carey in 'The Secret Man' at Strand Today," *Augusta Chronicle* (October 8, 1917): 8.

24. One Saturday at the Strand Theater in Portland, Oregon, *The Secret Man* "broke all box office records"—Abraham Nelson, "A Few Oregon Personals," *Moving Picture World* (November 3, 1917): 746.

25. "Manufacturers' Advance Notices," *Moving Picture World* (November 3, 1917): 752.

26. Robert C. McElravy, "A Marked Man," *Moving Picture World* (November 10, 1917): 875; Genevieve Harris, "The Marked Man," *Motography* (November 17, 1917): 10567.

27. "Loaned as Wife for Two Weeks," *Salt Lake City Telegram* (December 26, 1917): 6.

28. Within months, in *"Blue Blazes" Rawden*, another mother similarly will remain ignorant of her son's disreputable past.

29. "Harry Carey Western Universals," *Moving Picture World* (December 15, 1917): 1658.

30. "Universal Specializes in Harry Carey Types," *Motion Picture News* (December 15, 1917): 4193.

31. Genevieve Harris, "The Phantom Riders," *Motography* (January 9, 1918): 281; "Film Reviews," *Variety* (February 1, 1918): 19. MacRae was a Canadian-born film director, producer, and scenario writer, who worked at Universal.

32. "Reviews and Advertising Aids," *Moving Picture World* (February 16, 1918): 1010.

33. Harris, "The Phantom Riders," 281.

34. "Reviews and Advertising Aids," 1010. According to Wikipedia, the Chicago Board of Censors required many cuts of scenes and intertitles, most of them involving violence.

35. "Stirring Western Film at Mission," *Seattle Times* (February 3, 1918): 3.2; and "Phantom Riders at Majestic Theater," *Pueblo Chieftain* (March 1, 1918): 9.

36. "Harry Carey's 'Hell Bent' Leads Universal July 1," *Moving Picture World* (June 29, 1918): 1870; "Hell Bent," *Moving Picture World* (July 6, 1918): 110; "Manufacturers' Advertising Aids," *Moving Picture World* (July 6, 1918): 115. Carey and Ford together wrote the scenario. In 2020, Kino Lorber released a DVD of the film, Universal's restoration of a 35mm nitrate print from the Národni filmov´y archive in the Czech Republic. Apparently, as much as 20 minutes are missing from this print.

37. These and the following quotes come from the translated intertitles of the Czech film print.

38. The Tartar chieftain suffered this fate in the climactic scene of the equestrian melodrama, *Mazeppa* (1831), and the figure also was depicted in paintings.

39. In an unusual move, Carey climbed a cliff to prepare for one stunt, only to tumble down 50 feet, scraping his face and then getting hit in the ribs by a boulder. "Press Sheet for the Harry Carey Special Attraction 'Hell Bent,'" *Moving Picture Weekly* (June 1, 1918): 30.

40. Peter Milne, "Hell Bent," *Motion Picture News* (June 29, 1918): 3949. See also "'Hell Bent,' Big Thriller Draws Crowds to Tudor," *Atlanta Journal* (September 17, 1918): 5.

41. This phrasing does its own "civilizing"—"Amusements," *Arizona Republican* (September 13, 1918): 9.

42. "Take a Drink Beforehand," *Pueblo Chieftain* (July 19, 1918): 7.

NOTES 213

43. Dorothy Day, "News of the Movies," *Des Moines Tribune* (March 11, 1919): 5.

44. Much of the available information comes from Paul E. Mix, *Tom Mix: A Heavily Illustrated Biography with a Filmography* (Jefferson: McFarland, 1995) and Olive Stokes Mix and Eric Heath, *The Fabulous Tom Mix* (Englewood Cliffs: Prentice-Hall, 1957). Both are heavily cited and are admitted as inaccurate, in Richard D. Jensen, *The Amazing Tom Mix: The Most Famous Cowboy of the Movies* (New York: Universe, Inc., 2005). The unattributed entry on Mix for Wikipedia actually seems more accurate than any of those three books. See also Andrew Brodie Smith, *Shooting Cowboys and Indians: Silent Western Films, American Culture, and the Birth of Hollywood* (Boulder: University of Colorado Press, 2003), 189–191; and Donald W. Reeves, "Mix, Thomas Edwin," Oklahoma Historical Society, undated.

45. "Selig Filming Lillie Buffaloes," *Motography* (January 10, 1914): 26; "A Selig Buffalo Picture," *Moving Picture World* (November 14, 1914): 949; Selig ad, *Motion Picture News* (November 28, 1914): 65.

46. The 2011 DVD of the film comes from Alpha Home Entertainment in Narberth, Pennsylvania.

47. C.J.C., "Selig Buffalo Picture to be Released," *Motography* (November 28, 1914): 732; James S. McQuade, "In the Days of the Thundering Herd," *Moving Picture World* (December 12, 1914): 1506.

48. "Screen," *Los Angeles Times* (April 6, 1919): 3.10.

49. Selig ad, *Moving Picture World* (March 6, 1915): 1543; "Licensed Film Stories," *Moving Picture World* (March 13, 1915): 1647. A 35mm print from an unknown source survives at the EYE Museum.

50. Besides the many shots of the racing stagecoach and pursuing outlaws, there are several unusual shots that dolly ahead of the stagecoach before it is attacked.

51. Genevieve Harris, "Starring in Western Stuff," *Motography* (January 13, 1917): 98.

52. "Brief Stories of the Week's Film Releases," *Motography* (July 13, 1916): 168. A 35mm print, from the US Library of Congress, is included in the *Treasures 5: The West, 1898–1938* DVD.

53. With opportunities closed to them in the East, many women attorneys moved west in the late 19th century—Scott Simmon, "Legal Advice (1916)," in *Treasures 5: The West, 1898–1938* (San Francisco: National Film Preservation Foundation, 2011), 76–77. For a final comic fall, Mix shoots himself in the empty courtroom.

54. Selig ad, *Moving Picture World* (March 27, 1915): 2035; Neil G. Caward, "Tom Mix in Another Daredevil Ride," *Motography* (March 27, 1915): 485.

55. Selig ad, *Moving Picture World* (July 3, 1915): 162.

56. Selig ads, *Moving Picture World* (July 24, 1915): 751, and *Motion Picture News* (July 24, 1915): 133.

57. See, for instance, *Pals in Blue* (1915) and *The Man Within* (1916). The first film begins in the present day with two cowpunchers in a Wild West show and then, puzzlingly, reverts to an earlier period when they join the US Army and are sent to Fort Apache. The second reenacts plot lines from earlier films: one repeats the frequent quest of white men searching for gold; the other has a flawed husband and sick child, as in *The Better Man* (1912), but its outcome initially is grim.

58. "Stories of the Films," *Moving Picture World* (September 25, 1915): 2230; "Comments on the Films," *Moving Picture World* (October 9, 1915): 252.

214 NOTES

59. "Manufacturers' Advance Notes," *Moving Picture World* (May 3, 1917): 709; and "Arcade Sunday," *Morgan City* [Louisiana] *Review* (July 7, 1917): 3. Bessie Eyton headed the cast, with Mix listed fourth—"The Heart of Texas Ryan," *Watertown* [New York] *Times* (June 14, 1917): 5. Three months later, when the film returned by popular demand to Mansfield (Ohio), Mix shared the lead with Eyton—"Opera House," *Mansfield News-Journal* (June 6, 1917): 9.

60. James S. McQuade, "The Heart of Texas Ryan," *Moving Picture World* (March 3, 1917): 1369.

61. William C. Esty, "The Heart of Texas Ryan," *Motion Picture News* (March 3, 1917): 1421. Another reviewer was dismissive: "It abounds in reckless riding, holdups and has the necessary Western atmosphere to make it interesting for patrons of the cheaper houses."—"Film Reviews," *Variety* (February 20, 1917): 24. The film was popular enough to screen one night for sailors at San Diego's Navy YMCA—"Army and Navy Activities," *San Diego Union* (July 21, 1917): 8.

62. Genevieve Harris, "The Heart of Texas Ryan," *Motography* (February 24, 1917): 427.

63. McQuade, "The Heart of Texas Ryan," 1369.

64. "January Brings Six Fox Films," *Motion Picture News* (January 12, 1918): 259.

65. "'Cupid's Round Up' With Fox Star, Tom Mix, Finished," *Exhibitors Herald* (January 12, 1918): 30.

66. "Cupid's Round Up," *Exhibitors Herald*, 30.

67. Hanford C. Judson, "Cupid's Round Up," *Moving Picture World* (February 2, 1918): 683. See also the attraction of "his clever horsemanship [and] stunts" in the publicity for *Western Blood*—"Tom Mix at Imperium," *Zanesville* [Ohio] *Times Recorder* (August 16, 1918): 5.

68. "Tom Mix to Star in Western Drama 'Cupid's Round Up,'" *Exhibitors Herald* (January 19, 1918): 17.

69. For relevant studies of the emergence of American consumer society, see William Leach, *Land of Desire: Merchants, Power, and the Rise of a New American Culture* (New York: Pantheon, 1993); and Jackson Lears, *Rebirth of a Nation: The Making of Modern America, 1877–1920* (New York: HarperCollins, 2009). "By 1915," Leach notes, "the fashion market [or] clothing trade was America's largest, ranked only by steel and oil."—Leach, *Land of Desire*, 93.

70. Fox Film ad, *Exhibitors Herald* (August 10, 1918): 7; "Ready-Made Ad Talks," *Motion Picture News* (June 15, 1918): 3564. A 35mm print survives at the US Library of Congress.

71. "Daredevil Actor at Lyric Today and Tomorrow in 'Treat 'Em Rough,' Fox Play," *Illinois State Journal* (January 12, 1919): 17. See also "Fox Analyzes 1919 Film Vogue," *Motion Picture News* (January 18, 1919): 384. Two reels of this five-reel film survive at the George Eastman Museum.

72. "'Treat 'Em Rough' at Modjeska Today," *Augusta Chronicle* (January 6, 1919): 8.

73. "Tom Mix in Treat 'Em Rough," *Baltimore American* (February 16, 1919): 2.3.

74. "Advertising Aids for Busy Managers," *Moving Picture World* (January 4, 1919): 116. Newspapers highlighted this bulldogging stunt—"Strand—Tom Mix," *Buffalo News* (March 8, 1919): 9; and "Flashes," *Los Angeles Times* (April 7, 1919): 18.

75. "Moving Pictures," *Variety* (January 17, 1919): 51.

NOTES 215

76. "'Flashbacks' on Earlier Releases," *Motion Picture News* (March 1, 1919): 1400.

77. Mae Tinée, "Mountains, Plains, Punch, Romance and Tom Mix Well 'Mixed,'" *Chicago Tribune* (January 10, 1919): 10.

78. "Heart Interest and Thrills Mark 'Fighting for Gold,'" *Moving Picture World* (April 5, 1919): 106; and "The Screen," *Wyoming State* [Cheyenne] *Tribune* (April 11, 1919): 5.

79. "Mix Popularity Grows Each Successive Release," *Moving Picture World* (April 12, 1919): 265; "Credits Tom Mix with Big Strides," *Motion Picture News* (April 12, 1919): 2293. As another sign, some of his earlier one-reel westerns circulated as re-releases, as extra attractions to Hart features. See, for instance, the Gaiety ads in the *Cleveland Plain Dealer*, from March 18, 1919, to May 2, 1919.

80. Edward Weitzel, "Reviews and Advertising Aids," *Moving Picture World* (April 12, 1919): 270; "Fighting for Gold—Fox," *Motion Picture News* (April 12, 1919): 2153; and "Fighting for Gold," *Exhibitors Herald and Motography* (April 12, 1919): 36.

81. Smith, *Shooting Cowboys and Indians*, 205–206.

82. "Daring Stunts in St. Regis Picture," *Trenton Times* (April 3, 1919): 7.

83. "Amusements," *Grand Forks Herald* (April 25, 1919): 2.7.

84. The Film Girl, "Seen on the Screen," *Syracuse Herald* (December 28, 1915): 5; Virginia Tracy, "The Dazzling Sameness of Douglas Fairbanks," *New York Sunday Tribune* (January 26, 1919): 46.

85. "Triangle's Auspicious Opening," *Moving Picture World* (October 9, 1915): 233. W. Christy Cabanne directed the film. Although a print of *The Lamb* supposedly survives at the George Eastman Museum, the only version that I've seen is a badly preserved, incomplete DVD, *The Actors: Rare Films of Douglas Fairbanks, Sr., volume 1*, from Classic Video Streams. The following quotes come from the intertitles in this print.

86. These scenes resemble some in Mack Sennett's *The Tourists* (1912), a Biograph "Farce Comedy," set in Albuquerque, New Mexico.

87. *The Lamb* makes a mockery of a concurrent historical event, "Le Matanza" or Massacre, in which the US Army killed hundreds of Mexicans and Mexican Americans in retaliation for an uprising against white settlers in south Texas—Kelly Lytle Hernández, *Bad Mexicans: Race, Empire, and Revolution in the Borderlands* (New York: W.W. Norton, 2022), 298–300. The film's comic send-up of border conflicts also stands in sharp contrast to the compilation films then being made in Mexico documenting and promoting the revolution—David M. J. Wood, "The Compilation Film of the Mexican Revolution: History as Catalogue and Monument," *Film History* 29.1 (2017): 30–56.

88. Devra Weber, "Keeping Community, Challenging Boundaries: Indigenous Migrants, International Workers, and Mexican Revolutionaries, 1900–1920," in *Mexico and Mexicans in the Making of the United States*, ed. John Tutino (Austin: University of Texas Press, 2012), 209, 217; and Evelyn Hu-DeBart, *Yaqui Resistance and Survival* (Madison: University of Wisconsin Press, 2016), 7–10. See also the earlier endnotes for *The Yaqui Cur* in Chapter 3.

89. Members of "tribes in Northwestern Arizona," the actors playing Indians were said to be scorned as "of lower type than the half-breed Mexicans and required careful handling"—"Douglas Fairbanks in a Real Thriller," *Baltimore American* (September 30, 1915): 21.

216 NOTES

90. See, for instance, "Chestnut St. Opera House," *Philadelphia Inquirer* (October 3, 1915): Feature 10; "Triangle Films Score Triumph at Vaudette," *Atlanta Journal* (November 9, 1915): 7; and "'Lamb' in Photoplay," *Trenton Times* (November 23, 1915): 7.

91. "Doug. Fairbanks' Personality Soon Wins Following," *Cleveland Plain Dealer* (June 24, 1916): 6.

92. Kitty Kelly, "Mr. Fairbanks Tries Writing His Scenario," *Chicago Tribune* (April 7, 1916): 20; Louis Reeves Harrison, "Triangle Program," *Moving Picture World* (April 22, 1916): 643; and Thomas C. Kennedy, "The Good Bad-Man," *Motography* (April 22, 1916): 938.

93. The quote comes from the first intertitle in the 2014 DVD, drawn from a restored 35mm print from the Cinémathèque française. That print is a 1923 Tri-Stone reissue, apparently revised with new translated intertitles.

94. An intriguing parallel to this opening comes in *The Lady of the Dugout* (October 1918), where real-life outlaws, Al and Frank Jennings, happen to meet two newspaper editors sitting outside a Beverly Hills Hotel who have been talking about them. Prodded, Al launches into a story that he has been thinking of making into a movie, which leads into a reenactment of that story. Despite the title, the film tracks the exploits of the Jennings brothers before and after they come across a dugout family, evidence of the desperate poverty of white settlers on the plains. *The Lady of the Dugout*, copied from a 16mm print at the US Library of Congress, is included in *Treasures 5: The West, 1898–1938* (National Film Preservation Foundation, 2011).

95. "Film Reviews," *Variety* (April 14, 1916): 25.

96. Pap is called "The Weasel" as a member of The Wolf's gang in a Triangle ad, *Variety* (May 5, 1916): 23. See also "Strand Features Douglas Fairbanks," *Montgomery Advertiser* (May 21, 1916): Society 31.

97. Dwan shot much of the film in the Mojave Desert.

98. See, for instance, the short notice on Fairbanks as "one of the big favorites of the screen," when the film appeared in Atlanta—*Atlanta Constitution* (September 24, 1916): 6. Harrison calls him "Phoebus Apollo Fairbanks" in his review. See, also, G. P. Harleman and Clarke Irvine, "News of Los Angeles and Vicinity," *Moving Picture World* (August 12, 1916): 1096.

99. Kitty Kelly remarks on Fairbanks's boyishness in her review.

100. "Fairbanks Finishes Cattle Rustling Subject," *Motion Picture News* (September 15, 1917): 1826; "Fairbanks Film Cut En Route," *Motography* (September 22, 1917): 596.

101. See also "Screen Examinations," *Motion Picture News* (October 20, 1917): 2769; "Reviews," *Exhibitors Herald* (October 20, 1917): 26; and "Current Releases Reviewed," *Motography* (October 27, 1917): 885. The only print I could view is a 2019 Grapevine Video DVD, which, unfortunately, gives no source.

102. Louis Reeves Harrison, "The Man from Painted Post," *Moving Picture World* (October 20, 1917). 400.

103. One review seems to forget this moment, writing that "Eileen Percy is pretty with little to do as the girl"—Dorothy Day, "News of the Movies," *Des Moines Tribune* (October 2, 1917): 9.

NOTES 217

104. One exhibitor wrote: "Picture as a whole poor. Too much padding. Direction and details poor."—"What the Picture Did for Me," *Motography* (December 22, 1917): 1275.

105. At least one reviewer wrote: "He has not given himself suitable opportunity" for comedy—Harrison, *"The Man from Painted Post,"* 400.

106. In the film's initial scene, before his sister is killed, Fairbanks is introduced climbing the side of a barn; then, with his trademark grin, he stands on its roof peak, shooting off a pair of guns.

107. Louis Reeves Harrison, "Three Strong Triangle Subjects," *Moving Picture World* (July 22, 1916): 649; Oscar Cooper, "The Half-Breed," *Motion Picture News* (July 22, 1916): 452. For one newspaper article that calls the film's chief attraction "his beaming personality," see "Fairbanks Now at Gaiety," *Illinois State Register* (August 10, 1916): 2. For another, however, the story is the real attraction and Fairbanks "does not need the center of the stage to hold the eye"—"Douglas Fairbanks at the Family," *Jackson* [Michigan] *Citizen Press* (September 4, 1916): 8.

108. The following quotes come from the version restored by the Cinémathèque française and San Francisco Silent Film Festival and included on a 2013 Kino Lorber DVD. The restored version draws on an incomplete damaged 35mm nitrate original print found in Dawson City in 1978; a 35mm diacetate Pathé print from the 1924 Tri-Stone re-issue, with rewritten intertitles, at the Cinémathèque française; and an abridged, retitled 16mm print at Lobster Films. At least one reviewer praised the captions that "flash like rapiers"—Julian Johnson, "The Shadow Stage," *Photoplay* (September 1916): 76.

109. Several newspaper articles label Teresa "a dance hall girl," mistaking her for the blonde—"Photoplays," *Oregon Journal* (August 6, 1916): 3.2); and "Douglas Fairbanks in a Bret Harte Story," *Tampa Tribune* (August 20, 1916): B6.

110. Kitty Kelly, "Fairbanks Minus His Smile," *Chicago Tribune* (August 5, 1916): 9. Kelly also missed the Fairbanks's penchant for comedy. One trade press review compared his character here with that of his "sympathy-compelling role" in *The Good-Bad Man*—"Film Reviews," *Variety* (July 14, 1916): 19.

111. Brief comments on the screening of *The Half-Breed* at the Metropolitan in Cleveland single out only two scenes, the climactic forest fire and Fairbanks's rare stunt of using a pliable sapling to pole vault from the ground to the top of a fallen tree—"Latest News of Photoplays and Players," *Cleveland Plain Dealer* (July 29, 1916): 4; and "Big Stars and Big Features Offered for All Tastes Are the First Run Attractions," *Cleveland Sunday Plain Dealer* (July 30, 1916): Metropolitan/Photo Plays, 4. Other newspapers also highlighted the dangerous forest fire—"Famed Carquinez Woods Set Afire for Fairbanks Play," *Anaconda Standard* (August 16, 1916): 8.

112. Despite the ending of the restored film print, many newspapers, perhaps drawing on advance publicity, claim that Lo "finds his own happiness" with Teresa (and she with him) and "continue their life together"—see, for instance, "The Half Breed," *Philadelphia Inquirer* (August 1, 1916): 4; "Fairbanks Now at Gaiety," *Illinois State Register* (August 10, 1916): 2; and "Local Stage," *Arkansas Gazette* (August 27, 1916): 9.

218 NOTES

113. "Reviews," *Exhibitors Herald* (June 30, 1917): 25. The only print I could view is a 2019 Grapevine Video DVD, which, unfortunately, gives no source. Carpenter initially was an actor then an important scriptwriter, and finally a minor director. Audiences convulsed with laughter at Loos's "wit and humor"—"Fairbanks Scores as Westerner," *Montgomery Advertiser* (August 31, 1917): 12. For more information on Anita Loos's life and career, see JoAnne Ruvoli, "Anita Loos," Women Film Pioneers website (2013).

114. "Douglas Fairbanks Is Pleasing Large Crowds at the Liberty," *San Jose Mercury News* (July 27, 1917): 5.

115. "Fairbanks Scores as Westerner," 12.

116. "Reviews of Current Productions," *Moving Picture World* (June 30, 1917): 2117; and "Douglas Fairbanks Is at the Plaza Today," *New Orleans Times-Picayune* (August 5, 1916): B13.

Afterword: Looking Backward to Look Ahead

1. Janet Flanner, "Comments on the Screen," *Indianapolis Sunday Star* (July 14, 1918): 14.

2. A 35mm print from the Museum of Modern Art (New York) is included in the *Treasures 5: The West, 1898–1938* DVD.

3. Scott Simmon, "The Tourists (1912)," in *Treasures 5: The West, 1898–1938* (San Francisco: National Film Preservation Foundation, 2011), 1–3. The quote comes from one of the film's intertitles.

4. Michelle H. Raheja makes a good case for Fatty and Minnie Ha-Haw (1914) in *Reservation Reelism: Redfacing, Visual Sovereignty, and Representations of Native Americans in Film* (Lincoln: University of Nebraska Press, 2010), 74–82. As the most interesting of the two main characters, the overweight and dark-skinned Minnie He-Haw (Minnie Deveraux) lives in a native community that welcomes Fatty as a potential husband, but his own character flaws thwart his assimilation through marriage.

5. Margaret I. MacDonald, "Out West," *Moving Picture World* (February 2, 1918): 688; "Manufacturers' Advance Notes," *Moving Picture World* (February 2, 1918): 691; Peter Milne, "Out West," *Moving Picture World* (February 9, 1918): 867. See also Buster Keaton's *Go West* (1925).

6. P .S. Harrison, "'Two-Gun Betty'—Hodkinson," *Motion Picture News* (December 14, 1918): 36–1.

7. Harrison, "'Two-Gun Betty'—Hodkinson," 361. See also the Knickerbocker ad, *Cleveland Plain Dealer* (January 21, 1919): 8.

8. Another feature to include would be a little-known Indian picture, *The Heart of Wetona* (1919), starring Norma Talmadge as a half-breed who, after a white lover abandons her, chooses to leave her native community and marry a protective white Indian agent. A 35mm print of this film, from George Eastman Museum, was shown at the 2022 Giornate del cinema muto, Pordenone.

9. Mae Tinee, "Right Off the Reel," *Chicago Tribune* (November 25, 1916): 14.

NOTES 219

10. Dorothy Day, "News of the Movies," *Des Moines Tribune* (March 11, 1919): 5.

11. A graph of this San Francisco survey, undated but probably in 1914 or earlier, appears in Rev. J. J. Phelan, "Motion Pictures as a Phase of Commercialized Amusement in Toledo, Ohio," *Film History* 13.3 (2001): 253. Other surveys are summarized from Providence, Cleveland, and Portland, Oregon.

12. Ken Wlaschin and Stephen Bottomore, "Moving Picture Fiction of the Silent Era, 1895–1928," *Film History* 20.2 (2008): 224.

13. An early example is *Ruth Fielding at Silver Ranch or Schoolgirls Among the Cowboys* (1913). See also Richard Abel and Amy Rodgers, "Early Motion Pictures and Popular Print Culture: A Web of Ephemera," in *The Oxford History of Popular Print Culture, vol. 6: US Popular Print Culture, 1860–1920*, ed. Christine Bold (Oxford: Oxford University Press, 2012), 191–209, 202–207.

14. American Record Company ad, *The Talking Machine* (March 15, 1906): inside front cover. The brief list of suggested tunes to accompany "Western pictures" comes from Clarence E. Sinn, "Music for the Picture," *Moving Picture World* (May 25, 1912): 717.

15. "MOVIES featuring Haphazard Helen in Her Desert Love," *Chicago Sunday Herald* (January 3, 1915): 6.1. The "Haphazard Helen" comic strip drew on the popularity of Kalem's long-running series, *The Hazards of Helen* (1914–1917).

16. Christine Bold, "Indigenous Presence in Vaudeville and Early Cinema," *Journal of Cinema and Media Studies* 60.2 (Winter 2021): 159.

17. Cedric J. Robinson, *On Racial Capitalism, Black Internationalism, and Cultures of Resistance* (London: Pluto Press, 2019). For earlier studies that do not explore the impact of removing Indigenous peoples from the South, see Eric Williams, *Capitalism and Slavery* (Chapel Hill: University of North Carolina Press, 1944); and Barbara Fields, *Slavery and Freedom on the Middle Ground* (New Haven: Yale University Press, 1984).

18. Quoted in Roxane Dunbar-Ortiz, *Not "A Nation of Immigrants": Settler Colonialism, White Supremacy, and a History of Erasure and Exclusion* (Boston: Beacon Press, 2021), 60.

19. Dunbar-Ortiz, *Not "A Nation of Immigrants,"* 19–20.

20. Dunbar-Ortiz, *Not "A Nation of Immigrants,"* 60. Her source is Walter Johnson, *River of Dark Dreams: Slavery and Empire in the Cotton Kingdom* (Cambridge: Harvard University Press, 2013).

21. For an excellent study of the forced deportation of Indigenous peoples from the South, see Claudio Saunt, *Unworthy Republic: The Dispossession of Native Americans and the Road to Indian Territory* (New York: W.W. Norton, 2020). The Cherokee owned 12% of Georgia; the Creek owned 20% of Alabama; the Choctaw and Chicksaw owned nearly half of Mississippi—Saunt, *Unworthy Republic*, 37–38. "The population of enslaved Africans in the Deep South states increased from 100,000 in 1800 to 250,000 in 1840"—Dunbar-Ortiz, *Not "A Nation of Immigrants,"* 60.

22. "The South's 'coloured population'—whether free, enslaved, African, or indigenous—must remain 'mere *inhabitants*,' *(not citizens,)* and peculiarly the subjects of *state municipal regulation*"—Saunt, *Unworthy Republic*, 40. Saunt is quoting a footnote to the reprinting of a Georgia, Alabama, and Mississippi committee report in *Southern Recorder* (April 9, 1827): 2–3. See also Saunt, *Unworthy Republic*, 318–320.

220 NOTES

23. The term Black rather than African American seems more appropriate in this part of the Afterword.

24. Bruce A. Glasrud and Michael N. Searles, eds., *Black Cowboys in the American West: On the Range, on the Stage, Behind the Badge* (Norman: University of Oklahoma Press, 2016); Alice L. Baumgartner, *South to Freedom: Runaway Slaves to Mexico and the Road to the Civil War* (New York: Basic Books, 2021)—reviewed by David S. Reynolds in "When Slaves Fled to Mexico," *New York Review of Books* (May 13, 2021): 51–52.

Bibliography

Abel, Richard. *Americanizing the Movies and "Movie-Mad" Audiences, 1910–1914.* Berkeley: University of California Press, 2006.

Abel, Richard. *The Red Rooster Scare: Making Cinema American, 1900–1910.* Berkeley: University of California Press, 1999.

Anderson, Robert. "The Role of the Western Film Genre in Industry Competition, 1907–1911." *Journal of the University Film Association* 31.2 (1979): 19–26.

Bernardi, Daniel, ed. *The Birth of Whiteness: Race and the Emergence of U.S. Cinema.* New Brunswick, NJ: Rutgers University Press, 1996.

Blight, David W. *Race and Reunion: The Civil War in American Memory.* Cambridge: Harvard University Press, 2001.

Bold, Christine. *Selling the Wild West: Popular Western Fiction, 1860–1960.* Bloomington: Indiana University Press, 1987.

Bollier, David. *Silent Theft: The Private Plunder of Our Common Wealth.* New York: Routledge, 2002.

Brownlow, Kevin. *The War, The West, and the Wilderness.* New York: Knopf, 1979.

Cavanagh, Edward, and Lorenzo Veracini, eds. *Routledge Handbook of the History of Settler Colonialism.* New York: Routledge, 2016.

Cherchi Usai, Paolo, ed. *The Griffith Project.* vol. 1, London: British Film Institute, 1997.

Cherchi Usai, Paolo, ed. *The Griffith Project.* vol. 3, London: British Film Institute, 1999.

Cherchi Usai, Paolo, ed. *The Griffith Project.* vol. 4, London: British Film Institute, 2000.

Cherchi Usai, Paolo, ed. *The Griffith Project.* vol. 5, London: British Film Institute, 2001.

Cherchi Usai, Paolo, ed. *The Griffith Project.* vol. 6, London: British Film Institute, 2002.

Cozzens, Peter. *The Earth Is Weeping: The Epic Story of the Indian Wars for the American West.* New York: Vintage, 2016.

Cronin, William, George Miles, and Jay Gitlin, eds. *Under an Open Sky: Rethinking America's Western Past.* New York: W.W. Norton, 1992.

Dippie, Brian W. *The Vanishing American: White Attitudes & U.S. Indian Policy.* Lawrence: University of Kansas Press, 1982.

Dunbar-Ortiz, Roxanne. *An Indigenous Peoples' History of the United States.* Boston: Beacon Press, 2016.

Dunbar-Ortiz, Roxanne. *Not "A Nation of Immigrants": Settler Colonialism, White Supremacy, and a History of Erasure and Extinction.* Boston: Beacon Press, 2021.

Frymus, Agata. "Pocahontas and Settler Colonialism in Early Film, 1907–1910." *Journal of Cinema and Media Studies* 60.3 (Spring 2021): 83–103.

Gilio-Whitaker, Dina. *As Long as Grass Grows: The Indigenous Fight for Environmental Justice, from Colonization to Standing Rock.* Boston: Beacon Press, 2019.

Glasrud, Bruce A. and Michael N. Searles, eds., *As Black Cowboys in the American West: On the Range, on the Stage, Behind the Badge.* Norman: University of Oklahoma Press, 2016.

BIBLIOGRAPHY

Gómez, Laura E. *Manifest Destinies: The Making of the Mexican American Race*. New York: New York University Press, 2007.

Green, Rayna. "The Pocahontas Perplex: The Image of Indian Women in American Culture." In *Native Women's History in Eastern North America before 1900*, edited by Rebecca Kugel and Lucy Eldersveld Murphy, 7–26. Lincoln: University of Nebraska Press, 2007.

Gunckel, Colin, and Kimberly Tomadjoglou, eds. *Film History Special Issue: Mexican Silent Cinema* 29.1 (2017).

Hämäläinen, Pekka. *Indigenous Continent: The Epic Contest for North America*. New York: Liveright, 2022.

Hearne, Joanna. *Native Recognition: Indigenous Cinema and the Western*. Albany: SUNY Press, 2012.

Hernández, Kelly Lytle. *Bad Mexicans: Race, Empire & Revolution in the Borderlands*. New York: W.W. Norton, 2022.

Hyde, Anne F. *Born of Lakes and Plains: Mixed-Descent Peoples and the Making of the American West*. New York: W.W. Norton, 2022.

Jay, Gregory S. "'White Man's Book No Good': D.W. Griffith and the American Indian." *Cinema Journal* 39.4 (2000): 3–26.

Johannsen, Albert. *The House of Beadle and Adams and Its Dime and Nickel Novels: The Story of a Vanished Literature*. vol. 1, Norman: University of Oklahoma Press, 1950.

Johnson, Walter. *The Broken Heart of America: St. Louis and the Violent History of the United States*. New York: Basic Books, 2020.

Kasson, Joy S. *Buffalo Bill's Wild West: Celebrity, Memory, and Popular History*. New York: Hill and Wang, 2000.

Kiehn, David. *Broncho Billy and the Essanay Film Company*. Berkeley: Farwell Books, 2003.

Koszarski, Diane Kaiser. *The Complete Films of William S. Hart: A Pictorial Record*. New York: Dover, 1980.

Marubbio, M. Elise. *Killing the Indian Maiden: Images of Native American Women in Film*. Lexington: University of Kentucky Press, 2006.

Merchant, Carolyn. *The Columbia Guide to American Environmental History*. New York: Columbia University Press, 2002.

Mitman, Gregg. *Reel Nature: America's Romance with Wildlife on Film*. Seattle: University of Washington Press, 1999.

Musser, Charles. *Before the Nickelodeon: Edwin S. Porter and the Edison Manufacturing Company*. Berkeley: University of California Press, 1991.

Musser, Charles. *The Emergence of Cinema: The American Screen to 1907*. New York, Charles Scribner's Sons, 1990.

Nivers, Kemp R., and Bebe Bergston, eds. *Biograph Bulletins, 1896–1908*. Los Angeles: Locare Research Group, 1971.

Orians, Harrison. *The Cult of the Vanishing American: A Century View, 1834–1934*, Toledo: H. J. Chittenden, 1934.

Pearl, Matthew. *The Taking of Jemima Boone: Colonial Settlers, Tribal Nations, and the Kidnap That Shaped America*. New York: HarperCollins, 2021.

Peterson, Jennifer Lynn. *Education in the School of Dreams: Travelogues and Early Nonfiction Film*. Durham, NC: Duke University Press, 2013.

Raheja, Michelle. *Reservation Reelism: Redfacing, Visual Sovereignty, and Representations of Native American in Film*. Lincoln: University of Nebraska Press, 2010.

BIBLIOGRAPHY   223

Reddin, Paul. *Wild West Shows*. Urbana: University of Illinois Press, 1999.

Reisler, Mark. *By the Sweat of Their Brow: Mexican Immigrant Labor in the United States, 1900–1940*. Westport, CN: Greenwood Press, 1976.

Rifkin, Mark. *Manifesting America: The Imperial Construction of U.S. National Space*. New York: Oxford University Press, 2009.

Rony, Fatimah Tobing. *The Third Eye: Race, Cinema, and Ethnographic Spectacle*. Durham, NC: Duke University Press, 1996.

Rydell, Robert W. *All the World's a Fair: Visions of Empire at American International Expositions, 1876–1916*. Chicago: University of Chicago Press, 1984.

Sagala, Sandra K. *Buffalo Bill on the Silver Screen*. Norman: University of Oklahoma Press, 2013.

Saunt, Claudio. *Unworthy Republic: The Dispossession of Native Americans and the Road to Indian Territory*. New York: W.W. Norton, 2020.

Schimmel, Julie. "Inventing the 'Indian.'" In *The West as America*, edited by William H. Truettner, 149–189. Washington, DC: Smithsonian Institution Press, 1991.

Schrad, Mark Lawrence. *Smashing the Liquor Machine: A Global History of Prohibition*. New York: Oxford University Press, 2021.

Shaffer, Marguerite S. *See America First: Tourism and National Identity, 1880–1940*. Washington: Smithsonian Institution, 2001.

Simmon, Scott. *The Invention of the Western Film: A Cultural History of the Genre's First Half-Century*. Cambridge: Cambridge University Press, 2003.

Simmon, Scott. *More Treasures from American Film Archives, 1894–1931*. San Francisco: National Film Preservation Foundation, 2004.

Simmon, Scott. *Treasures 5: The West, 1898–1938*. San Francisco: National Film Preservation Foundation, 2011.

Slotkin, Richard. *Gunfighter Nation: The Myth of the Frontier in Twentieth-Century America*. New York: Atheneum, 1992.

Smith, Andrew Brodie. *Shooting Cowboys and Indians: Silent Western Films, American Culture, and the Birth of Hollywood*. Boulder: University of Colorado Press, 2003.

Smith, Henry Nash. *Virgin Land: The American West as Symbol and Myth*. Cambridge: Harvard University Press, 1970 [1950].

Smits, David D. "The 'Squaw Drudge': A Prime Index of Savagism." In *Native Women's History in Eastern North America Before 1900*, edited by Rebecca Krugel and Lucy Eldersveld Murphy, 27–49. Lincoln: University of Nebraska Press, 2007.

Spence, Mark David. *Dispossessing the Wilderness: Indian Removal and the Making of the National Parks*. New York: Oxford University Press, 1999.

Takaki, Ronald. *Iron Cages: Race and Culture in 19th-Century America*. Rev. ed. New York: Oxford University Press, 2000.

Tompkins, Jane. *West of Everything: The Inner Life of Westerns*. New York: Oxford University Press, 1992.

Trachtenberg, Alan. *The Incorporation of America: Culture and Society in the Gilded Age*. New York: Hill and Wang, 1982.

Truettner, William H., ed. *The West as America: Reinterpreting Images of the Frontier, 1820–1920*. Washington, DC: Smithsonian Institution Press, 1991.

Tutino, John, ed. *Mexico and Mexicans in the Making of the United States*. Austin: University of Texas Press, 2012.

Veracini, Lorenzo. *Settler Colonialism: A Theoretical Overview*. New York: Palgrave Macmillan, 2010.

BIBLIOGRAPHY

Verhoeff, Nana. *The West in Early Cinema: After the Beginning.* Amsterdam: University of Amsterdam Press, 2006.

Welling, William. *Photography in America: The Formative Years, 1839–1900.* New York: Crowell, 1977.

Witgen, Michael. *An Infinity of Nations: How the Native New World Shaped Early North America.* Philadelphia: University of Pennsylvania Press, 2012.

Wolfe, Patrick. *Settler Colonialism and the Transformation of Anthropology: The Politics and Poetics of an Ethnographic Event.* London: Cassell, 1999.

Wolfe, Patrick. "Settler Colonialism and the Elimination of the Native." *Journal of Genocide Research* 8.4 (2006): 387–409.

Worster, Donald. *Rivers of Empire: Water, Aridity, and the Growth of the American West.* New York: Oxford University Press, 1985.

Index

For the benefit of digital users, indexed terms that span two pages (e.g., 52–53) may, on occasion, appear on only one of those pages.

Figures are indicated by *f* following the page number

African Americans, 25–26, 53, 66, 154–55, 161–62, 164, 193n.17
airplane, 149
American Progress, concept, 2, 8–10, 33, 34, 157, 159–60
archives
    Academy Film Archive, 118
    Cinémathèque Suisse, 111
    Museo del cine Pablo C. Ducrós Hicken, Argentina, 118
    New Zealand Film Archive, 95–96
    Smithsonian Institution, 200n.1
    US Library of Congress, 35–36, 118
artists
    Adams, Cassilly, 31
    Fuller, William, 169n.26
    Gast, John, 3–4, 119–21
    Hoskins, 87–88
    Leutze, Emanuel, 6–8
    Remington, Frederic, 77–79, 87–88, 98, 135–37, 156–57
    Schreyvogel, Charles, 75
    Wimar, Carl, 21, 40–41
authenticity, concept, 17, 26–27, 30, 31, 43–44, 72–73, 95–96, 97–98, 101, 110–11, 121, 174n.28
automobile, 69–71, 126, 148–49

cameramen
    August, Joe, 207n.70
    Clark, James L., 94
    Hemment, J.C., 94–95
    Kearton, Cherry, 94
    Wyckoff, Alvin, 199–200n.72
cameras
    Bell and Howell, 95–96
    Biograph, 12, 35–36

Chicago censors, 131–33, 152–53, 154–55, 212n.34
Chinese/Chinaman, 6–9, 21, 25, 112–13, 117–18, 152–53, 154–55, 159–60, 161–62, 170n.29, 187n.62
Christian Doctrine of Discovery, 6–8
Civil War films, 164, 200n.78
    Broncho
        Pride of the South (1913), 92–93
        Sundered Ties (1912), 92–93
    Epoch Producing
        Birth of a Nation (1915), 92–93, 121, 149
    Kay-Bee
        Blood Will Tell (1912), 92–93
    Lubin
        Reunited at Gettysburg (1913), 92–93
    Mutual
        Battle of Gettysburg (1913), 92–93
    Universal-Bison
        Light in the Window (1913), 92–93
Civil War re-enactments, 121
consumer society, concept, 67, 145, 159
costume changes, 44–45, 48–49, 60–62, 74–75, 91–92
cowgirl films, 1–2, 8–10, 17–18, 20, 62–66, 121, 159–60

environmental/ecological studies
    Merchant, Carolyn, 168n.15
    Spence, Mark David, 35–36, 172n.42
European film imports
    Dante's Inferno, 72
    Notre Dame de Paris, 72
    Temptations of a Great City, 72
    Zigomar, 72

226   INDEX

film actors
  Anderson, G.M., 8–9, 17–18, 57, 58–60, 66, 177n.62, 184n.23
  Aoki, Tsuru, 197n.43
  Arbuckle, Fatty, 160–61
  Barricale, Bessie, 160–61
  Bosworth, Hobart, 40–41
  Carey, Harry, 8–10, 128–38, 159–60, 161–62
  Darkfeather, Mona, 81–82, 185n.34
  De Grasse, Sam, 156–57
  Eastwood, Clint, 103–4
  Eyton, Bessie, 142–44, 214n.59
  Fairbanks, Douglas, 8–10, 127, 128, 137–38, 144, 145–47, 148–57, 159–61, 163–64
  Farnum, Dustin, 90, 92
  Fielding, Romaine, 88–89
  Ford, Francis, 74–75
  Gebhardt, George, 189n.91
  Gibson, Hoot, 128, 133–34
  Glaum, Louise, 204n.32
  Golden, Olive, 128
  Goodboy, Joe, 197n.43
  Hart, William S., 8–9, 93, 97–121, 106f, 127, 128, 129–30, 134, 140, 145–47, 150–51, 154–55, 159–60, 162–63
  Hayakawa, Sessue, 197n.43
  Herron, Robert, 47–48
  Hooker, George, 193n.17
  Jones, Buck, 161–62
  Joyce, Alice, 44–45
  Keaton, Buster, 160–61
  Kurihara, Thomas, 203n.16
  Little, Anna, 195n.16
  Love, Bessie, 118–19, 149–50
  Markey, Edith, 102–3
  Marsh, Mae, 208n.91
  Maynard, Ken, 161–62
  McDowell, Claire, 57–58
  Michelina, Beatriz, 198n.58
  Mix, Tom, 68–69, 88, 97, 127, 128, 129–30, 137–48, 143f, 150–51, 157, 159–60, 161–63
  Normand, Mabel, 160–61
  Owen, Seena, 148–49
  Percy, Eileen, 156–57
  Perry, Pansy, 17–18

  Pickett, Bill, 161–62
  Pickford, Mary, 43–44, 57–58
  Red Wing (Lillian St. Cyr), 44–45, 53–56, 90
  Rubens, Alma, 153–54
  Schaeffer, Anne, 191n.127
  Sweet, Blanche, 41
  St. John, Al, 160–61
  Thomson, Fred, 161–62
  Walthall, Henry, 128
  West, Charles, 41
  Williams, Kathlyn, 142–44
  Wolfe, Jane, 49–51
film companies
  AM&B, 12–13, 35–36
  American Film, 15–16, 38, 46–47, 49–51, 74–75, 191n.120
  Biograph, 20, 24–25, 26–29, 30, 31, 38, 41, 45–46, 48–49, 57–58, 83–84, 128–29, 160–61, 197n.37
  Champion, 51–53
  Edison, 12, 15–17, 29–30, 33, 34, 35–36, 70–71
  Essanay, 20, 23–25, 30, 38–40, 53, 57, 58, 59–64, 67–68, 87–88, 98, 126
  Famous Players-Lasky, 90
    Apfel, Oscar, 90
    Lasky, Jesse L., 90, 92
  Fine Arts, 127
  Fox, 127, 145–47
  Frontier, 46
  Gaumont, 123–24
  Kalem, 38, 44–45, 51, 53, 67–68, 186n.42, 186n.45, 191n.120, 219n.15
  Keystone, 140, 148–49
  Kinemacolor, 70–71
  Kleine, 34–35
  Lubin, 12, 88–89, 92–93
  Motion Picture Patents Company (MPPC), 38
  Mutual, 98, 102–3, 104–5, 123–25
    Freuler, J.R., 123
  New York Motion Picture (NYMP), 38, 72, 79, 113, 195n.2, 196n.20
    Ince, Thomas, 72, 97–98, 105–6, 113, 195n.3, 203n.15
  Paramount, 98
  Paramount-Artcraft, 97, 113, 127, 148

Pathé, 34–35, 38, 44–45, 46–47, 53–56, 70–71, 123–24
Rex, 70–71
Rothacker, 123–25
Selig, 12, 17–18, 20, 21, 22–24, 25–26, 27–28, 29–30, 35–36, 38–41, 42–43, 45–46, 48–49, 67–69, 72, 84–86, 87–88, 94, 127, 138–39, 140, 145
Solax, 191n.120
Thanhouser, 51–53
Triangle, 81–82, 97, 105–6, 113, 127, 148, 149, 206n.61
Universal, 79, 92–93, 128, 129–45
Vitagraph, 21–22, 25–26, 30–31, 47–48, 49–51, 64–66
W.H. Productions, 113
filmmakers
Anderson, G.M., 17–18, 177n.62
Barker, Reginald, 202n.3
Birch, Harry, 123–24
Boggs, Francis, 67–68, 184n.25
Bruce, Robert C., 124–25
Buckwalter, H.H., 17–18, 21, 33
Cabanne, W. Christie, 215n.85
Campbell, Colin, 138–39
Chaplin, Charlie, 126
Chester, C.L., 124–25
Cowling; H.T., 123
Curtis, Edward S., 124–25, 184n.18
DeMille, Cecil B., 90–92
Ditmar, Raymond L., 124–25
Dwan, Alan, 149–51, 154–55, 187n.57, 187n.60, 188n.67, 191n.122
Earle, Ralph Radnor, 123–24
Emerson, John, 148
Emerson, W.D., 196n.28
Fielding, Romaine, 88–89
Ford, Francis, 84–86, 128
Ford, Jack, 127, 128, 131, 133–35
Griffith, D.W., 25–30, 41, 42–44, 128, 148, 149, 184n.19, 197n.37
Hart, William S., 2, 9–10, 149, 202n.10
Hitchcock, Alfred, 114–15
Holmes, Burton, 126
Jenkins, C. Francis, 70–71
Keaton, Buster, 218n.5
Klingensmith, W.B., 123–24
Méliès, Georges, 157

Montgomery, Frank, 81–82
O'Brien, John B, 193n.20
Rainey, Paul, 94–95
Rothacker, Watterson, 70–71
Rau, William, 70–71
Salisbury, Edward A., 95
Sennett, Mack, 215n.86
Sturgeon, Rollin S., 188n.65
Thompson, E.B., 67–68
Turner, Otis, 184n.18
Young Deer, James, 38, 44–45, 53–54, 55–56, 86, 189n.86
film reviewers
Bush, W. Stephen, 49–51, 86–87, 95–96, 98, 124–25
Day, Dorothy, 47–48, 162–63
Delluc, Louis, 208n.91
Flanner, Janet, 100–1, 159
Harris, Genevieve, 134–35, 144
Harrison, Louis Reeves, 75–76, 77–79, 105–6, 111, 117–18, 202n.10
Kelly, Kitty, 95–96
Mae Tinée, 162–63
films other than early westerns
Edison
The Great Train Robbery (1903), 174n.20
Essanay
The Tramp (1915), 126
Kalem
Hazards of Helen (1914-1917), 163–64, 219n.15
Malpaso
High Plains Drifter (1973), 103–4
MGM
Greed (1924), 103–4
Selig
Coming of Columbus (1912), 72
Frederick Warde theater company, 148

geographical regions and sites, selected
California, 12–13, 23–24, 38, 42–43, 48–49, 51, 72, 89–90, 92, 95–96, 113–14, 139–40, 153–54, 174n.29, 185n.29, 198–99n.59
Colorado, 17–19, 21, 23–24, 29–30, 34–35, 40–41, 176n.52
Kentucky, 15–16, 89–90
Little Big Horn, 30–31, 77–79

228 INDEX

geographical regions and sites, selected
(*cont.*)
  Oregon Trail, 12–13, 45–46
  Santa Fe Trail, 12–13, 45–46, 86–87,
    116–17, 139, 172n.2, 187n.52,
    198n.47
Giornate del cinema muto, 2, 97, 105–6,
    110–11, 118
good badman, concept, 8–10, 59–60, 104,
    106–7, 121, 128–29, 131, 159–60

half-breed, concept, 22, 23–25, 27–28,
    29–30, 31–32, 40–41, 44–45,
    49–51, 55–57, 111–12, 116, 150–
    51, 152–53, 177n.55, 177n.57,
    185n.34, 186n.45, 202n.10,
    215n.89, 218n.8
Historians of American culture and
    society
  Adamson, Glenn, 17
  Clements, Frederic, 3–4
  Coleman, Jon, 15–16
  Cronon, William, 3–4
  Faragher, John Mack, 4–6
  Gitlin, Jay, 4–6
  Johnson, Walter, 164
  Limerick, Patricia Nelson, 4–6
  Robinson, Cedric, 164
  Schrad, Mark Lawrence, 45–46
  Shaffer, Marguerite, 67, 123–24
  Slotkin, Richard, 121
  Snyder, Timothy, 10–11
  Truettner, William H., 169n.26
  Turner, Frederick Jackson, 3–4, 6–8
  Webb, Walter Prescott, 3–4
historians of Indigenous peoples
  Dippie, Brian, 56–57, 171n.38
  Dunbar-Ortiz, Roxanne, 2, 164
  Hämäläinen, Pekka, Co14 n.27
  Hyde, Anne F., 171n.40
  Orions, R. Harriosn, 46–47
  Saunt, Claudio, 192n.130
  Schimmel, Julie, 171n.40
  Smith, Paul Chaat, 31, 35–36
  Spence, Mark David, 35–36, 172n.42
  Witgen, Michael, 169n.27
historians of Mexicans and Mexican
    Americans
  Gómez, Laura A., 169–70n.28

Hernández, Kelly Lyttle, 169–70n.28
Tutino, John, 169–70n.28
historians of silent film
  Anderson, Robert, 38
  Brewster, Ben, 27–28
  Brownlow, Kevin, 68–69, 111
  Cherchi Usai, Paolo, 172n.42
  Gunning, Tom, 28–29, 83–84, 178n.69
  Hearne, Joanna, 31–32, 40–41, 44–45,
    53–54, 91–92
  Higashi, Sumiko, 43–44
  Horak, Laura, 62–64
  Keil, Charlie, 44–45, 57–58
  Koszarski, Diane and Richard, 2, 97,
    119–21, 206n.61, 208n.87
  Musser, Charles, 173n.17, 174n.20
  Peterson, Jennifer Lynn, 67, 69–70,
    123–24, 194n.23
  Raheja, Michelle, 30–31, 43–44, 54–55,
    176n.50
  Rony, Fatimah Tobing, 38
  Sagala, Sandra, 86–87, 198n.46
  Salt, Barry, 190n.111
  Simmon, Scott, 107–8, 176n.45,
    195n.16, 196n.18
  Smith, Andrew Brodie, 184n.18,
    195n.3, 202n.2
  Thompson, Kristin, 190n.111
  Verhoeff, Nanna, 8–9, 191n.120
  Wexman, Virginia Wright, 211n.15
historical events
  Calgary Stampede, Canada (1912), 138–39
  Cherokee Land Rush (1893), 64–66
  Civil War (1861-1865), 67, 149
  Golden Jubilee (1911-1915), 92–93
  Greater Colorado Industrial Parade,
    Denver (1911), 194n.23
  Jamestown Exposition (1907), 29–30
  Mariposa Indian Wars (1850-
    1851), 42–43
  Prescott Frontier Days, Arizona
    (1911), 138–39
  Revolutionary War (1775-1783), 15–16
  Seven Years War (1754-1763), 15–16,
    186n.42
  Trail of Tears, 141–42
historical figures
  Astor, John Jacob, 45–46
  Berra, Yogi, 165

INDEX 229

Black Hawk, 44–45, 184n.24
Boone, Daniel, 15–16
Bridger, Jim, 188n.76
Brunswick, H.A., 164
Carnegie, Andrew, 192n.1
Carrington, Reginald, 94–95
Carson, Kit, 12–15
Chief Little Turtle, 186n.50
Cody, Buffalo Bill, 77–79, 86–87
Cook, General George, 196n.18
Custer, Lieutenant Colonel George
    Armstrong, 22–23, 77–79
Davis, Jefferson, 44–45
Edison, Thomas, 34
Frémont, John Charles, 12–13
Fuqua, Chas., 68–69
Grammer, Henry, 68–69
Harris, Fisher Sanford, 72–73
Hill, George H., 3–4
Hooker, George, 193n.17
Jennings, Al and Frank, 216n.94
Leupp, Francis E., Commissioner of
    Indian Affairs, 56–57
Lincoln, Abraham, 79, 161–62
Long, Pat, 68–69
McCandell, Buck, 86–87
Marshall, Chief Justice John, 6–8
Mather, Stephen Tyng, 123
Mullens, Johnny, 68–69
O'Sullivan, John L., 3–4
Parker, Col. Edward Justus, 67–68
Pocahontas, 53–54, 180n.96, 180n.97
Scott, General Winfield, 79
Sioux Chief Gall, 77–79
Sioux Chief Sitting Bull, 77–79
Sommers, A.L., 69–70
Standing Bear, Luther, 163–64
Taft, President Howard, 38–40
Taylor, Zachary, 79
Thorpe, Jim, 25–26
Yellow Hand, 86–87
historical institution/organizations
    Carlisle Indian Industrial School, 25–26
    Hampton Normal and Agricultural
        Institute, 25–26
    Isalat Indian School, 33
    Ku Klux Klan, 134–35
    National Museum, Washington,
        D.C., 67, 94

New York Child Welfare
    Committee, 38–40
See America First Association
    (1911), 69–70
See America First League (1907-1909),
    35–36, 67–68
Smithsonian Institution, Washington,
    D.C., 67
Trams-Mississippi Commercial
    Congress, 69–70
Vassar College, 144

in-between figures, 8–9, 60–62, 83, 84–86,
    154–55, 159–60
Indian maiden, concept, 13, 15–17, 19–20,
    22, 28–30, 44–45, 81–82, 86,
    139–40, 177n.62
Indian pictures, 1–2, 8–11, 23–24, 26–29,
    30–31, 38, 43–49, 53–57, 60–62,
    66, 72–86, 92–93, 121, 159–60,
    162–63, 200n.82
Irish, 161–62
Italian, 161–62

Jewish character, 82–83

landscape, concept, 2–4, 18–19, 23–24,
    29–30, 40–41, 42–43, 46–48,
    67, 81–82, 86, 88–89, 98, 102–4,
    106–8, 116–17, 118–19, 121,
    128–29, 131–33, 137–38, 140,
    150–51, 154–55, 157
liquor trade, 45–46, 79, 153–55, 196n.31
Lost Cause, concept, 92–93, 121

Manifest Destiny, concept, 3–4, 10–11,
    19–20, 67, 92, 107–8, 159–60
Media History Digital Library, 9
Mexico and Mexicans, 2, 19–20, 21, 24–25,
    30–31, 47–51, 88–89, 92, 100–1,
    102–3, 104–5, 110–12, 117–21,
    128–30, 131–33, 140, 144, 147–
    49, 150–51, 152–54, 156–57,
    159–60, 164, 175n.36, 177n.53,
    215n.88
Diaz, President Portifio, 51, 83–84, 149
Magonistas, 83–84
Mexican Revolution, 83–84, 140,
    215n.88

230 INDEX

miscegenation, concept, 25–26, 27–28,
  29–30, 31–32, 51–54, 55–57,
  74–75, 179n.89, 187n.55,
  189n.90
mixed-race/mixed-descent, concept,
  29–30, 31–32, 46, 53–56, 91–92,
  171n.40
musicians
  National Film Preservation Foundation,
    9, 202n.17
  Schertzinger, Victor L., 204n.38
  Simm, Charles E., 189n.92

national parks
  General Grant, 123–24
  Glacier, 70–71
  Grand Canyon, 35–36, 70–71, 98
  Great Crater Lake, 70–71
  Mesa Verde, 123–24
  Mount Lassen, 123–24
  Rainier, 69–70
  Rocky Mountain, 123
  Sequoia, 123–24
  Yellowstone, 35–36, 67–68, 70–71
  Yosemite, 35–36, 42–43, 67, 70–
    71, 124–25
Native Americans/Indigenous peoples,
  19–20, 30, 67, 100–1, 116, 121,
  129–30, 131–33, 139–40, 141–
  42, 150–51, 152–55, 156–57,
  159–60, 161–62, 172n.7, 202n.9
  Apache, 12–13, 22, 45–46, 81–82, 86,
    102–3, 104, 116–17, 172n.2
  Arapaho, 13, 38–40
  Blackfoot, 13, 70–71
  Cherokee, 15–16, 64–66, 164
  Cheyenne, 13, 38–40, 76–77, 81–82,
    86–87, 161–62
  Chickasaw, 163–64
  Choctaw, 163–64
  Creek, 163–64
  Crow, 35–36, 194n.29
  Flathead, 188n.76
  Hopi, 46–47
  Kiowa, 12–13
  Miami Confederacy, 186n.50
  Navajo, 12–13, 35–36, 58–59, 160–61
  Pawnee, 139
  Shawnee, 15–16

Shoshone, 38–40, 188n.76
Sierra Miwok, 35–36, 42–43, 67
Sioux, 22–23, 26–28, 40–41, 44, 72–
  73, 75, 76–79, 81–82, 84–87,
  176n.52
Ute, 90
Yaqui, 83–84, 148–49
Zuni, 35–36
Noble Savage, concept, 8–9, 26–27, 43–44,
  171n.40

photographers
  Curtis, Edward S., 26–27, 46–47
  Dixon, Joseph K., 179n.83
popular arts and entertainments
  comic strips
    "Haphazard Helen," 163–64
  dime novels/pulp fiction
    Boone, the Hunter (1873), 15–16
    *Fighting Trapper, Kit Carson to the
      Rescue* (1874), 12–13, 14f
    *Kit Carson, the Prince of the Gold
      Hunters* (1849), 12–13
    Life & Times of Danel Boone
      (1859), 15–16
    *Life and Adventures of Kit Carson,
      Nestor of the Rocky Mountains*
      (1858), 12–13
    Motor Boys Across the Plains
      (1907), 163–64
    Motor Maids Across the Continent
      (1911), 163–64
    Moving Picture Boys in the West
      (1913), 163–64
    *Prairie Flower, or Adventures of the
      Far West* (1849), 12–13
    Ranch Girls juvenile series, 66
    Rover Boys Out West (1900), 163–64
    *Ruth Fielding at Silver Ranch or
      Schoolgirls Among the Cowboys*
      (1913), 163–64
    Seth Jones (1860), 154–55
  Hale's Tours, 34–36
  lithographs/paintings/murals
    "A Misdeal" (?), 135–37
    "American Progress" (1872), 3–4,
      3f, 119–21
    "Attack on an Emigrant Train
      (1856), 21

"Cowboy on Horseback" (1908), 87–88
    "Crow Creek Agency, Dakota
        Territory" (1884), 169n.26
    "Custer's Last Stand," 22–23
    "Defending the Stockade" (1905), 75
    "The Last Stand" (1890), 77–79
    "Westward the Course of Empire
        Takes Its Way" (1862), 6–8, 7f
magazines
    Independent, The, 92–93
    National Geographic, 1
    Outing Magazine, 124–25
    Popular Magazine, 163–64
    See America First, 70–71
newspapers
    Chicago Tribune, 162–63
    Cleveland News, 133–34
    Des Moines Tribune, 162–63
novels/short stories
    Highgrader, The (1915), 147
    In the Carquinez Woods
        (1883), 153–54
    "Salomy Jane's Kiss" 89–90
    Smoke Bellew (1912), 115–16
    Two-Gun Man, The (1911), 145–47
    Virginian, The (1902), 92
photographs
    "Vanishing Race" (ca. 1900), 46–47
popular songs
    "Cheyenne" (1906), 163–64, 174n.25
Selig Jungle Zoo, 142–44
stage productions
    Barrier, The (1908), 97–98
    Ben-Hur (1899), 97–98
    Bertha, the Sewing Machine Girl
        (1906), 87–88
    On the Trail (1907), 15–16
    Gentleman from Mississippi, A (1908-
        1909), 148
    Mazappa (1884), 21, 137–38
    Montana (1907), 128
    New Henrietta, The (1913), 148–49
    Squaw Man, The (1905), 90, 97–98
    Trail of the Lonesome Pine
        (1912), 97–98
    Virginian, The (1903-1904), 92, 97–98
Wild West shows
    Buffalo Bill's Wild West, 6–8, 20, 22–
        23, 172n.43

Great Wild West Indian
    Vaudeville, 163–64
Miller Bros. 101 Ranch Wild West,
    66, 72, 138–40
World's Fairs
    1893 Chicago World's Columbian
        Exposition, 34
    1901 Pan-American Exposition,
        Buffalo, 34
    1904 Louisiana Purchase Exposition,
        St. Louis, 34, 138–39
    1909 Alaska-Yukon Exposition,
        Seattle, 67–68
    1914 Panama-Pacific
        International Exposition,
        San Francisco, 123

"race theory," concept, 6–8
    African American, 6–8
    Chinese, 6–8
    Indigenous Peoples/Native Americans/
        Indians, 6–8
    Mexicans, 6–8
    Whites/Anglos, 6–8
railroads, 3–6, 161–62
    Central Pacific, 161–62
    Colorado and Southern, 194n.23
    Northern Pacific, 70–71, 70f
    Oregon Truck Railway, 126
    Santa Fe, 160–61, 176n.52
    Union Pacific, 67–68, 161–62
redface, concept, 21–22, 176n.50, 179n.82,
    197n.32
    cf. Blackface, concept, 21–22
Robin Hood, 128–29, 150–51

scenario writers
    Carey, Harry, 129–30, 212n.36
    Emerson, John, 148
    Fairbanks, Douglas, 149–50, 152
    Fielding, Romaine, 88–89
    Ford, Jack, 212n.36
    Hart, William S., 113–14, 119–21
    Loos, Anita, 148, 153–54, 156–57
    MacRae, Henry, 134–35
    Rector, Josephine, 58, 163–64
    Sullivan, C. Gardner, 119–21
    Willets, Gilson, 138–39
"See America First" campaign/slogan, 123

232 INDEX

settler colonialism, concept, 2–3, 9–10,
40–41, 67, 86, 99–100, 114–15,
119–21, 127, 159–64
Rifkin, Mark, 2–3
Veracini, Lorenzo, 2–3
Wolfe, Patrick, 2–3
Shakespeare, William, 97–98, 112–13
Richard III, 111–12
Spanish-American War films
Universal-Bison
Battle of Manila (1913), 92–93
Grand Old Flag (1913), 92–93
Stars and Stripes Forever
(1913), 92–93

theaters
Lyceum, New York, 94–95, 201n.10
Metropolitan, Cleveland, 206n.59,
217n.111
Royal, Des Moines, 138
Studebaker, Chicago, 95
Tivoli, San Francisco, 201n.14
trade press
Motion Picture Magazine, 97
Motion Picture News, 38
Moving Picture World, 40, 41, 49–
51, 72–73
New York Dramatic Mirror, 72–73
Nickelodeon, 38–40
Photoplay, 77–79
Variety, 29–30, 38–40, 43–44
travel films
AM&B
Asia in America (1904), 34
Coaching Party Yosemite Valley
(1902), 35–36
Devil's Slide (1901-1902), 35–36
Frazer Canon (1901-1902), 35–36
The Gap, Entrance to Rocky
Mountains (1901-1902), 35–36
Circle Ranch Film
Life on the Circle Ranch in California
(1912), 68–69
Edison
California Orange Groves, Panoramic
View (1897), 33
Coaches arriving at Mammoth Hot
Springs (1899), 35–36

Copper Mines at Bingham, Utah
(1912), 70–71
Indian Day School (1898), 33
Pan-American Exposition at Night
(1901), 34
Panorama of the Esplanade by Night
(1901), 34
Phantom Ride on Canadian Pacific
(1903), 33
Tourists going around Yellowstone
Park (1899), 35–36
Trip Through the Yellowstone Park,
U.S.A. (1907), 35–36
Waterfall in the Catskills (1897), 33
Educational Films
Alaskan Wonders (1918), 124–25
Bruce Scenics series, 124–25
Deschutes Driftwood (1916), 126
Valley of the Hoh (1917), 124–25
Essanay
Lake Tahoe, Land of the Sky (1916),
125f, 126
Wonders of Nature in the Twin
Falls Country, Southern Idaho
(1909), 67–68
Kalem
Trip to the Wonderland of America,
Yellowstone National Park
(1909), 67–68
Lady McKenzie's Big Game Pictures
(1915), 201n.10
Mutual
Heart of the Blue Ridge (1917), 123–24
Outing-Chester series, 124–25
Pines Up and Palms Down
(1918), 68–69
See America First series, 123–24
Paramount
Among the Geysers of the Yellowstone
(1917), 126
Beaver, The (1917), 124–25
Life in the Insect World
(1918), 124–25
Living Book of Nature series, 124–25
Tree Animals (1917), 124–25
Pathé
Blazing a New Trail through Glacier
National Park (1913), 70–71

INDEX 233

Glacier National Park (1917), 123–24
Our National Parks series, 123–24
"America First" series, 70–71
Trip to Mount Ranier (1912), 70–71
Waterfalls of Idaho (1913), 70–71
Paul Rainey's African Pictures
    (1912), 94–95
Rex
    Picturesque Colorado (1911), 70–71
Roosevelt in Africa (1910), 94
Seeing America (1916), 124–25
Seeing Yosemite with David A. Curry
    (1916), 126
Selig
    Columbia River (1906), 34–35
    Georgetown Loop (1902), 182n.15
    Grand Canyon of Arizona and the
        Cliff Dwellers (1907), 35–36
    Hunting Big Game in Africa
        (1909), 94
    Outing Pastimes in Colorado
        (1909), 67–68
    Panoramic View of Royal Gorge
        (1902), 182n.15
    Ranch Life in the Great Southwest
        (1910), 68–69
    Trip Through the Black Hills
        (1906), 34–35
    Trip Through the Coeur d'Alene
        Mountains (1906), 34–35
    Trip Through Utah (1906), 34–35
    Trip Through Yellowstone Park, A
        (1907), 35–36
    Ute Pass (1902), 182n.15
Union Pacific
    Frontier Day at Laramie
        (1909), 67–68
US Department of Agriculture
    Little Journeys in the National Forest
        of Colorado (1920), 126
    Trails That Lure (1920), 126
    Wild Animal Life in America
        (1915), 95–96

US court rulings, legislation, policies
    1787 Northwest Ordinance, 180n.100
    1823 Supreme Court decision, 6–8
    1862 Railroad Act, 3–4

    1863 Homestead Act, 3–4, 6–8
    1882 Exclusion Act, 6–8
    1887 Dawes Act, 51–53, 179n.89
    Jim Crow laws, 6–8, 51–53
US government
    Biological Survey Reservations, 95
    Department of Agriculture, 126,
        194n.25
    Department of Interior, 35–36, 51–53,
        67–68, 70–71, 123, 194n.25
    National Park Service, 123
    Reclamation Service, 123
    US Army/cavalry, 20, 21–23, 44, 53,
        84–86, 116–17, 138–39, 159–60,
        185n.29, 197n.37, 215n.87

"Vanishing American," concept, 8–10, 20,
    28–29, 30–31, 46–47, 56–57,
    70–71, 75–77, 84–86, 90, 99–
    100, 108–10, 159–60, 171n.38

West, The, concept, 1, 4–6, 175n.37
westerns (1903-1910)
    AM&B
        From Leadville to Aspen, Hold-up in
            the Rockies (1906), 18*f*, 174n.29
        Kit Carson (1903), 12–13, 16–17
        Pioneers, The (1903), 12–15, 16–17
    Biograph
        Call of the Wild, The (1908), 25–27,
            30–32, 45–46
        Comata the Sioux (1909), 27–
            28, 30–32
        Fight for Freedom (1908), 24–25
        Greaser's Gauntlet (1908), 25
        Mended Lute, The (1909), 26–27, 27*f*
        Red Girl, The (1908), 24–25, 28–
            29, 31–32
        Redman's View, The (1909), 28–29
    Bison
        Iona, the White Squaw (1909), 176n.48
        Ranchman's Wife, The (1909), 177n.57
    Edison
        Daniel Boone (1907), 15–17
        Life of a Cowboy, The (1906), 16–17,
            18–19
        Pioneers Crossing the Plains in '49
            (1908), 21

234   INDEX

westerns (1903-1910) *(cont.)*
   Pocahontas, Child of the Forest (1907),
      29–30, 51–53
  Esannay
   Indian Trailer, The (1909), 24–25
   Mexican's Gratitude, A (1909), 25
   Road Agent, The (1909), 23–24
  Selig
   Bandit King, The (1907), 17–18
   Cattle Rustlers, The (1908), 23–24,
      24f, 31–32, 178n.66
   Cowboy's Baby, The (1908), 21
   Girl from Montana, The (1907), 17–18
   Hold-Up of the Leadville Stage, The
      (1905), 17
   In Old Arizona (1909), 22, 176n.52
   On the Border (1909), 180n.99
   On the Little Big Horn (1909), 22–23
   On the Warpath (1909), 22, 25–26,
      27–28, 31–32, 176n.52
   Squawman's Daughter, The (1908),
      29–30, 31–32
   Western Justice (1907), 17–18
  Vitagraph
   Children of the Plains (1909), 21–
      22, 25–26
westerns (1910-1913)
  single reels
   American film
    Outlaw's Trail, The (1911), 62
    Poisoned Flume, The (1911),
      187n.60
    Ranchman's Vengeance, The (1911),
      49–51, 50f, 189n.94
    Vanishing Race, The (1912), 46–
      48, 57–58
    Ammunition Smuggling on the
      Mexican Border (1914), 188n.70
   Biograph
    Broken Doll, The (1910), 46,
      185–86n.38
    Female of the Species, The
      (1912), 57–58
    Fighting Blood (1911), 184n.19
    Gold-Seekers, The (1910), 57–58
    Heart of a Savage, The (1911),
      43–44, 46
    In Old California (1910), 48–49

Iola's Promise (1912), 38, 42–43,
  186n.43
Last Drop of Water, The (1911), 41,
  42–43, 57–58
Ramona (1910), 42–43, 184n.24
Romance of the Western Hills
  (1910), 42–43, 184n.24
Song of the Wildwood Flute, The
  (1910), 43–44
That Chink at Golden Gulch (1910),
  187n.62
Bison
  Little Dove's Romance (1911),
   185n.34
  Range Romance, A (1911), 62–64
Champion
  Indian Land Grab (1910), 51–
   53, 54–55
Essanay
  Bad Man's Last Deed (1910), 38–40
  Bearded Bandit (1910), 38–
   40, 60–62
  Broncho Billy character, 3–4, 66,
   93, 99–100, 159–60
  Broncho Billy series, 58, 66, 159–
   60, 162–63
  Broncho Billy's Christmas Dinner
   (1911), 62–64, 63f
  Broncho Billy's Narrow Escape
   (1912), 191n.119
  Broncho Billy's Redemption
   (1910), 58–59
  Cowboy and the Squaw, The
   (1910), 53
  Deputy's Love, The (1910), 60–62
  Little Prospector, The (1910),
   190n.100
  Loafer, The (1912), 190n.111
  Pal's Oath, A (1911), 51–53, 59–
   60, 60f
  Stage Driver's Daughter, The
   (1911), 62–64
  Under Western Skies (1910),
   184n.23
  Way Out West (1910), 57
  Western Chivalry (1910), 62
  Westerner's Way, A (1910), 58–
   59, 98

INDEX 235

Wife of the Hills, A (1912), 59–
   60, 60*f*
Frontier
   Maya, Just an Indian (1913), 46,
     187n.53
Kalem
   Blackfoot Half-Breed, The
     (1911), 44–45
   Conspiracy of Pontiac, The (1910),
     186n.42
   Girl Deputy, The (1912), 191n.120
   Jim Bridger's Indian Bride
     (1910), 53
   Mexican Joan of Arc, The (1911),
     51, 52*f*
   When California Was Won
     (1911), 51
Pathé
   Flag of Company H, The (1910),
     185n.27
   For the Papoose (1912), 55–56, 55*f*
   For the Squaw (1911), 54–55
   Legend of Lake Desolation, The
     (1911), 46, 47*f*
   Red Deer's Devotion (1911), 54–55
   Red Girl and the Child, The
     (1910), 44–45
   Romance of the Desert, The (1911),
     189n.90
   White Fawn's Devotion
     (1910), 53–54
Selig
   Across the Plains (1910), 40–41, 44
   Curse of the Red Man (1911), 45–
     46, 48–49, 84–86, 183n.10
   Daughter of the Sioux, A
     (1910), 44, 46
   Early Settlers (1910), 183n.17
   Girls on the Range (1910), 38–40
   In Old California, When the
     Gringos Came (1911), 48–49
   Sallie's Sure Shot (1913), 191n.122
   Saved by the Pony Express (1911),
     139–40, 198n.52
   Sergeant, The (1910), 42–43, 42*f*
Solax
   Two Little Rangers (1912),
     191n.120

Thanhouser
   Pocahontas (1910), 51–53
Vitagraph
   Better Man, The (1912), 49–51, 49*f*,
     64–66, 213n.57
   Bit of Blue Ribbon, A (1913),
     187n.61
   Craven, The (1912), 64–66, 64*f*
   End of the Trail, The (1912), 47–
     48, 49–51
   How States Are Made (1912), 64–
     66, 65*f*
westerns, multiple reels (1912-1914)
   American film
     Fall of Black Hawk, The
       (1912), 75, 79
     Geronimo's Last Raid (1912),
       196n.28
   Biograph
     Battle of Elderbush Gulch (1914),
       197n.37
     Massacre, The (1914), 197n.37
     Yaqui Cur (1913), 83–84, 86
   Bison-101
     Blazing the Trail (1912), 72–
       73, 77–79
     Deserter, The (1912), 77–79, 195n.6
     Indian Massacre, The (1912), 75–
       76, 76*f*, 162–63
     Lieutenant's Last Fight, The (1912),
       73–75, 74*f*, 82–83
     War on the Plains, The
       (1912), 72–73
   Broncho
     Man They Scorned, The
       (1912), 82–83
     Vengeance of Fate (1912), 83
   Buffalo Bill and Pawnee Bill Film
     Life of Buffalo Bill, The
       (1912), 86–87
   Essanay
     Broncho Billy Gets Square
       (1913), 87–88
   Kay-Bee
     Altar of Death, The (1912), 83
     Custer's Last Fight (1912), 77–
       79, 78*f*
     Invaders, The (1912), 76–79, 77*f*

236 INDEX

westerns (1910-1913) (*cont.*)
    Last of the Line, The (1914), 84–
      86, 85*f*
  Lubin
    Rattlesnake—A Psychical Species,
      The (1913), 198n.56
    Toll of Fear, The (1913), 88–89
  Selig
    Cowboy Millionaire, The
      (1913), 87–88
    Escape of Jim Dolan, The (1913), 88
    Law and the Outlaw, The (1913), 88
  Universal-Bison
    Flaming Arrow, The (1913), 92–93
    Massacre of the Fourth Cavalry, The
      (1912), 81–82, 81*f*
    Star Eye's Strategy (1912), 81–82
westerns (1914)
  features
    California Motion Picture
      Salomy Jane (1914), 89–90
    Essanay
      Indian Wars, The (1914), 199n.61
    Famous Players-Lasky
      Squaw Man, The (1914), 90–92, 91*f*
      Virginian, The (1914), 92, 98, 121
    Selig
      Spoilers, The (1914), 199n.60
westerns (1914-1919)
  Douglas Fairbanks
    Good Bad-Man, The (1916), 149–51,
      151*f*, 152–53
    Half-Breed, The, The (1916), 153–57,
      154*f*, 155*f*, 162–64, 217n.111
    Lamb, The (1916), 144, 148–49, 152,
      215n.87
    Man from Painted Post, The
      (1917), 152–53
    Mark of Zorro, The (1920), 148
    Wild and Wooly (1917), 156–
      57, 160–61
  Harry Carey
    Feature films
      Cheyenne Harry character, 128,
      129–30, 131, 133, 134–35
      Hell Bent (1918), 135–38, 136*f*, 157

      Knight of the Range, The (1916),
        129–30, 134
      Marked Man, A (1917), 134
      Phantom Riders, The
        (1918), 134–35
      Secret Man, The (1917), 133
      Straight Shooting (1917), 128, 130*f*,
        131–33, 132*f*, 134–35, 137–38
    Two- and three-reel films
      As It Happened (1915), 128
      Canceled Mortgage (1915), 128
      Drifter, The (1917), 128
      Goin' Straight (1917), 128
      Heart of a Bandit, The (1915), 128–
        29, 131–33
      Outlaw and the Lady, The (1917), 128
      Sheriff's Dilemma, The (1915), 128
      Six-Shooter Justice (1917), 128
Tom Mix
  Feature films
    Ace High (1918), 145–47
    Cupid's Round Up (1918), 145
    Fighting for Gold (1919), 147–48
    Heart of Texas Ryan, The (1917),
      143*f*, 144, 148–49
    In the Days of the Thundering Herd
      (1914), 138–39
    Treat 'Em Rough (1919), 145–
      47, 146*f*
  Two- and three-reel films
    Auction of the Run-Down Ranch,
      The (1915), 144
    Legal Advice (1916), 140, 141*f*
    Ma's Girls (1915), 141–42
    Man Within, The (1916), 213n.57
    Pals in Blue (1915), 213n.57
    Six-Cylinder Love (1918), 145
    Soft Tenderfoot, A (1918), 145
    Stagecoach Driver and the Girl, The
      (1915), 145
    Starring in Western Stuff
      (1916), 140
William S. Hart
  Feature films
    Aryan, The (1916), 9–10, 118–21,
      119*f*, 120*f*

Bargain, The (1914), 98, 100, 105–6
"Blue Blazes" Rawden (1918), 105–6, 115–17
Bucking Broadway (1918), 116–17
Captive God, The (1916), 202n.9
Darkening Trail, The (1915), 105–6
Dawn Maker, The (1916), 202n.9
Devil's Double, The (1916), 162–63
Disciple, The (1915), 105–6
Gun Fighter, The (1917), 111–12, 118
Hell's Hinges (1916), 106–8, 107f, 114–15
Narrow Trail, The (1917), 113–15, 114f, 115f, 154–55
On the Night Stage (1915), 98, 102–3, 203n.20
Poppy Girl's Husband, The (1919), 116–17
Return of Draw Egan, The (1916), 108–10, 109f, 121
Selfish Yates (1918), 117–18
Silent Man, The (1917), 99–100, 99f, 113, 118–19
Tiger Man, The (1918), 116–17
Truthful Tulliver (1917), 110–11, 145
Wagon Tracks (1919), 207n.78
Wolf Lowry (1917), 112–13
Saga of William S. Hart, The (1959), 118
Two-reel films: Broncho and Kay-Bee
"Bad Buck" of Santa Ynez (1915), 104
In the Sage Brush Country (1915), 99–101, 108–10
Keno Bates, Liar (1915), 104–5
Knight of the Trails, A (1915), 104–5, 204n.29
Man from Nowhere, The (1915), 103–4
Passing of Two-Gun Hicks, The (1915), 100
Pinto Ben (1915), 104–5, 204n.29
Sheriff's Streak of Yellow, The (1915), 99–100, 101–2

Taking of Luke McVane, The (1915), 102–3, 104–5
westerns, other
Al Jennings
Lady of the Dugout, The (1918), 216n.94
Biograph
Tourists, The (1912), 160–61, 161f, 215n.86
Fox
Iron Horse, The (1924), 161–62
Keystone
Fatty and Minnie He-Haw (1914), 218n.4
MGM
Go West (1925), 218n.5
Paramount
Covered Wagon, The (1923), 161–62
Out West (1918), 160–61
Pathé Exchange
Devil Horse, The (1926), 161–62
Two-Gun Betty (1918), 160–61
Vanishing American, The (1925), 161–62
westerns, serials
Galloping Hooves (1924-1925), 161–62
Go-Get-Em Hutch (1922), 161–62
In the Days of Buffalo Bill (1922-1923), 161–62
Ruth of the Rockies (1921-1922), 161–62
Timber Queen, The (1922), 161–62
white masculinity, concept, 8–10, 93, 98, 105–6, 127, 142–44, 159–60
white supremacist entertainments, concept, 9–10, 172n.43
wilderness, concept, 6–8, 13, 18–19, 42–43, 56–57, 67, 69–70, 98, 115–16, 139–40, 161–62, 168n.12
World War I/Great War, The, 121, 123, 127, 159
writers
Beach, Rex, 97–98
Bower, B.M., 163–64
Carpenter, Horace B., 156–57
Carter, Lincoln, 92–93

238 INDEX

writers (*cont.*)
    Crofutt, George A., 3–4
    Dench, Ernest A., 72–73
    Dumas, Alexandre, 97–98
    Harte, Bret, 41, 89–90, 153–55
    Kenyon, Charles, 113
    La Shelle, Kirke, 92
    Leupp, Francis E., 56–57
    Lindsay, Vachel, 205n.51
    London, Jack, 115–16

Longfellow, Henry Wadsworth, 26–27
McDowell, Lloyd W., 194n.27, 194n.28
Mooney, James, 56–57
Raine, William Mcleod, 147
Rising, Will, 29–30
Royle, Edwin Milton, 90, 97–98
Seltzer, Charles Alden, 145–47
Sigourney, Lydia, 188n.71
Wister, Owen, 16–17, 20, 22, 23–24, 91–
    92, 97–98, 147, 169n.24